Getting Started with

Microsoft
Word 5.5
for IBM® PCs and Compatibles

Getting Started with

Microsoft® Word 5.5

for IBM® PCs and Compatibles

Janet Rampa

PUBLISHED BY
Microsoft Press
A Division of Microsoft Corporation
One Microsoft Way, Redmond, Washington   98052-6399

Library of Congress Cataloging-in-Publication Data
Rampa, Janet, 1948–
    Getting started with Microsoft Word 5.5 / Janet Rampa.
        p.   cm. -- (Getting started right)
    Includes index.
    ISBN 1-55615-354-6
    1. Microsoft Word (Computer program)   2. Word processing -- Computer
programs. I. Title. II. Series
    Z52.5.M52R34   1991
    652.5'.536--dc20
                                                            91-9708
                                                            CIP

Printed and bound in the United States of America.

2 3 4 5 6 7 8 9   AGAG   6 5 4 3 2 1

Distributed to the book trade in Canada by Macmillan of Canada, a division
of Canada Publishing Corporation.

Distributed to the book trade outside the United States and Canada by Penguin Books Ltd.

Penguin Books Ltd., Harmondsworth, Middlesex, England
Penguin Books Australia Ltd., Ringwood, Victoria, Australia
Penguin Books N.Z. Ltd., 182–190 Wairau Road, Auckland 10, New Zealand

British Cataloging-in-Publication Data available.

Project Editor: Mary Renaud
Technical Editors: William Teel, Randy Thompson
Acquisitions Editor: Marjorie Schlaikjer

To my husband,
Haluk Ozdemir

Contents

Introduction

A Word Before Getting Started

Word processing is the most widely used application for personal computers. You might think that you don't have time to stop and learn how to use the latest word-processing technology. This book shows you how to use Microsoft Word—a powerful yet friendly word-processing program—without investing a lot of time and effort. Whether you've never touched a computer before or are an old hand at operating one, this book will help you get started with Word as quickly as possible.

THE LATEST WORD

Today's software is becoming friendlier and more visual. An industry standard for operating personal computers is emerging: Among the leading software applications, you'll now find more consistency in how you interact with programs, how commands are named, how the keyboard is used, and how information and text are displayed and manipulated. The latest version of Microsoft Word, version 5.5, clearly embraces that standard to give you a word processor for DOS systems that looks and feels like software found in the Windows, OS/2, and Macintosh environments. The skills you learn with Word 5.5 can be used with other software applications and in other operating system environments.

If you have an earlier version of Word, it's well worth the cost to replace it with an updated copy. Word 5.5 is more in tune with the way most people work and is more responsive to specific needs. The new, more graphical interface of Word 5.5 provides more visual prompts and feedback to keep you on track. Graphical interfaces have been proven to boost productivity and to lower frustration and fatigue. With the new look of drop-down menus and dialog boxes comes better organization of command groups, which makes learning, remembering, and using the program easier and faster. Because everything is within easy reach, you are more likely to use advanced capabilities of the program that were harder to access in earlier versions.

HOW THIS BOOK IS ORGANIZED

This book is designed to help you quickly find the information you need. The first part of the book, "A Short Course in Word," screens out all but the most essential features so that you can begin using Word right away. If you have minimal word-processing needs, you might not need to read any further. If you expect more from a word processor, Part I prepares you for the more sophisticated tools presented in the second and third parts of the book, "Advanced Word" and "Super Word."

Part I: A Short Course in Word

The first four chapters ease you into Word. In Chapter 1, you learn what word processing is, why Microsoft Word stands out among other word-processing programs, and what kind of equipment you need to work with Word. To demonstrate how easy it is to start working with Microsoft Word, the next three chapters walk you through the steps of processing a document from start to finish. In Chapters 2, 3, and 4, you learn how to create, revise, store, retrieve, and print a document. When you finish reading Part I, you'll be ready to put Word to work for you.

Part II: Advanced Word

After you're comfortable with the basics of the program, Part II gently introduces you to the extra speed and power that Microsoft Word offers. Chapter 5 provides an overview of Word's menus (lists of commands) and teaches you how to choose commands from a menu and respond to dialog boxes.

Chapters 6 through 12 explain how to use advanced commands and special techniques to revise documents, find and replace text, format documents, manage files, and print documents with more control over what is printed and how it is printed. Throughout this book, you'll find step-by-step explanations of how to use each key feature of Word.

Part III: Super Word

The third part of the book introduces you to the special features and capabilities that make Microsoft Word an exceptional word processor. You learn about merge printing, the spelling checker, the built-in thesaurus, automatic hyphenation, document retrieval, macros, and style sheets. With these features, you'll be able to reduce complicated or time-consuming tasks that require many keystrokes to simple tasks that require few keystrokes.

Part IV: Appendixes

In the fourth part of this book, you'll find six appendixes for quick reference when you need help with using DOS (the disk operating system), setting up Word to fit your computer system, or remembering which commands, keys, or mouse maneuvers to use for a particular task.

Finally, at the end of the book, a comprehensive index quickly directs you to the correct page when you want help with any of Word's features.

And now, let's learn Word.

Part I

A Short Course in Word

Chapter 1

Getting Acquainted

With Microsoft Word, you can use your computer to prepare any kind of document, from memos and letters to reports, brochures, and even entire books. When you use a computer to prepare a document, you type on a keyboard much like the keyboard of a typewriter, but your words appear on a TV–like screen instead of on paper. As you type, a blinking underscore called a cursor (or insertion point) marks your place in the document on the screen. Whenever you like, you can tell the computer to print what you've typed, but typing on the keyboard and printing on paper are separate events.

WHY USE A WORD PROCESSOR INSTEAD OF A TYPEWRITER?

A word processor is much more forgiving than a typewriter. You can review and easily change what you type *before* you print it on paper. You can move words or large sections of text from one place to another. Your paper copy of a document is always free from erasures, strips of correction tape, and blotches of white-out.

Typing a document on a word processor is easier than typing it on a typewriter. For example, you don't need to worry about typing beyond the edge of the paper. When it's time to start a new line or a new page, a word processor automatically starts it for you, while you continue typing.

You can change the appearance of a document, reshaping it to fit your needs or tastes, as easily as you can change the words. You can reset the margins, adjust the spacing between lines, or justify the text (to make the right edge as straight as the left). You can also choose special printing effects, such as boldface or underlined text.

Compared to what a typewriter can do, these word-processing features are marvels. Today, however, they are commonplace marvels. You can expect to get them with any reasonably good word-processing program.

WHAT MAKES WORD SPECIAL?

Microsoft Word is an extremely versatile and powerful word-processing program. It offers much more than most word processors. Word's friendliness and intuitive design make it easy to learn and easy to use. Its formatting abilities and graphics integration power approach those of desktop publishing programs.

The Visual Interface: A Friendly Face

A program's interface refers to the contact points it creates between you and the computer. How does it ask you for information? How do you tell it what to do? How does it display what you've done? How forgiving is it?

Word 5.5 presents you with an attractive, clean, uncluttered screen. Like a good work buddy, it provides plenty of clues and help when needed, leads you through tasks, gives you lists of choices, uses graphics and familiar words, tries to follow your thinking and way of working, lets you see what your documents look like before you print them, and helps you avoid and recover from mistakes.

Flexibility

Whatever the task at hand, Word offers you a variety of ways to accomplish it. Word strives to accommodate your preferences and work habits rather than forcing you to adapt to it. More than any other word processor, Word lets you control what you see, what you do, and how you do it.

You can give instructions to Word by choosing commands in plain English from lists called menus that drop down on the screen. Or, instead of using menus, you can use function keys or other special-purpose keys to perform word-processing tasks. You can even decide what each special-purpose key will do if you don't like Word's key assignments. If you purchase a mouse—a hand-held pointing device—you can do most of your work by pointing to what you want and clicking a mouse button.

Powerful Editing

Whether you use the keyboard, the menus, or the mouse to make changes to a document, Word safeguards your work each step of the way by making text difficult to lose and easy to recover. An Undo command lets you undo most changes, not only deletions.

Commands that let you move quickly to any part of a document make it easy to work with long documents. You can even look at different parts of the same document at the same time. You can view as many as nine documents in separate windows simultaneously, and you can easily move text from one document to another.

Instead of retyping frequently used names, phrases, or paragraphs, put them in a special storage area called a glossary. Then you can copy these pieces of text at any time, to insert in any document.

Are you a poor speller? Want some help in finding typing errors? With Word's built-in Spell program, you can check a single word or an entire document for spelling errors and typos without leaving the Word program. Unsure where to hyphenate a word? Let Word do it for you. It will hyphenate a single word or all the words in a document that need to be hyphenated. Trying to think of a better word choice? Use the built-in thesaurus to find a good alternative.

Word can search through an entire document for anything you want to find, and it can replace each occurrence with something else. Every imaginable safeguard is built into Word's search-and-replace feature to help you avoid finding or replacing the wrong text. In addition to searching for text, you can search for and replace formatting instructions or search for entire documents.

Exceptional Formatting

Word is unmatched in the formatting features it offers. Your control over the appearance of a printed document is limited more by the capabilities of your printer than by the capabilities of Word. Although all formatting parameters have been conveniently preset, you can view the settings and easily change them. As soon as you make a formatting change, you see the results on the screen. You're free to experiment with different formats, polishing the appearance of a document before you print it.

Some formatting features make typing easier. If you type a word and then decide you want it to appear in uppercase (capital) letters, you can reformat the word without retyping it. You can automatically indent the first line of each paragraph in a document without once pressing the Tab key, or you can insert a blank line after each paragraph with a single formatting command.

Word lets you tap your printer's power to produce characters from different fonts (styles) and of different sizes. Special effects such as boldface text, underlining, italics, double underlining, small capitals, strikethroughs, subscripts, and superscripts are within easy reach.

You can tell Word to add headings in the top and bottom margins of each printed page. Word allows you to specify different headings for alternate pages and to control the exact positions of both headings and page numbers. Word makes it easy to add footnotes and annotations to a document, and it keeps track of them for you.

You can set tabs anywhere and control how text is aligned in the columns of a table. For example, you can ask Word to line up the decimal points in a column of numbers or to center the column headings in a table. Need to rearrange a table? You can delete, move, or copy entire columns.

To reduce time spent formatting documents, you can record and store often-used formats in style sheets and then apply the styles to any document.

Merge Printing

Word's Print Merge feature makes mass mailings easy and lets you control what goes in each letter. If you want to send the same (or a similar) letter to a number of people, simply type the letter once. Then give Word a mailing list of names and addresses, and it produces a letter for each person on the list.

Document Retrieval

Word doesn't limit you to an eight-character filename for identifying and finding files. You can append a summary sheet to each document, which contains information such as the name of the person who wrote or prepared the document, the creation date, the revision date, and keywords and comments that identify the document. Then you can search for the document based on this information or on text in the document itself.

Macros

With macros, complicated tasks can be reduced to a few keystrokes. Word lets you record any sequence of keystrokes or commands that you use repeatedly. When you need to repeat the task they perform, you can play back the entire sequence by pressing a few keys.

Help Is Never Far Away

If you forget how to do something, you can get help without leaving the computer. When help is summoned, Word displays instructions, reminders, and explanations about almost every aspect of itself. You can get help with a specific command or task when you need it. And you can ask for a tutorial that guides you through each step as you try out a feature.

The List Goes On

The list of features seems endless: line and box drawing; math and sorting capabilities; indexing; outlining; inserting pictures made by other programs; wrapping text around pictures and special paragraphs; linking Word with spreadsheets and other programs. And the makers of Word aren't done yet. Microsoft is committed to keeping Word a state-of-the-art word processor. As computing power continues to grow, word-processing power with Word will grow too.

WHAT DO YOU NEED TO USE WORD?

To use Word, you need a computer with a hard disk and one floppy-disk drive or with a minimum of two floppy-disk drives. You must also have a keyboard, a display unit, a printer, disk operating system software, and several blank disks for storing documents.

The computer must be a member of the IBM family of personal computers, or it must be an IBM compatible (a computer that works like an IBM personal computer). Once you have Word up and running on one of these computers, Word manages the computer for you. You don't need to know how a computer works in order to use Word, but it's helpful to have a general understanding of what the various components do and the role each plays in word processing.

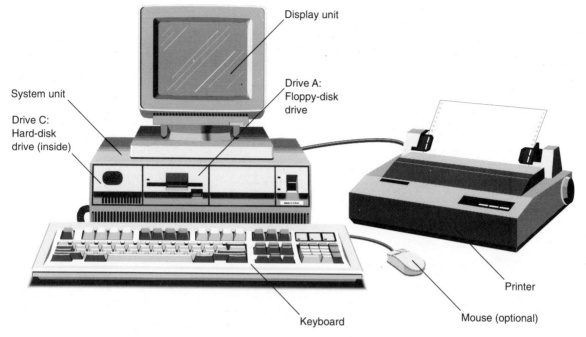

Figure 1-1. *A complete personal-computer system.*

Figure 1-1 shows a complete personal-computer system. Your computer might not look exactly like the one pictured here, but the basic components will be the same.

The Keyboard and the Mouse

You talk to your computer through the *keyboard* or the *mouse*. By pressing keys or maneuvering the mouse, you can tell the computer when to start and stop the Word program, what words you want processed, and how you want them processed. The keyboard comes with the computer; the mouse is an optional device that is purchased separately.

The mouse, which fits neatly under the hand, lets you give most commands without using the keyboard. As you slide the mouse around your desktop, a pointer moves in a similar fashion around the screen. The text, icon, or command you point to determines the instruction you give to the computer when you press a button on top of the mouse.

The mouse needs a clean, dry surface to glide over. If the rotating ball on the underside of the mouse gets clogged with desktop debris, it stops rotating freely. If this happens, refer to the *Microsoft Mouse User's Guide* for instructions on removing and cleaning the ball.

The Display Unit

What you type on the keyboard shows up on the *display unit*. Also called a monitor, CRT (cathode-ray tube), VDU (visual display unit), or screen, the display unit lets you see your words before you commit them to paper.

The display unit is connected to a *video adapter card,* which is inserted in a slot in the computer. A video adapter is a printed-circuit board that interprets your computer's electronic signals for your display unit. The quality and the graphics capabilities of the display depend on both the type of monitor and the type of video adapter attached to it. The *Getting Started* booklet that comes with Word contains a list of possible combinations, with specific brand names identified.

The various combinations of display units and video adapter cards fall into two main categories: those that have graphics capabilities and those that don't. If you have a graphics monitor and adapter, you'll be able to use Word in either graphics mode or text mode. In *graphics mode,* you are treated to some special graphics that Word uses to illustrate what the mouse is doing. Special printing effects, such as italics and small caps, are displayed on the screen. In *text mode,* Word's operating speed increases, but you forfeit the special graphics capabilities of the monitor. With Word, you can easily switch from one mode to the other.

Some display units are automatically turned on when you turn on the computer; others must be switched on separately. You'll spend many hours looking at the display unit, so find the controls and adjust the brightness and contrast to comfortable levels.

The Printer

The *printer* delivers the final product—a paper copy of your document. Printers come in two basic varieties: serial and parallel. Word needs to know which kind you have. They differ in how they receive signals from the computer, but in terms of word-processing capabilities, parallel and serial printers perform equally well.

Printers also differ in how they put images on paper. *Impact printers,* the most common and economical, employ mechanisms that strike the paper through an inked ribbon. Dot-matrix and formed-character printers are impact printers. *Dot-matrix printers* form characters out of dots. Individual pins in the print head strike the paper to print dots in various patterns. Dot-matrix printers are usually faster and less expensive than formed-character printers, but their print quality is generally not as good. *Formed-character printers,* like typewriters, strike the paper with preformed characters on a printing element, usually a daisy wheel or a thimble. A *daisy wheel* is a round, flat disk with spokes radiating from its center. At the end of each spoke is a character. A *thimble* is a cup-shaped printing element similar to a daisy wheel.

Among *nonimpact printers,* laser printers and ink-jet printers are becoming increasingly popular. Much more expensive than dot-matrix or formed-character printers, they combine the best features of those two types: speed and quality of printing. *Laser printers* use light beams to produce images on paper, much as photocopiers do. *Ink-jet printers* print characters by spraying dots of ink onto the paper through a print head. Both laser printers and ink-jet printers offer quiet operation and a wide selection of fonts, styles, and sizes. With them, you can produce text that approaches typeset quality.

Your printer plays a key role in the word-processing cycle. Get to know it well by reading the manual that comes with it.

The Computer Itself

At the center of a computer system is the computer itself. In most personal computers, the vital electronic parts that make the computer seem intelligent are housed in a flat case called the *system unit.* Within the system unit are the CPU (*central processing unit*) and the *memory.* The CPU enables the computer to interpret and follow instructions, carry out commands, perform calculations, and manipulate text. But the CPU can handle only one instruction or a small amount of information at a time. So the memory helps out by storing the instructions and information that either are waiting in line to be processed or have already been processed.

What you type on the keyboard goes to the computer's memory, where the CPU can access it. From the memory, it can be sent to the display unit, to the printer, or to permanent storage on a disk.

The part of the memory that is available to you is called RAM (*random access memory*). Its size is measured in bytes; 1 byte is the amount of storage needed to hold one character. RAM is a temporary storage place. Each time you turn off the power, the contents of RAM disappear. If you want to keep what you've typed, you must remember to store your work on a disk before you turn off the power.

The amount of memory in your computer depends on how much memory you originally purchased or have added to your computer. To use Word version 5.5, you need at least 384 kilobytes (384 KB) of RAM; 512 KB are recommended. (1 KB = 1024 bytes.)

The Disks and Their Drives

You create or edit a document in the computer's temporary memory and then copy it onto a disk, where it can be stored permanently. Transferring a copy of a document from memory to a disk is called *saving* the document. Transferring a copy of a document from a disk back to memory is called *opening* (or *loading*) the document.

Programs are also stored on disks and are usually purchased on disks. Before you can use a program, a copy of it must be loaded into the computer's memory. A *program* is a set of instructions that tell the computer how to perform specific tasks. The Microsoft Word program tells the computer how to process the words you type.

Documents and programs are stored in *files* on a disk, much as papers are organized in folders in a filing cabinet. Each file is given a name and usually holds one document, one program, or one section of a large program. The length of a file and the number of files you can store on a disk are limited primarily by how much space is available on the disk. The total amount of space available depends on the type of disk.

Two types of disks can be used with personal computers: *floppy* (or flexible) *disks,* and *hard* (or fixed) *disks*. Both types have a magnetic recording surface on which information can be recorded as well as erased. Floppy disks are enclosed in covers and are either 5¼ inches or 3½ inches in diameter. (See Figure 1-2 on the following page.) Hard disks, housed in a rigid metal structure and permanently fixed in place inside the system unit, have much higher storage capacities and are much faster than floppy disks.

The standard 5¼-inch floppy disk is double sided (has a recording surface on both sides) and double density (holds twice as much information as older-style disks). It holds about 360,000 characters (360 KB). Higher-capacity floppy disks can hold much more—5¼-inch high-density disks, for example, hold 1.2 million characters (1.2 megabytes, or 1.2 MB). The 3½-inch floppy disks can hold either 720 KB or 1.44 MB. Most hard disks currently being sold hold from 40 to 100 MB.

The type of disk you need depends on the type of disk drive you have. A *disk drive* is the device that writes information on disks and reads information from them. Disk drives are identified by letters. The top or left-hand floppy-disk drive on a two-drive system is usually called drive A, and the second floppy-disk drive is called drive B. If you have only one floppy-disk drive, it is both drive A and drive B. Drive C refers to a hard disk.

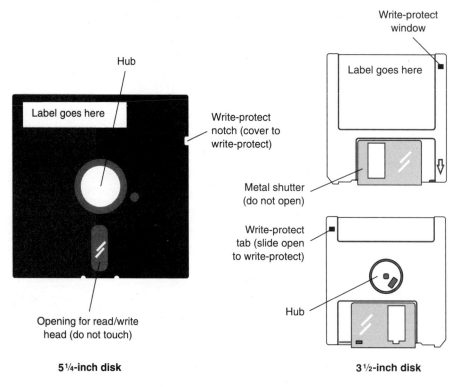

Figure 1-2. *A 5¼-inch floppy disk and a 3½-inch floppy disk.*

Because the Word program has grown to include so many features, operating Word with two standard (360-KB) 5¼-inch floppy-disk drives is becoming impractical. To take full advantage of Word's features and to avoid awkward disk switching, you need to use the higher-capacity floppy disks or a hard disk.

Handling floppy disks

All disks must be protected from temperature extremes, moisture, smoke, and magnetic fields. Floppy disks that are not encased in a rigid sleeve need extra care. Do not bend them, press them, or touch their exposed surfaces. Keep their dust jackets on when the disks are not in use. Use a soft felt-tip pen when writing on their labels.

You can erase what's recorded on a disk, and you can write over a previous recording. If you want to prevent files stored on a floppy disk from being accidentally erased or changed, it's a good idea to *write-protect* the disk. The computer can read information from a write-protected disk but cannot write on the disk. To write-protect a 5¼-inch disk, put a write-protect tab or a piece of opaque tape over the write-protect notch found on the side of the disk. To write-protect a 3½-inch disk, slide the tab in the write-protect window until the window is open. (See Figure 1-2.)

A 5¼-inch floppy-disk drive has a *door* or a *latch* that must be opened before you insert the disk and closed afterward. A light on the disk drive indicates when it's in use. If you remove a disk when the light is on, you can damage the disk and lose the information stored on it. To insert a 5¼-inch disk in a disk drive, gently hold the disk by its edge and insert it, label side up, with the long oval access slot pointing toward the rear of the drive and the write-protect notch on the left, as shown in Figure 1-3 on the following page. (With a vertical drive, insert the disk with the label facing left and the write-protect notch on the bottom.) Slide the disk all the way into the drive, and then close the door.

A 3½-inch disk will go in only one way. Hold the disk with the circular hub facing down and the arrow stamped on the disk pointing toward the drive (as illustrated in Figure 1-4 on the next page). Push the disk into the drive until it clicks into place. To remove the disk, press the eject button on the drive.

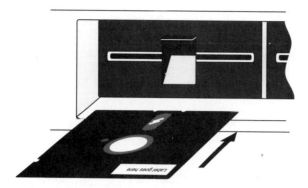

Figure 1-3. *Inserting a 5¼-inch floppy disk.*

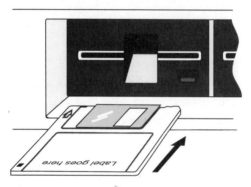

Figure 1-4. *Inserting a 3½-inch floppy disk.*

The Disk Operating System

When you purchase a computer system, you also purchase disk operating system software. If your computer has a hard disk, the disk operating system needs to be installed on the hard disk. The documentation that comes with the operating system tells you how to do this, but your computer dealer will usually install it for you.

Referred to as DOS (pronounced ''doss''), the disk operating system is a complex set of instructions that tell the computer how to perform basic tasks: how to read other programs found on disks, how to organize disk space, and how to work cooperatively with all the other components of the system—including you. In short, DOS makes your computer operable. Before you can start Word, you must start DOS. Microsoft Word must be run with version

2.11 or later of MS-DOS, the Microsoft version of DOS. (To find out what version you have, start DOS, type *ver*, and press the Enter key.)

In addition to making your computer operable, DOS comes with a tool kit of commands and small programs that are helpful in word processing. If you're not familiar with DOS, read Appendix A to learn about the most useful DOS commands. If you have a hard disk or the higher-capacity floppy disks, be sure to learn the directory and path commands that help you organize and access your storage space.

The Word Package

When you open the Word package, you'll find a handful of floppy disks, in addition to an array of documentation. You won't be juggling all of these disks every day. Several of them are used only to set up Word to fit your system and to teach you how to use the Word program. After you set up your copy of the Word program and learn how to use it, you need only one or two Word program disks to run Word and do most of your work. If you have a hard disk, everything you need can probably be put on your hard disk.

Appendix B contains a description of each disk you receive with the Microsoft Word 5.5 package.

BEFORE YOU USE WORD

Before you use Word, be sure to make backup copies of the disks in the Word package. No matter how careful you are in handling floppy disks, accidents do happen. With daily use over a long period of time, a disk becomes worn and therefore less reliable. Protect your software by copying the contents of each disk onto a second disk and storing the originals where they won't be damaged. To make backup copies of Word disks, use the DOS command DISKCOPY, described in Appendix A.

After you make backup copies of Word, you need to run the Setup program. This program enables Word to make the best use of your equipment. In most cases, you'll use the Setup program only once—before you use Word for the first time. If your copy of Word has not been set up for your system, turn to Appendix B to find out what setup tasks are necessary. Once these initial preparations are out of the way, you'll find that starting Word is a simple ceremony and that using Word requires minimal disk handling.

Chapter 2

Starting Word and Creating a Document

After you've made backup copies of the Word disks and run the Setup program, you're ready to start using Word. In this chapter, you learn how to start the Word program and how to create a document.

HOW TO START WORD

The Setup program creates a working copy of the Word program and, if necessary, modifies your working copy of DOS. Always use these working copies to start DOS and then Word.

For those who have a computer system with a hard disk, this discussion assumes that both DOS and Word have been installed on your hard disk in drive C. The copy of DOS and the copy of Word that reside on your hard disk are your working copies.

Starting DOS

Before you can start Word, you must first start DOS. Ordinarily, if DOS is already up and running, you don't need to restart it. But if DOS was not started with your *working copy* (as modified by Word's Setup program), you must restart DOS. In particular, the first time you use Word after running the Setup program, you must restart DOS so that the computer will be notified of any changes made to DOS files during setup.

To start DOS:

1. If you have a floppy-disk system and if you do not have DOS on your working copy of the Word Program (Startup Word) disk, put your *working copy* of the DOS disk in drive A. (This disk was altered during setup.) If you do have DOS on your Word Program (Startup Word) disk, insert that disk in drive A. (Recall that drive A is the left-hand or top drive of a two-drive system.)

   If you have a hard-disk system, leave drive A empty with the door open.

2. If your computer is off, turn it on. If your computer is already on, restart it by holding down the Control (Ctrl) and Alternate (Alt) keys as you press the Delete (Del) key.

3. If the current date displayed by DOS is correct, press the Enter (↵) key to confirm it. If the date needs to be changed, type the correct date and then press the Enter key. Use hyphens or slashes to separate parts of the date.

4. If the current time displayed is correct, press the Enter key to confirm it. If the time needs to be changed, type the correct time and then press the Enter key. Use colons to separate units of time.

When you see the *A>* prompt (on a floppy-disk system) or the *C>* prompt (on a hard-disk system), you know that DOS is running and ready for you to give the command to start Word.

Starting Word on a Floppy-Disk System

To start Word on a two-drive, floppy-disk system after you've started DOS:

1. When you see the *A>* prompt, remove your DOS disk, and insert your working copy of the Word Program (Startup Word) disk in drive A (if it isn't already there). Put a formatted disk for storing documents in drive B. For systems with 360-KB or 720-KB disks, use a document disk that contains a copy of the printer information file created during setup.

2. If you have multiple directories, change to the directory where Word is stored. For example, if you told the Setup program to copy the Word program files to a directory called *word,* type

   cd \word

   and press the Enter key. (As explained in Appendix A, this step isn't necessary if you include the Word program directory in the DOS PATH command within your AUTOEXEC.BAT file.)

3. At the *A>* prompt, type

   word

   and press the Enter key to start Word.

Word prompts you to insert additional disks if necessary. If you see the message *Bad command or file name,* try again. Take care to insert the correct disk and, if you have multiple directories, be sure to type the correct directory name.

 REMINDER: When you give commands and information to DOS or Word, you can type either uppercase or lowercase letters. It's usually easier to type lowercase letters.

Starting Word on a Hard-Disk System

To start Word on a hard-disk system after you've started DOS:

1. When you see the *C>* prompt, change to the directory where Word is stored. For example, if you told the Setup program to copy the Word program files to a directory called *word,* type

   cd \word

   and press the Enter key. (As explained in Appendix A, this step isn't necessary if you include the Word program directory in the DOS PATH command within your AUTOEXEC.BAT file.)

2. When the *C>* prompt reappears, type

   word

   and press the Enter key to start Word.

If you see the message *Bad command or file name,* try again. Be sure to type the correct directory name so that DOS can find the Word program.

What You See After You Start Word

After you start Word, the program introduces itself and draws a box, called a *window,* on the screen:

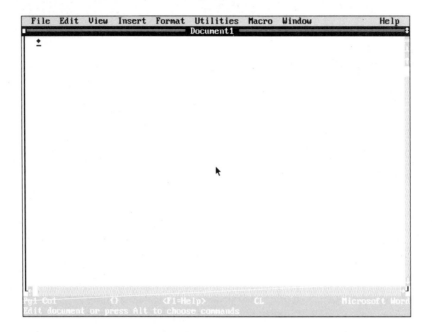

You look through this window to see what you type with the keyboard. When you first start Word, the program displays a blank document in the window and temporarily calls it *Document1,* displaying that title in the top window border. The blinking underscore in the upper left corner of the window is called a *cursor.* It moves along as you type, marking the place where the next typed character will appear. The diamond above the cursor marks the end of the document and is called the *endmark.* When there is no text in the document, the endmark appears directly above the cursor. The lines of text above and below the window remind you what to do, explain your options, tell you where you are, and notify you if something goes wrong.

You'll take a closer look at these symbols and the text above and below the window later on, in Chapter 3. But first you need to know how to create a document.

HOW TO CREATE A DOCUMENT

Because word processing makes it so easy to change a document without retyping it, it's easier to compose while you're typing. You don't need to worry about getting it right the first time because you can polish and refine your words later. You can spend more time creating and less time typing and retyping. Whether you compose as you type or whether you type from prewritten copy, the method for typing a document with Word is the same.

You can start typing as soon as you start the program. Word formats the document as you type it. Margins and tabs have already been set to meet most word-processing needs. If they don't meet your needs, you can change them either before or after you type the document.

You'll learn about formatting alternatives in later chapters. For now, let Word do the formatting for you.

About the Keyboard

Personal-computer keyboards have a lot of special-purpose keys, but you can ignore most of them for now. If you're familiar with a typewriter, you already know all the keys you need to type a document. The keys used to type text are the unshaded keys shown in Figures 2-1 and 2-2. Some of them—the Shift keys, the Caps Lock key, the Tab key, the Spacebar, the Backspace key, and the Enter key—look a bit different or behave differently from similar keys on a typewriter.

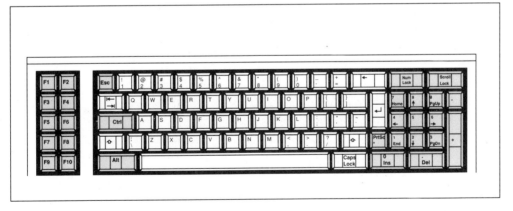

Figure 2-1. *The typing keys as they appear on the 83-key keyboard.*

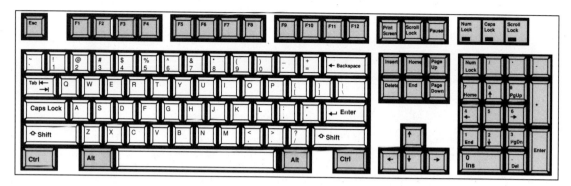

Figure 2-2. *The typing keys as they appear on the 101-key extended keyboard.*

The Shift keys

Although the two Shift keys don't look exactly like the shift keys on a typewriter, they behave the same. Use a Shift key in combination with other keys to type uppercase letters and any symbol or other character shown on the upper half of a key top. (Note that if the Caps Lock key is on, using the Shift key produces *lowercase* letters.)

The Caps Lock key

When you want to type words in all uppercase (capital) letters, press the Caps Lock key so that you don't need to hold down the Shift key. Unlike the shift-lock key on a typewriter, the Caps Lock key affects the letter keys only. Caps Lock is a toggle key: Press it once, and it's turned on. Press it again, and it's turned off.

The Tab key

Use the Tab key as you would on a typewriter to type tables or to type facts and figures arranged in columns. You can also use the Tab key to indent the first line of a paragraph. (In Chapter 9, you'll learn how to have Word automatically indent the first line of each paragraph in a document.)

On a typewriter, the Tab key simply moves the typing element (or carriage) to a fixed position, skipping over any previously typed letters on the way. With Word, you cannot use the Tab key to skip over characters because the Tab key inserts a tab character at the cursor location. A tab character is a special space-making character that can be deleted like any other character.

The Spacebar

Use the Spacebar as you would on a typewriter to add space after words or punctuation. Like the Tab key, the Spacebar cannot be used to skip over previously typed characters as it can on a typewriter. Pressing the Spacebar inserts a space at the cursor location. In Word, a space is a character that can be deleted like any other character.

The Backspace key

Unlike the backspace key on a typewriter, the Backspace key in Word erases characters as you back up over them. It's useful for correcting an error while you're typing, right after you make a mistake.

The Enter key

On an electric typewriter, you press a carriage-return key at the end of each line in order to start a new line. On most computer keyboards, the return key is called the Enter key. When using Word, you do not press the Enter key at the end of each line. Word knows where the right-hand margin is set and automatically starts a new line when you reach that location. (If you press the Enter key at the end of each line, you could end up with some very short lines when you revise what you've typed.)

When you're typing short documents or documents that won't need extensive formatting, it's easiest to use the Enter key as follows:

- Press Enter to end a paragraph. Do not press Enter to end each line in a paragraph.

- Press Enter twice to create a blank line between paragraphs. (In Chapter 9, you'll learn how to have Word automatically insert extra space between paragraphs.)

- Press Enter to end a line at a definite place. For example, when you're typing a table, a poem, or the address in a letter, you want to end each line after a particular word or number, regardless of how far it is from the right-hand margin. (You can also end each line by pressing Enter while holding down the Shift key. This enables you to treat the separate lines of closely related text as a single paragraph, making the text easier to format.)

The Enter key inserts a nonprinting character called a *paragraph mark*, which can be deleted like any other character. (Similarly, the Shift-Enter key combination inserts a *newline mark*.)

The New Page keys

When using a typewriter, have you ever typed off the bottom edge of a sheet of paper? With Word, you don't have to worry about when to start new pages. Just keep typing. When printing your document, Word automatically starts a new page when the current page is filled.

Occasionally, you might want to begin a new page at a particular place, before the current page is filled. For example, if you're typing a letter that includes a list of employee names on a separate page, you'll want to start a new page for the list immediately after the letter ends.

Two keys are used together to start a new page at a specific place: Hold down the Ctrl key while you press the Enter key.

These keys insert a character called a *manual* (or *hard*) *page break,* which appears as a dotted line across the window, showing where the new page starts. The dots of a manual page break are close together, whereas the dots of an *automatic* (or *soft*) *page break* are more widely spaced. You can move the cursor to a manual page break and delete it, copy it, or move it. You cannot move the cursor to an automatic page break.

What You Do

Just start typing. Try out Word by typing the letter shown in Figure 2-3 on the following page. Remember these guidelines:

- Don't press Enter at the end of each line in a paragraph. Keep typing until you get to the end of the paragraph.

- To create a blank line between paragraphs, press Enter twice.

- When you get to the bottom of the screen, keep typing. Word moves your text up on the screen so that you always see what you are currently typing.

- No loitering is allowed on any of the keys when you're typing. If you hold down a key, it repeats itself until you release it.

- If you make any errors, try using the Backspace key to correct a few of them. But save some errors to correct later.

In the next chapter, you'll learn how to correct mistakes and revise the letter you've just typed. If you want to take a break now before you start editing the letter, skip to Chapter 4 to learn how to save your document, quit Word, and start again later.

August 18, 1990

Mallory Steiger
Microsoft Press
One Microsoft Way
Redmond, WA 98052-6399

Dear Mallory,

I took a preliminary look at Word 5.5, and I'm sending some
ideas about what it will take to revise the Learn Word Now
book.

Overall Organization: Can stay the same.

Organization Within Chapters: Some restructuring will be
required to reflect new menu organization. Chapter 5 needs a
complete rewrite.

How-To Details: Need to be changed throughout the book.

Command-Related Terminology: Changes throughout. For
example, command fields become dialog boxes.

Command Names: Most change. For example, Delete becomes Edit
Cut.

Screen Terminology: New concepts and some changes.

In general, I hope to stay away from the trend toward mega-
books in this industry. The new screen dumps will require
more space because of the new drop-down menus, dialog boxes,
and message boxes. To compensate for the additional space
they require, I plan to streamline the text to reflect the
improved ease of use of the program. Some text in the
original book can be cut because of improvements in the
program.

Sincerely,

Janet Rampa

Figure 2-3. *A sample letter.*

Chapter 3

Revising a Document

So far, nothing you've done is very different from typing on a typewriter. Not having to press a return key at the end of each line saves time and effort, but the real value of word processing lies in being able to make changes to a document without retyping it. Before word processing, the only way to revise a document without retyping it was to pick up your scissors and cut out the parts you wanted to delete or move. You saved any scraps of paper that you could use elsewhere. When you wanted to insert a scrap of text, you pasted, glued, or taped it in place and hoped that your cut lines wouldn't show on the photocopy.

Electronic cut-and-paste is a lot easier, and the seams never show. In this chapter, you learn how to correct errors, revise wording, move and copy text, add new text, and make some pleasing formatting changes by using the keyboard, the mouse, or a combination of both. Before you start editing, let's take a closer look at the Microsoft Word editing screen.

THE EDITING SCREEN

The basic editing screen, shown on the following page, includes the window in which the text you type appears, the menu bar above the window, the title bar in the top window border, the status bar below the window, and the message bar below that.

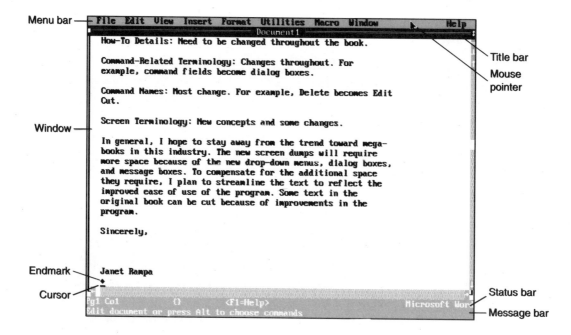

Menu bar — Title bar
Mouse pointer

How-To Details: Need to be changed throughout the book.

Command-Related Terminology: Changes throughout. For example, command fields become dialog boxes.

Command Names: Most change. For example, Delete becomes Edit Cut.

Screen Terminology: New concepts and some changes.

Window —

In general, I hope to stay away from the trend toward mega-books in this industry. The new screen dumps will require more space because of the new drop-down menus, dialog boxes, and message boxes. To compensate for the additional space they require, I plan to streamline the text to reflect the improved ease of use of the program. Some text in the original book can be cut because of improvements in the program.

Sincerely,

Endmark —
Janet Rampa

Cursor —

Status bar
Message bar

Pg1 Co1   {}   <F1=Help>   Microsoft Wor
Edit document or press Alt to choose commands

The Window

In addition to the text you type, the window displays these symbols:

— The *cursor* is a blinking underscore that marks the spot where the next character you type will appear. You can move the cursor anywhere in a document, and you can extend the cursor to become a block of light that highlights what you want to change.

▶ *or* ▮ If you have a mouse installed, you also see a *mouse pointer*. The shape of the mouse pointer depends on your system's graphics capability. When you start Word, the mouse pointer is either an arrow pointing up and to the left or a bright rectangle.

◆ The *endmark* is a diamond-shaped symbol that marks the end of your document. When you start Word, or when the cursor is at the end of a document, the endmark is above the cursor: ♦

The corners and borders of the window, as well as the column of space between the left border and your text, are sensitive places for the mouse. The corners and borders contain a number of symbols called *icons*. You can point to these places or icons with the mouse pointer to perform a variety of tasks. For example, the up and down arrows in the right window border are icons that allow you to scroll up and down to see more of a long document. Until you learn what all the icons and special tasks are, avoid pressing the mouse button when the mouse pointer is on an icon, in a corner, in a border, or in the left margin.

The Menu Bar

Commands, which are tools used to perform word-processing tasks, are listed on menus. The *menu bar* at the top of the screen lists the names of menus.

```
File  Edit  View  Insert  Format  Utilities  Macro  Window          Help
```

When you choose a menu name, that menu drops down to reveal a list of related commands. For example, choosing the Format menu leads to a list of the commands that help you change the appearance of a document.

The Title Bar

The *title bar* tells you the name of the document you see in the window. If you haven't saved the document and given it a filename yet, Word assigns it a temporary name such as *Document1*.

```
Document1
```

The Message Bar

The *message bar* at the bottom of the screen tells you what Word is doing (saving, printing, searching, and so on), reminds you what to do (press the Alt key to choose a command, for example), or briefly describes what tasks can be done with the menu or command you've chosen.

```
Edit document or press Alt to choose commands
```

The Status Bar

The *status bar,* the line above the message bar, offers assorted information about the document you're working on and what you're doing.

The status bar shown here provides this information:

Pg1 Co7

The *page and column indicator* tells you the number of the page and the number of the column in which the cursor is currently located. (By using the View Preferences command, you can tell Word to include the line number in the status bar.)

{las..ece}

The last piece of text you deleted or copied is shown in braces and is called the *scrap.* You see only the first few and the last few characters; an ellipsis (...) represents the omitted characters. Nonprinting characters appear as special symbols—for example, a space is shown as a raised dot (·), a tab is shown as an arrow (→), and a paragraph mark as ¶. (For a list of symbols that appear in the scrap, see Appendix F.)

<F1=Help>

Whenever you have a question about how things work, refer to the *Help button.* To get help, press the F1 key, or move the mouse pointer to <F1=Help> and then press and release the mouse button.

SAVE

When the word SAVE appears in the status bar, it's time to do just that—save your work. The *SAVE indicator* warns you when you're running out of working space in memory or on the Word Program disk.

CL

If you turn on a *toggle key,* the key's abbreviation (such as CL for the Caps Lock key) appears as a reminder that the key is on. (See Appendix D for a complete list of toggle keys and commands and their abbreviations.)

THE EDITING KEYS

Even if you plan to use the mouse for most of your editing, familiarize yourself with the editing keys so that if you accidentally press one, you'll understand what's going on. You'll find most of the keys you need to edit a document on the sides and top of the keyboard. They are the unshaded keys in Figure 3-1 (which shows the 83-key keyboard) and in Figure 3-2 (which shows the 101-key keyboard). In this book, most references to keys are based on the 101-key extended keyboard, but the differences between individual keys on the two keyboards are minor.

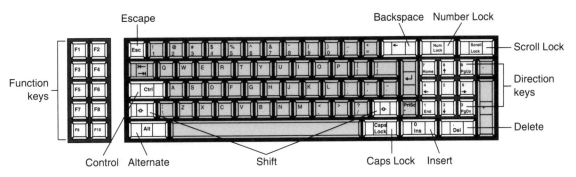

Figure 3-1. *The editing keys on the 83-key keyboard.*

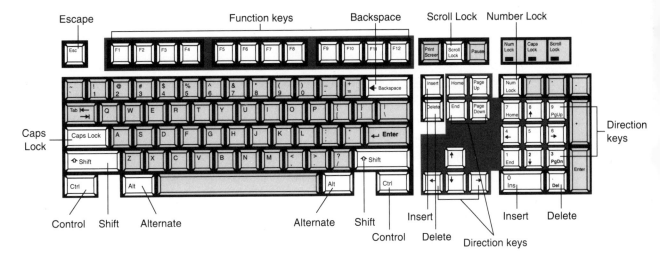

Figure 3-2. *The editing keys on the 101-key extended keyboard.*

The Function Keys

On the left side of the 83-key keyboard is a block of 10 *function keys,* labeled F1 to F10. The 101-key extended keyboard has a row of 12 function keys at the top of the keyboard. Each of these keys has more than one function. Just as you can get a different result from a letter key by holding down the Shift key as you press the letter key, you can also shift a function key to perform a different task. You can alter the purpose of a function key with the Control (Ctrl) key or the Alternate (Alt) key as well as with the Shift key.

The Shift, Control, and Alternate Keys

When coupled with other keys, the Shift key, the Control key, and the Alternate key change the behavior of the other keys. The Control key and the Alternate key can be used exactly like the Shift key: Press Ctrl or Alt first, and hold it down while you press the second key.

When using the Alternate key in combinations, take care not to release it until you press the second key. Pressing and releasing the Alternate key alone takes you to and from the menu bar at the top of the screen, where you can then choose a menu by typing the letter that is highlighted in the menu name. If you accidentally press and release the Alternate key, press it again or press the Escape (Esc) key to leave the menu bar so that you can resume typing.

 KEYBOARD TERMINOLOGY: The instruction Press Alt, E, S *means press and release the Alt key, then press and release the letter E key, and then press and release the letter S key. Press them in the order given, as rapidly or slowly as you like. The instruction* Press Alt-F2 *means press and hold down the Alt key, and then press the F2 function key while you continue to hold down the Alt key.*

The Direction Keys

On the right side of your keyboard are number keys, arranged as they appear on a 10-key adding machine. The keys on this number (or numeric) keypad are great for typing numbers when you're typing more numbers than words.

But their primary role is to help you edit. They are called *direction keys* because the arrows and words on the key tops (↑, ↓, ←, →, PgUp, PgDn, Home, and End) indicate the direction in which these keys move the cursor or scroll the text. The extended keyboard includes an extra set of direction keys, which is closer to the letter keys and easier to use.

The direction keys can be altered with the Shift key, the Control key, the Number Lock (Num Lock) key, or the Scroll Lock key to perform different tasks. When you combine the Shift key with one of the direction keys, the cursor not only moves in the indicated direction but also highlights everything it passes over. Using the Control key amplifies the effect of a direction key, allowing you to move through the text farther and faster. The Number Lock key allows you to type numbers with the direction keys in the number keypad. The Scroll Lock key lets you use the cursor-moving keys to flip through a document so that you can view all parts of it. As explained in the next section, the Number Lock key and the Scroll Lock key are toggle keys and are used like the Caps Lock key.

The Toggle Keys

The Number Lock, Scroll Lock, Caps Lock, and Insert keys are called *toggle keys* because they alternate between turning a function on and turning it off, the way a light switch does. Press a toggle key once to turn a function on, and press it again to turn the function off.

Toggle keys usually change the behavior of other keys. Caps Lock, for example, turns all the letters you type into uppercase letters. And the Insert key switches between *overtype mode* (in which you type new text directly over old text) and *insert mode* (in which old text moves over to make room for newly typed text). It's easy to forget to turn toggle keys off. On some computers, you can't tell whether a toggle key is on or off until you press one of the keys it affects. Word helps you by displaying an abbreviation in the status bar for any toggle key that is on—for example, NL for Number Lock. Some keyboards have indicator lights to remind you that a Caps Lock, Number Lock, or Scroll Lock key is on.

Later in this book, you'll learn about several other toggle keys. In the meantime, you need to know how to turn off toggle keys in case you accidentally turn one on. If typing or editing keys aren't doing what you think they should, check the status bar for a two-letter abbreviation. If you find an unfamiliar abbreviation in the status bar, look it up in Appendix D to find out which key(s) to press to turn the toggle key off.

The Insert and Delete Keys

Below the number keypad are the Insert (Ins) key and the Delete (Del) key. For convenience, the 101-key extended keyboard has an additional set of Insert and Delete keys to the right of the Backspace key. In addition to being a toggle key for typing over text, the Insert key can be combined with the Shift key or the Control key to move and copy text. The Delete key erases text.

THE MOUSE

Except for adding new text, you can do all your editing with the mouse. It offers greater speed and flexibility, and it's often easier to use than the keyboard. The mouse, shown in Figure 3-3, usually has either one or two buttons on top and a rotating ball underneath. (Word treats a three-button mouse like a two-button mouse, ignoring the middle button.)

Figure 3-3. *A one-button mouse and a two-button mouse.*

What the mouse does depends on where you position the mouse pointer on the screen and on how you use the mouse button—whether you press and release the button once or twice or whether you hold it down and release it later. To move the pointer around on your screen, slide the mouse around on your desktop. You can move the mouse in any direction. If the mouse runs off the edge of your desk before you get where you want to go, pick it up and put it down again—farther from the edge this time. Then continue moving it until you reach your destination.

To tell you which mouse technique to use, the following terms are used in this book. (For a two-button mouse, the term *mouse button* refers to the left mouse button, unless the right button is specified. A two-button mouse allows you to take some shortcuts that aren't available with a one-button mouse.)

Click	Press and release the mouse button. The instruction *Click the down arrow* means point to the down arrow with the mouse pointer and then press and release the mouse button.
Double-click	Click the mouse button twice quickly.
Click both mouse buttons	Click both buttons of a two-button mouse simultaneously.
Drag	Press the mouse button and hold it down while you move the pointer. Then release the mouse button.

In the next sections, you can try out some of these techniques.

COMMAND BASICS

When you start Word, you're in the window, where you can type or revise text. If you press and release the Alternate key, you move to the menu bar, where you can choose a menu by typing the boldface (highlighted) letter from the menu name.

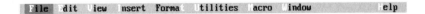

With the mouse, you don't need to press the Alternate key to move to the menu bar. Simply point to the name of the menu you want and click. Try choosing the Edit menu now: Using the keyboard, press the Alt key, and then press E (Alt, E). Using the mouse, point to Edit and click the mouse button.

After you choose a menu name from the menu bar, Word shows you the list of commands on that menu. For example, after choosing the Edit menu, you see a list of commands that can help you revise the text in a document:

Commands are chosen the same way menus are chosen—by typing the bold letter from the command name or by pointing and clicking with the mouse. Some commands are carried out as soon as you choose them, such as the Cut command on the Edit menu, which erases text. But if a command needs extra information from you, it displays a dialog box in which you supply the information needed or choose among available options. To see what a dialog box looks like, choose the Search command from the Edit menu. With the Edit menu in view, press S, or point to Search and click the mouse button. You see this dialog box:

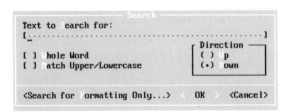

NOTE: To clearly and briefly identify commands, menu names are combined with command names. The Edit Cut command refers to the Cut command on the Edit menu, for example, and the instruction Choose the Edit Search command means first choose Edit from the menu bar and then choose Search from the Edit menu.

Choosing menus and commands and working with dialog boxes are covered in detail in Chapter 5. In the meantime, it's important to know how to cancel a menu or command you've chosen by mistake or out of curiosity. Press the Esc key whenever you want to retreat from the menu bar, a menu, or a dialog box. Press the Esc key now so that you'll be ready to try out the keys and mouse techniques explained in the next sections.

JUST LOOKING

To decide what editing changes you want to make, you must be able to review your work. The letter you typed in Chapter 2, as well as most documents you create, can't be viewed all at once through the window. When you *scroll* through a document, the document rolls by as if it were on one long, continuous sheet of paper—a scroll—instead of on separate sheets. To see those parts of the document that don't fit in the window, you must scroll (move the text) to the part you want to see. Word lets you scroll vertically (up and down) or horizontally (left and right). Horizontal scrolling is used only when your text is wider than the window.

Scrolling Up and Down with the Keyboard

Using scroll keys, you can scroll one line at a time, one windowful at a time, or all the way to the beginning or end of a document in one step.

To scroll one line at a time, press and release the Scroll Lock key to turn it on. (The abbreviation SL appears in the status bar.) Then press the Up or Down direction key to move to another line. When you're finished, don't forget to turn off Scroll Lock by pressing it again.

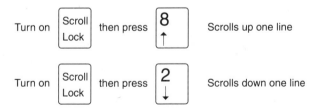

Try out all of the vertical scroll keys to find out how they work. Simply press them to see what they do.

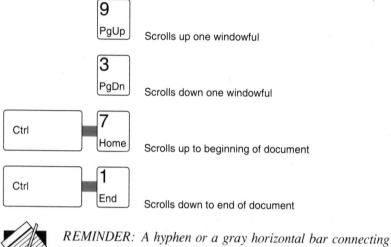

9 PgUp   Scrolls up one windowful

3 PgDn   Scrolls down one windowful

Ctrl — **7** Home   Scrolls up to beginning of document

Ctrl — **1** End   Scrolls down to end of document

 REMINDER: A hyphen or a gray horizontal bar connecting two or more keys indicates that those keys are held down at the same time.

Scrolling Up and Down with the Mouse

To scroll up or down with the mouse, move the mouse pointer to the *vertical scroll bar* (the right window border). Point to the up or down arrow on the scroll bar and click the mouse button to scroll up or down one line. To scroll window by window, place the pointer above the scroll box (to scroll up) or below the scroll box (to scroll down) and click. To scroll continuously, hold down the mouse button instead of clicking it when the mouse pointer is on the scroll bar.

Try scrolling to different places in the letter you typed by clicking the up and down arrows on the scroll bar or by clicking the scroll bar above and below the scroll box, as illustrated on the next page.

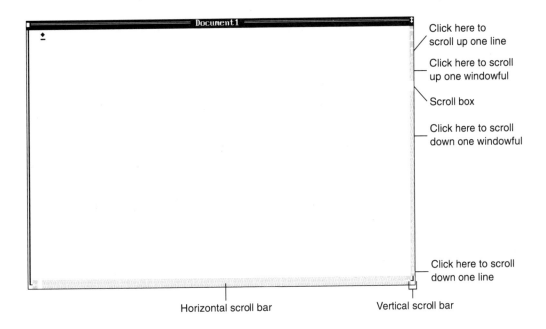

Scrolling Sideways with the Keyboard

Word lets you create documents that are wider than the window. When working with a wide document, you must scroll horizontally to see the part of the document that doesn't fit in the window.

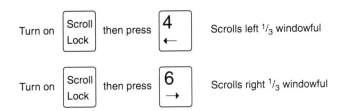

Because the sample letter you typed isn't wider than the screen, you won't be able to try out these keys yet.

Scrolling Sideways with the Mouse

You can also scroll sideways with the mouse when you have a document wider than the window. To scroll sideways, use the *horizontal scroll bar* in the bottom window border in much the same way you use the vertical scroll bar.

Point to the left or right scroll arrow and click to scroll one column to the left or right. To scroll one-third windowful at a time, position the pointer to the left or the right of the scroll box in the horizontal scroll bar and click.

Scrolling to a General Location with the Mouse

The top of the vertical scroll bar represents the beginning of the document, and the bottom of the scroll bar represents the end. (Similarly, the left end of the horizontal scroll bar represents the left border of a wide document, and the right end represents the right border.) The location of the scroll box on a scroll bar tells you what part of a document currently appears in the window. If, for example, the scroll box is in the middle of the vertical scroll bar, you're looking at text from the middle of the document.

By pointing to the scroll box and holding down the mouse button, you can drag the scroll box up and down the vertical scroll bar to quickly scroll to a general location in a document. Drag the scroll box to a position on the scroll bar that represents the part of the document you want to see. For example, if you want to move to the end of the document, drag the scroll box to the bottom of the vertical scroll bar. This feature is especially useful for lengthy documents.

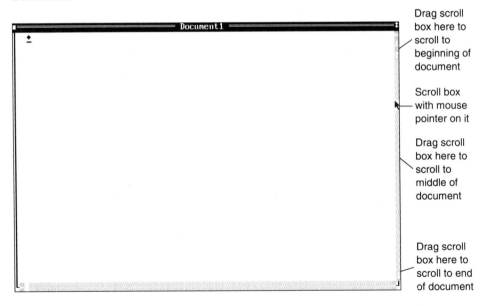

Drag scroll box here to scroll to beginning of document

Scroll box with mouse pointer on it

Drag scroll box here to scroll to middle of document

Drag scroll box here to scroll to end of document

Try dragging the scroll box to various positions on the vertical scroll bar. Although scrolling to a general location isn't really necessary in a short document like the sample letter, you'll nevertheless be able to see that it is a fast and easy way to move directly to the beginning or end of a document.

MOVING THE CURSOR

While you were typing the sample letter, you probably noticed the cursor jumping ahead with every keystroke, moving to where the next character would appear. You can move the cursor to any place in the document where you want to make a change. As you move the cursor, Word scrolls the document if necessary so that the cursor is always in view.

Moving the Cursor with the Keyboard

To move the cursor one character or one line at a time, use the Up, Down, Left, and Right direction keys, which are marked with arrows:

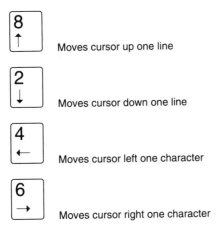

Moves cursor up one line

Moves cursor down one line

Moves cursor left one character

Moves cursor right one character

All keys repeat themselves when held down. Try holding down each direction key to see what happens.

Add the Control key to the direction keys to take bigger steps:

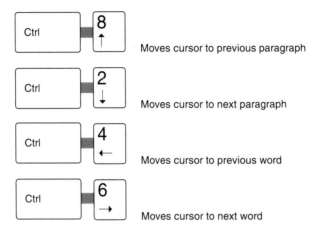

Ctrl 8 ↑   Moves cursor to previous paragraph

Ctrl 2 ↓   Moves cursor to next paragraph

Ctrl 4 ←   Moves cursor to previous word

Ctrl 6 →   Moves cursor to next word

To move to the beginning of a line with one keystroke, press the Home key; to move to the end of a line, press the End key:

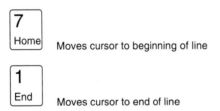

7 Home   Moves cursor to beginning of line

1 End   Moves cursor to end of line

To move quickly to the top or bottom of the window, use the Control key in combination with the PageUp (PgUp) key or the PageDown (PgDn) key:

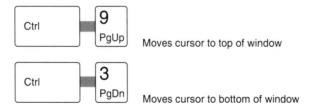

Ctrl 9 PgUp   Moves cursor to top of window

Ctrl 3 PgDn   Moves cursor to bottom of window

To move all the way to the beginning or the end of the document, use the Control key in combination with the Home key or the End key:

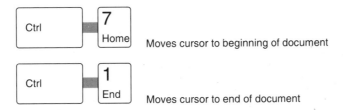

Moves cursor to beginning of document

Moves cursor to end of document

Test-drive the cursor-moving keys until you feel comfortable steering your way around a document. Don't be too concerned if you can't remember all the ways to move the cursor. The Up, Down, Left, and Right direction keys ($\uparrow$, $\downarrow$, $\leftarrow$, $\rightarrow$) are easy to remember, and they take you everywhere.

Moving the Cursor with the Mouse

To move the cursor with the mouse, just point to where you want the cursor to be and click the mouse button. If the place where you want to move the cursor is not in the window, scroll to bring it into view.

SELECTING WHAT YOU WANT TO CHANGE

Before you can change anything in a document, you must first *select* what you want to change. You indicate your selection by moving the cursor to it or by highlighting it with the cursor. You can stretch the cursor so that it highlights any amount of text: whole words, parts of words, lines, sentences, paragraphs, or even an entire document.

Selecting Text with the Keyboard

Think of the text you want to select as a block, and stretch the cursor from one end of the block to the other. To select text with the keyboard:

1. Move the cursor to one end of the block.

2. Hold down the Shift key.

3. Using the direction keys, move the cursor to the other end of the block. If you go too far, you can back up to reduce the amount of text highlighted.

When the Shift key is held down, the Home or the End key extends the cursor to the beginning or the end of the line, and the Page Up or the Page Down key extends the cursor up or down one windowful.

Try selecting different bits of text. Notice that when you extend the cursor *forward,* Word includes the character above the cursor in the selection, but when you move *backward,* it does not. To shrink the cursor back to a blinking underscore, release the Shift key and press any direction key.

Selecting Text with the Mouse

The mouse lets you select any character, word, sentence, or larger piece of text with greater ease and flexibility than the keyboard allows. To select a block or sequence of any length, use the dragging technique:

1. Move the mouse pointer to one end of the block, and hold down the mouse button.

2. Move the pointer to the other end of the block, and then release the button.

If part of the block is outside the window, you can find it by dragging the mouse pointer across the window border while holding down the mouse button. The text will scroll as you cross over the border.

Practice highlighting text with the mouse until you have a good feel for this technique.

MAKING CHANGES

Now that you know how to scroll to any part of a document and highlight what you want to change, you're ready to learn the most essential editing features of any word processor: inserting and deleting text. Other, more powerful editing features are simply faster and easier ways to insert and delete. Eventually, you'll want to use these more advanced features; for now, let's stick to the basics.

Inserting New Text

When you want to insert new text, just move the cursor to where the text should be added and start typing. The new text is inserted *to the left* of the cursor, pushing the cursor and any text that follows to the right. Let's add another paragraph to the end of the sample letter.

To insert text with the keyboard:

1. Press Ctrl-End to move the cursor to the end of the document.

2. Use any of the direction keys to move the cursor to the "S" in "Sincerely."

3. Type the new text:

   My guess is that it will take three months to prepare a new manuscript.

   Press the Enter key twice to leave a blank line above "Sincerely."

To insert text with the mouse:

1. If the end of the document is not in view, point to the down scroll arrow and hold down the mouse button until you can see the end of the document.

2. Point to the "S" in "Sincerely," and click the mouse button to move the cursor there.

3. Type the new text:

   My guess is that it will take three months to prepare a new manuscript.

   Press the Enter key twice to leave a blank line above "Sincerely."

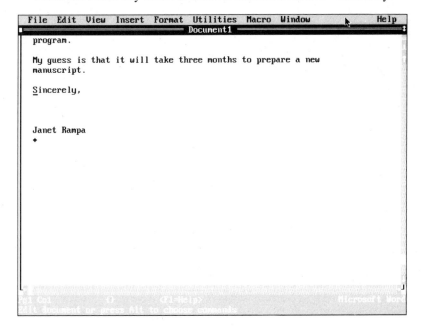

Deleting Text by Backspacing

Pressing the Backspace key once deletes one character to the left of the cursor. You might have already used the Backspace key to erase errors when you were typing the letter. To see how it works when you're editing, let's change the last word in the third paragraph from "rewrite" to "revision":

1. Move the cursor to the period (.) after "rewrite."

2. Press the Backspace key until "rewrite." is changed to "re."

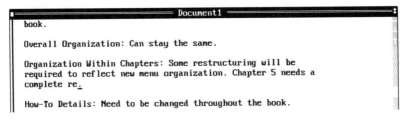

3. With the cursor still under the period after "re," type *vision* to make the word "revision."

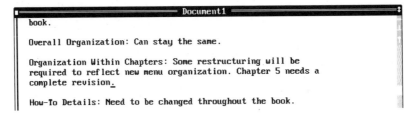

Deleting Selected Text

You can use either the Delete key or the Edit Cut command to delete the character above the cursor or whatever is highlighted by the cursor. Let's use the Delete key to erase a word in the first sentence:

1. Use the direction keys to move the cursor to the "p" in the word "preliminary" in the first sentence.

2. Hold down the Shift key, and press the Right direction key until "preliminary" and the space after it are highlighted.

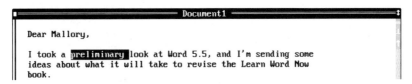

3. Press the Del key to delete the selected word.

Notice that the surrounding text immediately adjusts itself, leaving no sign that text was erased.

If you have a mouse, try out the Edit Cut command on any word or group of words in the sample letter:

1. Point to the first character of the text you want to delete, and hold down the mouse button while you drag the pointer to the last character you want to delete. When all the text you intend to delete is highlighted, release the mouse button.

2. Point to Edit in the menu bar and click.

3. Point to Cut in the Edit menu and click.

After you erase text with the mouse, undo the deletion with the Edit Undo command, which is explained in the next section.

Changing Your Mind

Suppose you change your mind about the last deletion. You can easily retrieve the deleted text and put it back where it was. The Edit Undo command reverses any kind of editing change. Use it freely whenever you change your mind about deleting, inserting, or moving text, typing new text, or typing over text. If the most recent change you made was with the Edit Undo command, you can even undo that. Edit Undo reverses the *last,* or most recent, editing change *only.*

Try reinserting the last deleted word with the Edit Undo command. To undo a change with the keyboard:

1. Press the Alt key to go to the menu bar.

2. Press E for Edit.

3. Press U for Undo.

The deleted word reappears in its original place. Or, instead of choosing the Edit Undo command, you can press Alt-Backspace to undo a change. (Hold down the Alt key while you press the Backspace key.)

To undo a change with the mouse:

1. Point to Edit in the menu bar and click.

2. Point to Undo in the Edit menu and click.

Typing Over Text

Sometimes it's easier to type over text that you want to replace instead of deleting the unwanted text and then typing in the new text. The Insert key lets you do that. The Insert key is a toggle key that turns overtype mode on and off. Let's use it to change the word ''some'' to ''many'' in the comment about screen terminology:

1. Using the mouse or the keyboard, move the cursor down to the paragraph that begins with ''Screen Terminology.'' Position the cursor on the ''s'' in the word ''some.''

2. Press the Ins key to turn on overtype mode. The abbreviation OT appears in the status bar.

3. Type

    many

4. Press the Ins key again to turn off overtype mode. The abbreviation OT disappears from the status bar.

Moving Text

To move text, you must cut it out of one place in the document and paste it in another. When you cut text, you delete it from the document and put it in the scrap. When you paste text, you take a copy of it from the scrap and put it in the document. The *scrap* is a temporary holding place for pieces of text. Although the scrap can hold text of any length, it can hold only one piece at a time. If you have text in the scrap and you then put in a second piece of text, the new text displaces the first piece. You can always see what's currently in the scrap by looking at the text enclosed in braces ({ }) in the status bar.

In order to save deleted text in the scrap, you must use the Edit Cut command or the Shift-Delete keys instead of the Delete key alone. (Text erased with the Delete key alone is *not* saved in the scrap.) If you don't have a mouse, using the Shift-Delete keys to delete text is faster and easier than choosing and carrying out the Edit Cut command. Word saves the contents of the scrap until you delete another piece of text with the Shift-Delete keys or the Edit Cut command.

To move any amount of text:

1. Select (highlight) the text you want to move.

2. Press Shift-Del, or choose the Edit Cut command.

3. Move the cursor to the new location.

4. Press Shift-Ins, or choose the Edit Paste command.

Let's try this out by moving a paragraph from the end of the sample letter to the beginning. To move the paragraph using the keyboard:

1. Move the cursor to ''I,'' the first character in the paragraph that begins with ''In general.'' Hold down the Shift key while you press the direction keys to move to the last character of the paragraph. Release the Shift key when the entire paragraph is highlighted, as shown in the first half of Figure 3-4. (See page 51.)

2. Press Shift-Del to delete the selected paragraph to the scrap. Look at the status bar to see a representation of the text you've just deleted enclosed in braces:

{In ...an.}

3. Press the Del key once or twice to delete any extra blank lines left between surrounding paragraphs. (Notice that using the Delete key alone does not change the contents of the scrap.)

4. Use the direction keys to move the cursor to the end of the first paragraph. You might need to use the Spacebar to add a space after the period at the end of the paragraph.

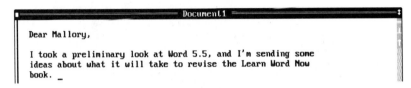

5. Press Shift-Ins to insert the text from the scrap in the new location, as shown in the second half of Figure 3-4.

If you have a mouse, select the block of text shown in the first half of Figure 3-4 and try moving it to another location. To move text using the mouse:

1. Move the mouse pointer to the first character of the text you want to move. Hold down the mouse button while you drag the pointer to the last character of the text to be moved. When all the text you want to move is highlighted, release the mouse button.

2. Choose the Edit Cut command: Point to Edit on the menu bar and click. Then point to Cut on the Edit menu and click.

3. Move the mouse pointer to the new location and click.

4. Choose the Edit Paste command: Point to Edit on the menu bar and click. Then point to Paste on the Edit menu and click.

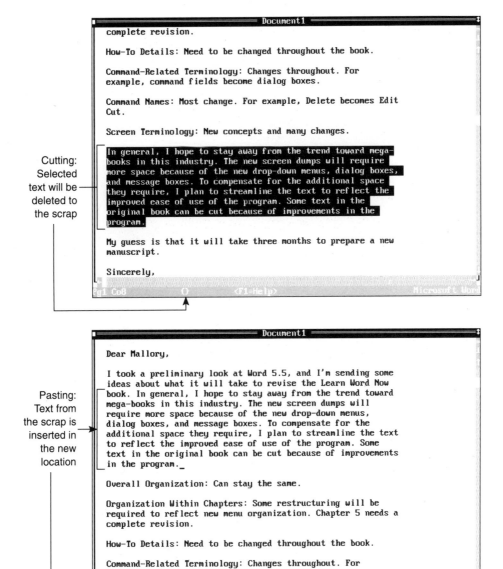

Figure 3-4. *Cutting and pasting to move text.*

Copying Text

Copying text is similar to moving text, except that you copy the text to the scrap without deleting it from its original location in the document. Once the text is in the scrap, you can retrieve a copy of it any number of times, to insert in any number of places.

To copy text:

1. Select (highlight) the text you want to copy.

2. Press Ctrl-Ins, or choose the Edit Copy command.

3. Move the cursor to the new location.

4. Press Shift-Ins, or choose the Edit Paste command.

A copy of the highlighted text appears in front of the cursor. You still have a copy of the text in the scrap, so you can insert another copy elsewhere in the document. Think of the Shift-Insert keys or the Edit Paste command as a duplicating machine that can produce as many copies of the text in the scrap as you need.

Try copying any piece of text using the mouse or the keyboard. Then use the Edit Undo command to erase all traces of your experiment.

What if you lose the scrap?

As you're moving through the document to find a new location for deleted text, you might spot something else that needs to be changed or an error that needs to be corrected. As long as you don't delete or copy anything else to the scrap, you can make other editing or formatting changes on the way. You can delete other text without changing the contents of the scrap if you use the Backspace key or the Delete key alone.

If you accidentally delete or copy other text to the scrap before you complete a move, the text you want to move disappears from the scrap. You can recover it if you can undo the command that put new text in the scrap. (Remember, you can undo only the last command carried out.) Undoing a command that changed the contents of the scrap also undoes the change to the scrap. After you carry out the Edit Undo command, the text that was previously in the scrap (the text you were planning to move) reappears in the scrap. Whenever you see valuable text in the scrap, you can salvage it by using the Shift-Insert keys or the Edit Paste command.

The Mouse Express for Moving and Copying Text

If you have a two-button mouse, you can use the mouse with the Control and Shift keys to directly move and copy text without going through the scrap. To move or copy text with lightning speed:

1. Select (highlight) the text you want to move or copy.

2. Move the mouse pointer to the new location.

3. To move the selected text, hold down the Ctrl key while you click the right mouse button. To copy the selected text, hold down the Ctrl key *and* the Shift key while you click the right mouse button.

Joining and Splitting Paragraphs

Recall that you pressed the Enter key twice after each paragraph to start a new paragraph and to leave a blank line. Each time you press the Enter key, it inserts a nonprinting character called a paragraph mark (¶) that can be deleted like any other character. When you delete the paragraph mark following one paragraph, that paragraph becomes joined to the next one. To join two paragraphs, move the cursor to the first character of the second paragraph and then press the Backspace key until the two paragraphs are joined. If necessary, press the Spacebar to insert a space between the sentences where the paragraphs are joined.

You can just as easily split a long paragraph into two shorter paragraphs. Move the cursor to where you want the new paragraph to start, and press the Enter key. Press it twice to separate the paragraphs with a blank line.

Try first joining and then resplitting any two paragraphs in the sample document.

MAKING IT LOOK GOOD

After you get the words in a document to say what you want them to say, you might want to improve the document's appearance to add clarity, emphasis, or visual appeal. Let's try making some easy and frequently desired formatting changes.

Changing the Margins

Although the margins that Word initially sets work for most documents, you might find that you need to change the margins for some documents. Let's increase the top margin of the sample letter to leave room for printing it on letterhead stationery.

To change a margin with the keyboard:

1. Press the Alt key to go to the menu bar.

2. Press T to choose the Format menu.

3. Press M to choose the Margins command.

4. Press Alt-T to go to the Top Margins box.

5. Type *2* and press the Enter key to change the top margin from 1 inch to 2 inches:

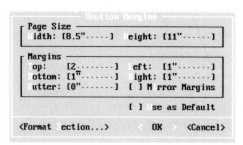

Changing the left, the right, or the bottom margin is just as easy. In step 4 above, press Alt-L for the left margin, Alt-R for the right margin, or Alt-B for the bottom margin, and then type in the new measurement.

To change a margin with the mouse:

1. Point to Format in the menu bar and click.

2. Point to Margins in the Format menu and click.

3. Point to the Top Margins box (between the brackets following Top) and click:

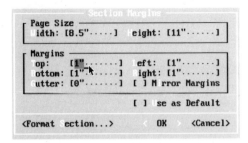

4. Type 2 for 2 inches. Then press the Enter key or point to <OK> at the bottom of the dialog box and click:

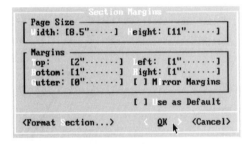

To change other margins, point to the margin you want to change and then click before typing in the new measurement.

Indenting Paragraphs

Let's indent the comments in the sample letter to set them off from the rest of the text and to improve the letter's overall appearance:

1. Using either the mouse or the keyboard, select (highlight) the text you want to indent. In this case, we'll indent several paragraphs, beginning with the one that starts with "Overall" and ending with the one that starts with "Screen." Only part of each paragraph you want to indent needs to be highlighted, as shown on page 56.

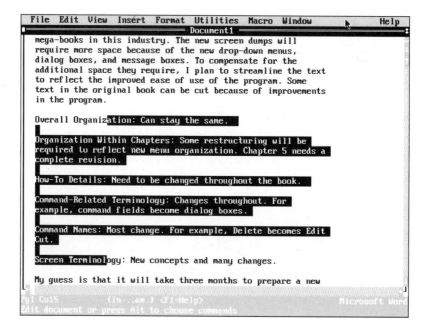

2. Press Ctrl-Q to indent the selected paragraphs.

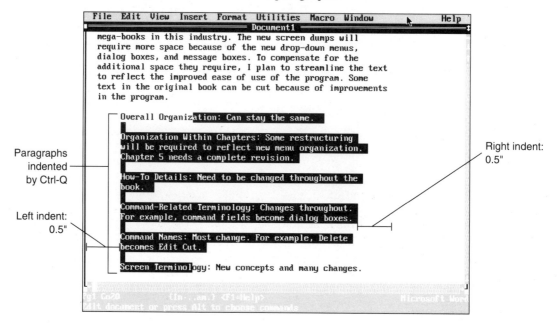

Paragraphs indented by Ctrl-Q

Right indent: 0.5"

Left indent: 0.5"

Each time you press Ctrl-Q, both the left and right margins for the high-lighted text increase by 0.5 inches—that is, both edges of the text move in toward the center of the page. If you indent too much, press Ctrl-M to de-crease the indents.

Adding Underlining, Boldface, and Italics

A little underlining, **boldface**, or *italic* can brighten up a document and emphasize key words. Let's underline the book title in the sample letter.

To underline words using the keyboard:

1. Select (highlight) the words of the title "Learn Word Now" in the first paragraph.

2. Press Ctrl-U.

The Control-U keys are toggle keys that turn underlining on or off. For ex-ample, if you reselect the underlined words "Learn Word Now" and press Ctrl-U again, the underline disappears.

Word also offers a convenient way to format characters with the mouse. Begin by choosing the View Ribbon command to turn on the formatting rib-bon. (Point to View on the menu bar and click, and then point to Ribbon on the View menu and click.) A line of text called the *ribbon* appears under the menu bar. The most frequently used character formats—boldface (Bld), Italics (Ital), and Underlining (Ul)—are listed on the right side of the ribbon:

```
Style:[Normal·········]↕  Font:[Pica·········]↕  Pts:[12·]↕  Bld Ital Ul
```

To underline words using the mouse and the ribbon:

1. Select (highlight) the words of the title "Learn Word Now" in the first paragraph.

2. Point to Ul (for Underline) on the ribbon and click.

On the ribbon, Ul brightens to indicate that underlining is turned on. To remove underlining, highlight the underlined words, point to Ul on the rib-bon, and click. Ul dims to indicate that underlining is turned off.

NOTE: If you are using Word in graphics mode with a graphics monitor and adapter, you can see the special effects on the screen as they will be printed. Otherwise, the words that have been assigned special formats simply appear brighter or in another color. To find out what display modes are available for your monitor, see the Getting Started *booklet that comes with your Word package. If you have a graphics monitor and adapter, you can easily switch from text mode to graphics mode (or vice versa) by pressing Alt-F9.*

You can apply more than one character format to text. Let's make the topics covered in the comments, starting with ''Overall Organization,'' appear in **bold and italics**.

To apply boldface and italics format using the keyboard:

1. Select the words ''Overall Organization,'' including the colon that follows them.

2. Press Ctrl-BI. (Hold down the Ctrl key while you press B for bold and I for italics.)

Like Control-U, the Control-B and Control-I keys are toggle keys that turn a character format for selected text on and off.

To apply boldface and italics format using the mouse and the ribbon:

1. Select the words ''Overall Organization,'' including the colon that follows them.

2. Point to Bld (for bold) on the ribbon and click.

3. Point to Ital (for italics) on the ribbon and click.

Practice moving and extending the cursor by highlighting the rest of the topics, each in turn. Press Ctrl-BI, or point to Bld and Ital on the ribbon and click to make each phrase appear in boldface italics.

When you finish working with the ribbon, you can turn it off to allow more room for text. The ribbon is turned off in the same way it is turned on— by choosing the View Ribbon command.

These few formatting changes do a lot to improve the appearance of the sample letter, as shown in Figure 3-5.

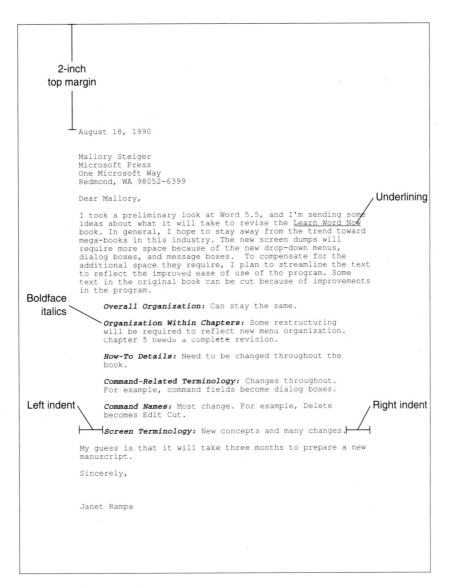

Figure 3-5. *The revised sample letter.*

Chapter 4

Saving, Retrieving, and Printing Your Words

If you've just finished creating or editing a document, your words are sitting somewhat precariously in the computer's electronic memory. They will be lost if the electricity goes off or if someone comes along and turns off your computer. To protect your work, make a habit of saving it on a disk every 15 minutes. Then, if a mishap occurs, you lose only what you have done since you last saved your document. (Word does have an *autosave* feature, which you can find by choosing the Utilities Customize command; see Chapter 11 for more information.)

In this chapter, you first learn how to save and name a document. Then you learn how to gracefully quit the Word program and how to restart it. You also find out how to open a previously created document and how to print a document.

SAVING A DOCUMENT

When you *save* a document, you transfer a copy of it from temporary memory to a more permanent storage place—a disk.

The First Time You Save

If you're saving a document for the first time, you must give it a filename, and you might need to tell Word where to save it. In addition, you have the option of supplying descriptive information about the file that will make finding it easier.

Let's save the sample letter you typed and name it SAMPLE.DOC. This time, let Word decide where to save it; you'll learn how to specify locations for files later.

To save a document for the first time:

1. Choose the File menu: Press the Alt key and then press F. Or, with the mouse, point to File on the menu bar and click the mouse button.

2. Choose the Save command: Press S, or point to the Save command and click the mouse button.

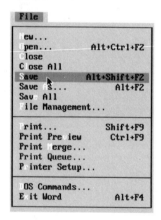

3. When you see the File Save As dialog box (shown on the next page), type a name for the file in the File Name box (using uppercase or lowercase letters). Then press the Enter key or point to <OK> and click the mouse button to save the file.

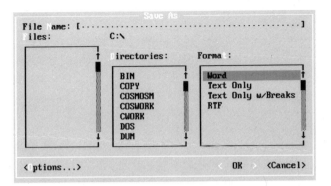

For the sample letter, type

sample

and press the Enter key or point to <OK> and click.

4. When you see a box labeled Summary, press the Esc key to skip the summary for now.

After Word saves the file, it displays the filename in the title bar at the top of the window. In the message bar at the bottom of the screen, Word tells you the drive and directory where the document was saved as well as how many characters were saved (including tabs and paragraph marks—each paragraph mark counts as two characters). If the file is saved on a floppy disk, Word tells you how many bytes of storage space are now available on that disk.

The Next Time You Save

If you revise a document that you have previously saved, you must save it again to preserve the changes. The next time you save it, you won't be asked any questions. After you choose the File Save command, the revised document is saved with the same name and in the same place as before. Word keeps the previous version of the document and renames it with the filename extension .BAK.

If you want to change a document's name or location, use the File Save As command, and specify the name and location in the File Name box of the File Save As dialog box, as if you were saving the document for the first time.

Naming Documents

You can make up any filenames that are meaningful to you. The same rules that apply to DOS filenames apply to Word filenames. Filenames can be one to eight characters long. You can use letters, numbers, and some symbols, but no spaces. Acceptable symbols include the following:

! @ # $ % & ( ) - _ { } ' ` ~

You'll find that it's easier to work with the commands that handle document files if you use the filename extension .DOC. No need to type it in, though: Word automatically appends .DOC to a document filename unless you type a filename extension of your own.

Telling Word Where to Save a Document

Unless you tell Word where to save a file, it assumes that you want to save the file in the *default drive* and *default directory*. Together, the default drive and directory are called the *default path*. Word displays the default path under the File Name box in the File Save As dialog box:

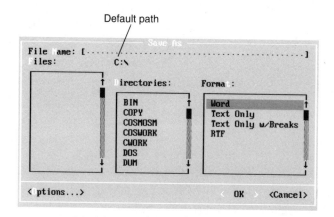

On a floppy-disk system, the default path is initially the root directory of drive B (indicated by *b:*). (If you're not maintaining multiple directories, you don't have to be concerned with directories.) On a hard-disk system, the default path is the drive and directory you were in when you started Word.

If you want to save a document in a different drive or directory, you can *override* the default path by specifying where you want to save an individual file when you type its filename in the File Name box. For example, if you want to save a document called SAMPLE.DOC in drive A, type

a:sample

Word observes the same conventions for specifying paths that DOS does. So if you're using multiple directories and you want to save a document in a directory called LETTERS rather than in the default directory, type

\letters\sample

Note that, in this example, the file will be saved in the default drive because no drive is specified.

You can specify both the drive and the directory where you want the file saved in this way:

b:\letters\sample

If the drive or directory you specify doesn't exist, this message appears:

The filename or path is not valid.

If you see this message, press Enter to acknowledge it and to remove it from the screen. If you typed the path incorrectly, retype the path and filename. Remember that before you can store files in a directory, you must create the directory with the DOS command MD (Make Directory).

If you are working with multiple directories, see Appendix A to familiarize yourself with DOS's terminology for paths and directories and to find out how to create, name, specify, and organize directories.

Using the Directories Box

Instead of typing the pathname with the filename, you can choose a drive and directory from the Directories box in the File Save As dialog box. This method is often easier than typing the names, and it is especially helpful when you're not sure of the directory name. The Directories box lists the subdirectories of the default directory as well as the available drives:

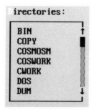

Disk drive names appear at the end of the list in this format:

[–A–] (for drive A)

To choose a drive or directory from the Directories box after you choose the File Save or the File Save As command:

1. Press Alt-D to move to the Directories box. With the mouse, simply point to the box.

2. Use the PgUp and PgDn keys to see more of the list. With the mouse, scroll through the list in the same way you scroll through a document: Point to the up or down scroll arrow, and click the mouse button to move up or down one line at a time. To scroll continuously, hold down the mouse button.

3. To choose a drive or directory from the list, move through the list with the direction keys until your choice is highlighted, and then press the Enter key. With the mouse, point to your choice and double-click the mouse button.

If the File Name box contains a filename when you press the Enter key, Word closes the dialog box and saves the file in the highlighted directory. If the File Name box is empty or if you chose a path from the Directories box using the mouse, the display in the Files box changes when you press Enter, to show the names of the files found in the chosen path. The display in the Directories box also changes to show the subdirectories, if any, of the drive or directory you chose.

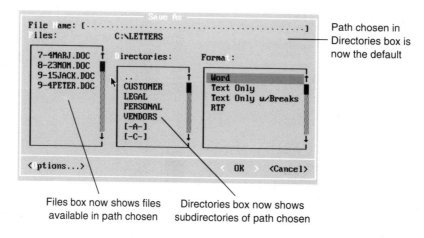

Path chosen in Directories box is now the default

Files box now shows files available in path chosen

Directories box now shows subdirectories of path chosen

The drive and directory chosen from the Directories box become the new default path until you quit Word—unless you designate another path to *always* be used as the default. To find out how to change the default path for all work sessions, see Chapter 11.

What if you don't see the directory you want?

If you don't see the directory you want in the Directories box, you might need to choose another drive, or you might need to look at a higher or lower level of directories.

If you choose another drive from the Directories box, Word displays the first level of subdirectories in that drive. If no subdirectories exist, you see only a list of disk drives.

To view a lower level of directories, choose a directory on the list. If that directory has subdirectories, they will appear in the Directories box. You might see two dots (..) as an entry in the Directories box. This symbol indicates that a higher level of directories exists. To view the next higher level of directories, choose the dots, just as you would choose a directory.

Once you learn to navigate around the Directories box, you won't need to worry about typing the wrong directory name when saving or opening files.

Summary Information

If you're saving a document for the first time, Word presents you with a summary questionnaire before completing the save. Summary information supplements the eight-character filename, which can be too cryptic to tell you what's in a document. You can search for a file or group of files based on the data you provide in the summary. If you produce a lot of documents or if you use a hard-disk system, summary information can be a big help in retrieving documents and keeping track of files. (More details on summary information sheets and file management are included in Chapter 15.)

QUITTING GRACEFULLY

When you quit Word, you exit the program and return to the DOS prompt (*A>* or *C>*). Let's walk through the steps of quitting, restarting, and opening a document.

To exit the Word program:

1. Choose the File menu: Press the Alt key and then press F. With the mouse, point to File on the menu bar and click the mouse button.

2. Choose the Exit Word command: Press X, or point to the Exit Word command and click the mouse button.

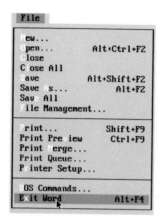

If you have not saved all your work, the following message appears:

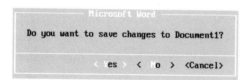

If you encounter this message, press Y (or point to <Yes> and click the mouse button) to save your work before quitting. Press N (or point to <No> and click) if you don't want to save the document or the changes made to a previously saved document. Press the Esc key (or point to <Cancel> and click) if you want to cancel the File Exit Word command.

After Word carries out the File Exit Word command, DOS takes over. (If you have a floppy-disk system and your computer can't find DOS in the A drive, it might ask you to insert the DOS disk before it displays the *A>* prompt.) When you see the *A>* or *C>* prompt, you can turn off the computer or load another program.

RESTARTING WORD

To resume working with Word after quitting, you need to restart the program. You can restart Word the same way you originally started it. At the DOS prompt *A>* or *C>*, type

> *word*

and press the Enter key. If you have multiple directories, you might need to change the directory before you type the startup command.

If you start Word this way, you see a blank window. You can then start typing to create a new document, or you can open a previously saved document. When you *open,* or *load,* an existing file, you transfer a copy of it from its permanent storage place—your document disk—to temporary memory.

You can open a document at the same time you start Word. To start the Word program and open the file you last worked on, type

> *word/l*

and press the Enter key. Word displays the file with the cursor where you left it when you quit working on the file.

To open a different file, include the filename with the startup command. For example, type

> *word yourfile*

and press the Enter key to start Word and open the file named YOUR-FILE.DOC. (If you don't type a filename extension, Word assumes that the filename has the extension .DOC.) As usual, you must include the path to the file if the file isn't stored in the default path.

Restart Word now by typing *word* so that you can try opening and printing a document in the next sections.

OPENING A DOCUMENT

To open a document, Word needs to know its filename and location. Unless you tell it otherwise, Word assumes that the document is in the default path. Let's open the sample letter you created and saved in the default path under the name SAMPLE.DOC.

To open a document:

1. Choose the File menu: Press the Alt key and then press F. With the mouse, point to File on the menu bar and click the mouse button.

2. Choose the Open command: Press O, or point to the Open command and click the mouse button.

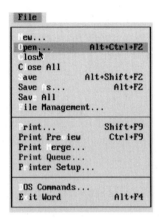

3. When you see the File Open dialog box, check to see where Word will look for the file. The default path is shown under the File Name box:

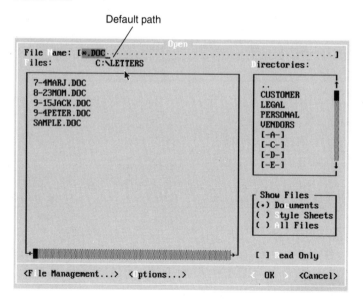

4. If the file you want to open is in the default path, type the filename in the File Name box and press the Enter key. If the file is not in the default directory, include the path to the file with the filename. To open the file containing the sample letter, type

   sample

   and press the Enter key.

After a document is opened, you see it in the window with its filename in the title bar (the top window border).

If Word can't find the file you request, it assumes that you want to create a new file and displays this message:

The file does not exist. Do you want to create it now?

If this happens while you're attempting to open an existing file, press the Esc key to remove the message. Then check to be sure that you typed the correct path and filename and that you have the correct floppy disk in place.

Using the Files Box

Instead of typing in the filename, you can choose it from the Files box, which appears in the File Open dialog box. The Files box lists all the files in the default path. To choose a file from the Files box after you choose the File Open command:

1. Press Alt-F to go to the Files box. With the mouse, simply point to the box and click the mouse button.

2. Use the direction keys to highlight the name of the file you want to open (as illustrated on the following page), and press the Enter key. With the mouse, point to the name of the file you want to open, and double-click the mouse button. (If necessary, use the Left and Right direction keys or scroll horizontally to see more of the list.)

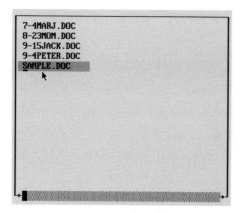

```
7-4MARJ.DOC
8-23MOM.DOC
9-15JACK.DOC
9-4PETER.DOC
SAMPLE.DOC
```

If the file you want to open is not in the default path, it will not be listed in the Files box until you choose a new path from the Directories box. The Directories box in the File Open dialog box works exactly like the Directories box in the File Save As dialog box. (See "Using the Directories Box" earlier in this chapter.) After you choose the correct drive and directory from the Directories box, you can choose the name of the file you want to open from the Files box.

PRINTING A DOCUMENT

A document must be open and visible in the window when you give the File Print command. If you've recently finished creating or editing a document, that's where it will be. But if you just started Word or if you're working with another document, you must open the document you want to print.

To print a document:

1. Open the document if it isn't already in the window.

2. Be sure your printer is ready: Is the paper in position? Is the printer plugged in? Is the printer connected to your computer? Are the power switch and the online switch turned on?

3. Choose the File menu: Press the Alt key and then press F. With the mouse, point to File and click the mouse button.

4. Choose the Print command: Press P, or point to the Print command and click the mouse button.

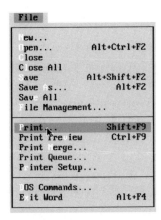

5. The File Print dialog box appears. (In Chapter 12, you'll learn what all the options in this dialog box mean.) To start printing, press the Enter key. Or, with the mouse, point to <OK> and click.

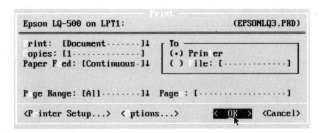

To interrupt printing, press the Esc key. Word then displays a message box that allows you to continue printing or to cancel the File Print command:

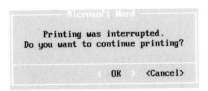

To restart printing where you left off, press the Enter key or point to <OK> in the message box and click the mouse button. To stop printing altogether, press the Esc key or point to <Cancel> and click the mouse button.

If you experience problems printing documents, Word might have incorrect information about your printer. Chapter 12 explains how to be sure that Word can communicate with your printer.

CLOSING ONE DOCUMENT
AND OPENING ANOTHER

As you will learn in later chapters, you can have more than one document open at the same time. But until you know how to work with multiple windows, it's a good idea to close each document before opening another.

To close a document:

1. Choose the File menu: Press the Alt key and then press F. With the mouse, point to File and click the mouse button.

2. Choose the Close command: Press C, or point to the Close command and click the mouse button.

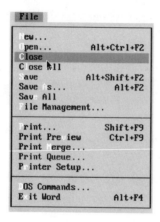

If you have not saved the changes you've made to the document, a message box appears, asking if you want to save the changes. Press Y, or point to <Yes> and click the mouse button, to save. Press N, or point to <No> and click, if you don't want to save. If you want to cancel the File Close command, press the Esc key or point to <Cancel> and click.

After you close a document, the document and the window framing it disappear from the screen. If no other files are open, fewer menus appear in the menu bar because most commands now have no text to work on. You can now open a new document or a previously saved document with the File Open command. To open a new document, type the name you want to give it in the File Name box of the File Open dialog box. When Word asks you to confirm that you want to create a new file, press Y, or point to <Yes> and click the mouse button. (You can also use the File New command to open a new file.)

WHERE TO GO FROM HERE

You might want to return to the sample letter and use it to practice the editing techniques you learned in this part of the book. Practice moving the cursor or moving the mouse pointer until it seems like second nature to you. Try correcting any typing errors you might have made. Practice inserting new text, selecting text, and deleting or moving parts of the letter. Don't be afraid to experiment. If you get stuck, you can reset the computer by holding down the Control, Alternate, and Delete keys simultaneously and then start over. All you can lose is some practice text, and you won't even lose all of that if it's been saved once.

Perhaps you don't have time to practice and experiment. If some urgent work is waiting for you, you're ready to start doing it. You can clear the sample letter out of the way and start creating your own document. Use the File Close command to close the document, and then use the File Open command (or the File New command) to give yourself a blank window for typing.

When you have more time, or when you find that you need more information or more tools, take a look at later chapters of this book. There you'll find out how to make editing changes faster and with more finesse. You'll also see that Word can check your spelling, hyphenate your words, and even suggest alternative words from its built-in thesaurus. You'll discover tricks that make creating a document easier and that reduce the amount of typing. You'll learn about formatting and printing alternatives, and you'll learn more about managing your files.

Part II

Advanced Word

Chapter 5

Selecting Text and Using Commands

Becoming well versed in selecting text and using commands enables you to tap the power of Word. The menus of commands that appear on the screen increase the scope of what you can do and the speed with which you can do it. The rest of this book is about using on-screen commands to process words more efficiently and to arrange them into attractive formats.

This chapter presents an overview of what commands can do; specific commands are explained in detail in later chapters. Here you learn how to precisely and quickly select text for commands to act on and how to choose menus, commands, and options in dialog boxes.

SELECTING TEXT

The first step in using some commands is to select, or highlight, the text you want the command to work on. Let's review what you already know about selecting text and add some more tricks. Start Word, and open any document to try out the selection techniques as you read about them. Remember that you can shrink the cursor back to its single-character size by pressing any direction key.

Selecting Text with the Keyboard

The keyboard method for selecting text that you learned in Chapter 3 is easy to remember: Hold down the Shift key while you press a direction key. Other methods initially take more time to learn, but if you do a lot of word processing, the time you spend learning will pay off in the long term.

Selecting a word, sentence, paragraph, or document

The key combinations Alt-F6, Alt-F8, and Alt-F10 extend the cursor to highlight the entire word, sentence, or paragraph that the cursor is in. Shift-F10 or Ctrl-5 (on the numeric keypad) highlights the whole document.

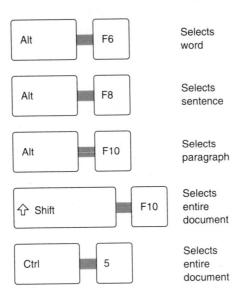

Alt	F6	Selects word
Alt	F8	Selects sentence
Alt	F10	Selects paragraph
⇧ Shift	F10	Selects entire document
Ctrl	5	Selects entire document

The Alt-F6, Alt-F8, and Alt-F10 keys can double as cursor-moving keys because repeated pressing moves the cursor to highlight the *next* word, sentence, or paragraph. For example, if you press Alt-F6 to highlight a word and then press it again, the cursor moves on to highlight the next word.

Selecting part of a word, paragraph, or document

If you hold down the Control key as well as the Shift key while you press a direction key, you can select the first or last part of the word, paragraph, or document in which the cursor is located. The highlight extends either forward or backward from the cursor location.

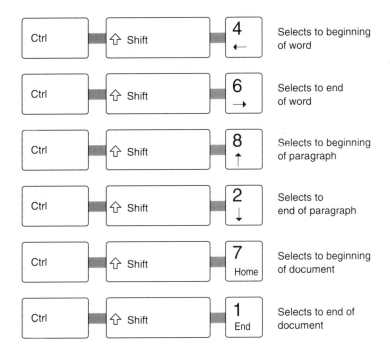

Ctrl	⇧ Shift	4 ←	Selects to beginning of word
Ctrl	⇧ Shift	6 →	Selects to end of word
Ctrl	⇧ Shift	8 ↑	Selects to beginning of paragraph
Ctrl	⇧ Shift	2 ↓	Selects to end of paragraph
Ctrl	⇧ Shift	7 Home	Selects to beginning of document
Ctrl	⇧ Shift	1 End	Selects to end of document

When you try these key combinations, notice that Word includes in the highlight the space (or spaces) after a word or paragraph. Remember that when you move forward from the cursor position, Word includes the character above the cursor in the selection, but that when you move backward, the character above the cursor is not included.

If you move the cursor to the beginning or end of a word or paragraph, you can use these key combinations to highlight the whole word or paragraph. Repeated pressing of the direction keys while the Control and Shift keys are held down continues to extend the cursor a word or paragraph at a time.

Using the Extend key to select text

Pressing and releasing the Extend key (F8)—that is, turning on the Extend function—is similar to holding down the Shift key. Like the Shift key, the F8 key can be used to highlight a block of text of any size:

1. Move the cursor to one end of the text block.

2. Press the F8 key.

3. Move the cursor to the other end of the block.

To move the cursor to the other end of the block, use any of the cursor-moving keys or the scroll keys. Or, instead, you can type the last character to be included in the block. If you type a character when the Extend function is on, Word extends the cursor to the first occurrence of that character. Typing the character again extends the cursor to the next occurrence. For example, you can press the F8 key and type a period to extend the cursor to the end of the sentence the cursor is in. Typing another period extends the cursor to the end of the next sentence.

The F8 key turns the Extend function on, and the Escape key turns it off. The abbreviation EX in the status bar tells you that the Extend function is turned on. Word turns it off after you make an editing change that affects the highlighted text. If you decide not to make a change, press Esc to stop the cursor from extending every time you try to move it.

If you press the F8 key more than once, it not only turns on the Extend function but also highlights text, highlighting increasingly bigger units of text each time you press it. Press F8 twice to highlight a word, three times to highlight a sentence, four times to highlight a paragraph, or five times to highlight an entire document. To reduce the size of the unit of text you select, press Shift-F8.

Experiment with the F8 key, but don't forget to press the Esc key when you're done. The EX abbreviation disappears from the status bar when the Extend function is turned off. As usual, press any direction key to shrink the cursor back to its single-character size.

Selecting Text with the Mouse

In Chapter 3, you learned to select a block of text by dragging the mouse pointer from one end of the text you want to highlight to the other end. Here you learn another way to select any block of text as well as some shortcuts for selecting defined units of text.

Selecting any block of text

Here's another way to highlight a block of text:

1. Move the mouse pointer to one end of the block and click.

2. Press F8, which turns on the Extend function. The abbreviation EX appears in the status bar.

3. Move the pointer to the other end of the block and click. If the other end is not in view, use the scroll bar to scroll to it.

Word turns off the Extend function after you carry out a command. If necessary, you can press the Esc key to turn it off.

Selecting a word or sentence

To select a word, point to any character in the word and double-click the mouse button. To select a sentence, point to any character in the sentence, hold down the Ctrl key, and click. If you have a two-button mouse, click the right mouse button to select a word, or click both buttons at the same time to select a sentence.

Point to a character and	to select a
double-click	word
click the right button	word
Ctrl-click	sentence
click both buttons	sentence

Selecting a line, paragraph, or document

The *selection bar* is the column of space to the left of your text, between the text and the left window border. (See Figure 5-1 on the next page.) When the mouse pointer is in the selection bar, you can highlight a line, a paragraph, or the whole document. When the mouse pointer is in the selection bar, it changes color (if it is a rectangular pointer) or changes direction (pointing up to the right instead of to the left, if it is an arrow).

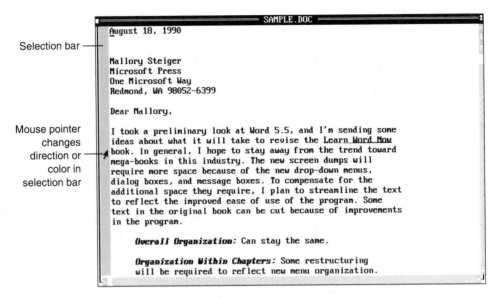

Selection bar

Mouse pointer changes direction or color in selection bar

Figure 5-1. *The mouse selection bar.*

With the mouse pointer in the selection bar, click once to highlight the line next to the pointer, double-click to highlight the paragraph next to the pointer, or hold down the Ctrl key and click once to highlight the entire document. With a two-button mouse, click the right mouse button to highlight the paragraph next to the pointer, and click both buttons simultaneously to highlight the whole document.

With the mouse pointer in the selection bar, point to a line and	to select a
click	line
double-click	paragraph
click the right button	paragraph
Ctrl-click	document
click both buttons	document

Selecting the last part of a word or sentence

If you have a two-button mouse, you can quickly highlight the last part of a word or sentence:

1. Move the mouse pointer to the beginning of the part you want to highlight, and click the left mouse button.

2. Press the F8 key. The abbreviation EX appears in the status bar.

3. Click the right mouse button to extend the cursor to the end of the word, or click both buttons to extend it to the end of the sentence.

WHAT'S ON THE MENUS?

A good way to get an overview of Word commands is to browse through the menus. Before you choose a command, you can view a brief message telling you what kinds of commands a menu includes. To do this, press the Alt key to activate the menu bar, and then move the highlight to the menu name by pressing the direction keys. After highlighting Edit on the menu bar, for example, you see the following message in the message bar:

```
Undo, delete, copy, insert, search, replace, and go to
```

To see the actual list of commands on a menu, choose the menu: Press the Alt key and then press the bold (highlighted) letter of the menu; or, with the mouse, point to the menu name and click. The menu drops down to display its contents. To see what a particular command on a menu does, highlight the command name by using the Up and Down direction keys. After you highlight Search on the Edit menu, for example, you see this message:

```
Finds text or formatting
```

To see a Help window containing a more descriptive explanation of what a command does, highlight the command and press the F1 key. Press the Esc key to clear the Help window from the screen.

The File Commands

The commands you use to work with files and to leave the Word program are found on the File menu. The first group of commands controls file storage. They let you open, save, and rename files or erase the contents of all or part of your work area in memory. In addition, the File Management command on this menu lets you search for, copy, or delete files.

The second group of commands controls everything related to printing. With them, you can print all or part of a document, peek at ''snapshots'' of entire pages before you print them to see how they will look on paper, merge documents while printing, line up a series of files to be printed while you continue working, or choose a printer.

With the last two commands on the File menu (Exit Word and DOS Commands), you can exit the Word program, or you can run DOS commands and other programs without exiting Word.

The Edit Commands

Commands on the Edit menu help you make changes to the text and graphics in a document. You can delete, move, or copy text; reverse or repeat your most recent typing, editing, or formatting change; find text or formatting and substitute other text or formatting; leap directly to a specific page, bookmark, footnote, or annotation; or store and retrieve frequently used pieces of text.

The View Commands

Commands on the View menu control what is displayed on your screen and how it is displayed. By changing the view, you can organize a document within an outline and see the outline. You can look at the layout of specially formatted text, such as graphics or paragraphs framed by surrounding text or text arranged in columns. You can turn the formatting ribbon, the ruler, and the status bar on or off.

The View Preferences command leads to a host of other options controlling the display in windows. You can choose to show or hide nonprinting characters, line breaks (as they will appear during printing), the menu bar, the window borders, the message bar, the scroll bars, and line numbers. You can change the cursor speed, choose another display mode, or change the colors of the display.

The Insert Commands

The Insert commands let you add a variety of items to a document: page, column, or section breaks; footnotes or annotations; another document or spreadsheet; location markers; page numbers; and graphics created with another program. The Insert Index and Insert Table of Contents commands create *and* insert an index or table of contents from coded entries in the document.

The Format Commands

The formatting commands help you change the appearance of a document. They determine the overall layout of a printed page and the appearance of particular paragraphs and characters.

The basic formatting commands allow you to change the type size and style of characters and add special effects such as boldface, italics, underlining, subscripts, and superscripts. You can justify, center, and indent lines; adjust spacing between lines; arrange text in columns; position footnotes; add line numbers; restart page numbering at a specific place; and adjust the page size and margins.

Miscellaneous formatting commands let you set and clear tab stops, draw lines or boxes around paragraphs and add background shading, position a paragraph or graphic in surrounding text, and print headings at the top or bottom of every page.

Instead of using individual formatting commands, you can format a document with style sheets that you create, apply, view, and edit with the group of style sheet commands on the Format menu.

The Utilities Commands

Commands on the Utilities menu include writing tools that check and correct spelling, look up definitions, find synonyms, and hyphenate words. Other commands on this menu let you automatically number items, mark changes made, count words, draw lines, sort text, and calculate numbers.

The Utilities Customize command allows you to change the way the program behaves. Using this command, you can have Word automatically save your work at specified time intervals, alter key assignments, choose another unit of measure for formatting text, and more.

The Macro Commands

With custom-made commands called macros, you can simplify your work by reducing complicated tasks to a few keystrokes, and you can remap your keyboard to make function keys do what you want them to do. The Macro commands let you create, revise, and run macros.

The Window Commands

With the Window commands, you can open, close, position, or change the size of multiple windows. You can also split a single window into two panes in order to view two distant parts of a long document simultaneously. Multiple windows can be overlapped or arranged side by side.

The Help Commands

The Help commands lead to tutorials and useful information about commands, procedures, the keyboard, the mouse, and making the transition from Word 5.0 to Word 5.5.

WORKING WITH MENUS

The procedure for using menu commands, with either the keyboard or the mouse, can be summarized in three steps:

1. Choose the menu.

2. Choose the command.

3. Respond to the dialog box, if one appears.

First let's go over the general rules for choosing menus and commands and for responding to dialog boxes. Then you can try out what you learn by choosing and carrying out a command that includes almost every kind of option you might encounter.

Choosing Menus and Commands

Menus are chosen from the menu bar at the top of the screen, and commands are chosen from menus. With the keyboard, press the Alt key to go to the menu bar. The mouse has free access to the menu bar whenever the bar is visible. If the menu bar has been turned off to allow more space for text (with the View Preferences command), press the Alt key to make it temporarily reappear.

After you press the Alt key, Word highlights the first menu name on the menu bar to let you know that you're in command mode:

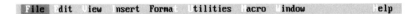

Being in *command mode* means you cannot enter text in your document by pressing the letter keys. While you are in command mode, the letter keys can be used only to choose menus, commands, or command options. To leave command mode without choosing a command, press the Esc key. Or, with the mouse, point to any place in the window and click the mouse button.

As you learned in Chapter 3, a command is usually identified by the name of the menu the command is chosen from, combined with the command name that appears on the menu. For example, the Edit Go To command refers to the Go To command on the Edit menu. The instruction *Choose the Edit Go To command* tells you to choose the Edit menu and then choose the Go To command.

To choose a menu and a command:

- With the keyboard, press the Alt key and type the bold letter from the menu name. When the menu of commands drops down, type the bold letter from the command name.

- With the mouse, point to the name of the menu and click the mouse button. When the menu of commands drops down, point to the command and click the mouse button.

When a command appears on a menu in a shade lighter or darker than that of the other commands, it can't be used. For example, the Calculate command on the Utilities menu shown in Figure 5-2 appears in gray rather than black to indicate that it is not available. If you give the Calculate command

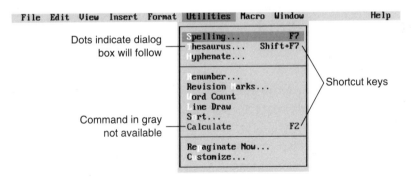

Figure 5-2. *The Utilities menu.*

something to calculate, however, Word makes the command available. If you type and highlight the mathematical expression

$49.32*23

you can then choose the Calculate command to perform the multiplication. Word will show you the result in the message bar.

Some commands also show *shortcut keys*. In Figure 5-2, for instance, Utilities Calculate is followed by F2, which means that you can press the shortcut key F2 to calculate instead of choosing the Utilities menu and the Calculate command.

Some commands toggle on or off each time you choose them. When a toggle command is turned on, a mark appears to its left. For example, when the status bar at the bottom of your screen is visible, the Status Bar command on the View menu is marked as shown in Figure 5-3. (The Outline, Layout, Ribbon, and Ruler toggle commands are turned off in Figure 5-3.) Choosing the Status Bar command when it is on turns off the status bar display.

Figure 5-3. *The View menu, with the Status Bar toggle command turned on.*

If Word needs to communicate with you before carrying out a command, a dialog box appears after you choose the command. An ellipsis (...) after a command name on a menu indicates that the command has a dialog box. Commands with dialog boxes are carried out after you respond to the dialog box. Commands that are not followed by an ellipsis do not have dialog boxes and are carried out as soon as they're chosen.

Responding to Dialog Boxes

When a command can be carried out in alternative ways, the dialog box tells you what your options are and provides a place for you to supply the information needed to carry out the command. Within dialog boxes, Word uses boxes and buttons to ask you for information and to display options. Depending on the type of information needed and the available options, you find the following kinds of boxes and buttons in dialog boxes:

- Text boxes

- List boxes

- Check boxes

- Option buttons

- Command buttons

Figure 5-4 points out each type of box or button that you might see in a Word dialog box.

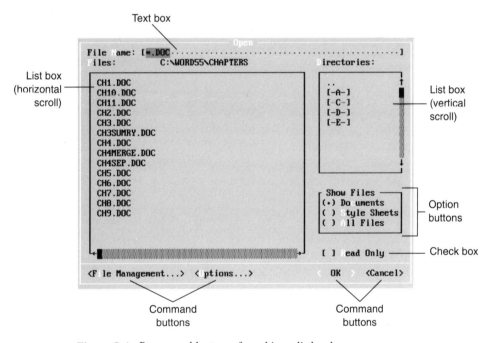

Figure 5-4. *Boxes and buttons found in a dialog box.*

To save you time, a *proposed response* (or *default answer*) for each box or button usually appears. If the proposed response is acceptable, simply skip that box or button.

After you've provided the necessary information and chosen your options, you must signal Word that it's time to close the dialog box and carry out the command. You usually do this by choosing the <OK> command button at the bottom of the dialog box. To choose the <OK> button, press the Enter key, or point to the button and click. If you want to close the dialog box without carrying out the command, choose the <Cancel> command button (press Esc, or point to <Cancel> and click).

Text boxes

Text boxes offer a place for you to type in information. In the File Name text box for the File Open command, for example, you can type the name of the file you want to open:

```
File  ame: [*.DOC · · · · · · · · · · · · · · · · · · · · · · · · · · · · · · · · · · · · · · · · · · · · · ]
```

A text box is identified by square brackets ([ ]) with a line of dots and, frequently, a proposed response between the brackets. Both the dots and the response disappear as you type over them. The cursor must be in the text box (between the brackets) before you can begin typing.

To move the cursor to a text box and type a response in it:

1. With the keyboard, hold down the Alt key while you type the bold letter of the box's name. Or tab to the box by pressing the Tab key to move forward or Shift-Tab to move backward until the cursor moves to the box. With the mouse, point to the box and click.

2. Type your response. You can correct errors with the Backspace key or the Delete key. If necessary, use either the direction keys or the mouse to move the cursor as you would in a document.

Sometimes a text box is linked to a separate list box that provides a list of possible answers. Instead of typing a response, you can choose a response from the linked list box. When you do so, the response instantly appears in the text box. For example, the File Name text box is linked to the Files list box. If you select a filename from the Files list box, it appears in the File Name text box. If a down arrow appears to the right of a text box, a list of possible responses is available.

List boxes

A list box encloses a list of choices. It is identified by the presence of a vertical or horizontal scroll bar:

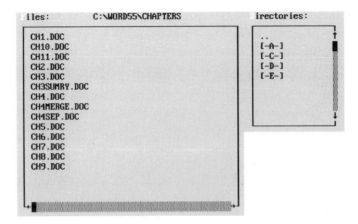

If you need to scroll to see more of the list, use the mouse and the scroll bar as you would in a document. If you're using the keyboard, press the PgUp and PgDn keys or any of the direction keys.

Some list boxes are drop-down boxes—that is, rather than seeing the list initially, you see a drop-down arrow to the right of a text box:

oint Size: [12····]↓

To view a drop-down list:

- With the keyboard, hold down the Alt key while you press the bold letter in the text box name, or tab to the text box. Then press the F4 key, or press Alt-Down direction key.

- With the mouse, point to the drop-down arrow next to the text box and click.

The list box drops down, allowing you to choose a response from the list:

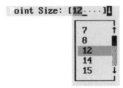

You choose a response from a list box by highlighting your choice. To move the cursor to a list box and highlight an item in the list:

- With the keyboard, hold down the Alt key while you press the bold letter in the list box name, or tab to the list box. Then use the direction keys (or type the first letter of the item you want) to highlight your choice in the list.

- With the mouse, point to your choice on the list and click.

A drop-down list disappears after you click an item on the list with the mouse or after you click the drop-down arrow again. With the keyboard, press the F4 key or Alt-Down direction key to make the list disappear.

Option buttons

Option buttons come in sets of two or more, with each set enclosed in a box. One—and only one—option button in a set is always turned on if the options are available. A mark between the parentheses to its left indicates which button is on:

To move the cursor to an option button and turn the button on:

- With the keyboard, hold down the Alt key while you press the bold letter of the option you want to turn on. Or tab to the box enclosing the option buttons, and use the Spacebar or the direction keys to move to the option you want.

- With the mouse, point to the option you want and click.

Turning on an option button turns off the button that was previously on.

Check boxes

A check box is identified by a set of square brackets to its left. It can be toggled on and off. When the check box is on, an X appears between the brackets; when it is off, the X disappears.

[ ] ead Only

To move the cursor to a check box and turn the check box on or off:

- With the keyboard, hold down the Alt key while you press the bold letter of the check box. Or tab to the check box, and press the Spacebar to turn it on or off.

- With the mouse, point to the box and click.

Like option buttons, related check boxes often appear in groups. Unlike option buttons, more than one check box in a group can be turned on.

Command buttons

Command buttons appear at the bottom of the dialog box. Each button is enclosed in angle brackets. Most dialog boxes have an <OK> button and a <Cancel> button. Choosing the <OK> button tells Word to carry out the command using the options shown in the dialog box. Choosing the <Cancel> button tells Word to close the dialog box without taking any action.

Notice that the File Open command has two additional command buttons, the <File Management> and <Options> buttons, each followed by an ellipsis:

If a command button is marked with an ellipsis, choosing that button leads to another dialog box with another set of options. Sometimes a command button is a duplicate of a command that appears on the same or another menu. It lets you take a convenient shortcut to choosing a related command without going back to the menu bar. For example, choosing the <File Management> command button in the File Open dialog box is the same as choosing the File Management command from the File menu.

If a command button is not followed by an ellipsis, the action described by the button's label is carried out as soon as you choose it. Word immediately acts on the options chosen in the dialog box. Take care not to choose this kind of command button unless you know what it does.

To move the cursor to a command button and choose it:

■ With the keyboard, hold down the Alt key while you type the bold letter of the command button. Or tab to the button and press Enter. If the angle brackets of a command button are highlighted, you can choose it by pressing Enter. The brackets of the <OK> button are usually highlighted to let you easily carry out a command.

■ With the mouse, point to the command button you want and click.

Traveling Through a Dialog Box

Take the "test drive" described here to learn to steer your way through dialog boxes. You need to select some text before choosing the Format Character command. With this command, you can then try changing the font style, size, position, and special attributes of the characters you selected. Don't worry if you don't understand all the terms and choices you see in the dialog box; you'll learn more about them in Chapter 9. For now, concentrate on the mechanics of moving around the dialog box and choosing options.

1. Press Alt, T, C to choose the Format Character command. Or, with the mouse, point to Format on the menu bar and click the mouse button, and then point to Character and click. You see the Format Character dialog box:

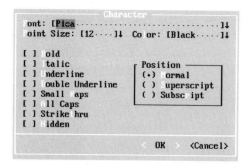

2. Press Alt-Down direction key (or the F4 key) to see the list of fonts available. With the mouse, point to the drop-down arrow next to the Font text box and click.

3. Use the direction keys to highlight any font on the list. With the mouse, scroll to see more of the list, if necessary, and then point to your choice and click.

4. If you're using the keyboard, press Alt-Down direction key to make the list disappear so that you can see what's beneath it.

5. Press Alt-P to move to the Point Size text box, and press Alt-Down direction key to see the list of available sizes. With the mouse, point to the drop-down arrow next to the Point Size box and click.

6. Use the direction keys to choose any size on the list. With the mouse, point to the size you want and click.

7. Press Alt-B and then Alt-I to move to the two check boxes labeled Bold and Italics and to turn them on. (Notice that the Size drop-down list disappears by itself when you press Alt-B to move on.) With the mouse, first point to the Bold box and click, and then point to the Italics box and click. You should see an X in each box.

8. Press Alt-S to move to the Superscript option button and to turn it on. With the mouse, point to Superscript and click. (When you choose Superscript, the dot next to Normal disappears because only one option button can be on.)

You can go back and change any of the options until you're satisfied. When everything is set the way you want, carry out the command: Press the Enter key or, with the mouse, point to the <OK> command button and click. If you'd rather cancel the command, press the Esc key or click the <Cancel> button. If you cancel the command, none of the changes indicated in the dialog box will take effect.

COMMAND SPECIALS

Word provides some special tools to help you work with commands. With these tools, you can repeat a command you've just carried out, cancel a command before you carry it out, undo a command after you carry it out, or get help with a specific command before you carry it out.

Repeating Commands

You can repeat many commands without working your way through menus and dialog boxes again. Before you repeat a command, you can move the cursor or highlight text. To repeat the last (most recent) command that was carried out, with all the same options, choose the Edit Repeat command or press the F4 key. To repeat the last Search command with all the same options, press Shift-F4.

The commands listed in the following table can be repeated using the Edit Repeat command or the F4 key:

Menu	Commands
File	New, Open
Edit	Repeat, Cut, Copy, Paste, Replace
Insert	Break, Footnote, File, Annotation, Picture
Format	Character, Paragraph, Section, Margins, Tabs, Borders, Position, Header/Footer, Apply Style, Record Style
Utilities	Spelling, Thesaurus, Hyphenate, Word Count, Sort, Calculate
Macro	Run, Edit
Window	New Window

Before repeating the Edit Replace, Utilities Spelling, Utilities Thesaurus, and Utilities Hyphenate commands, Word displays their dialog boxes so that you can reset the options.

Canceling Menus and Commands

With the keyboard, you can cancel most commands that display a dialog box by pressing the Esc key. If you want to choose another command, you must press the Alt key again to return to command mode. As an alternative, you can press Ctrl-Esc to cancel a dialog box without leaving command mode. To cancel a command with the mouse, click the <Cancel> or <Close> command button in the dialog box.

To cancel Help commands, press Esc or choose the <Exit> command button. To cancel the File Print Preview command, press Esc or choose the File Exit Preview command (which is available only when needed). To cancel the Format Define Styles command, close the style sheet window with the File Close command or the Window Close command.

Undoing Commands

If you carry out a command by mistake, or if you change your mind, reach for the Edit Undo command. It reverses the last editing or formatting change.

For example, if you deleted text, Edit Undo inserts it back in place. If you inserted text, Edit Undo deletes it. If you replaced text, Edit Undo restores the original wording. If you changed a word from boldface to italics, Edit Undo changes it back to boldface.

Edit Undo works with the following commands:

Menu	Commands
Edit	Undo, Repeat, Cut, Copy, Paste, Replace, Glossary
Insert	Break, Footnote, File, Bookmark, Page Numbers, Annotation, Picture, Index, Table of Contents
Format	Character, Paragraph, Section, Margins, Tabs, Borders, Position, Header/Footer, Apply Style, Record Style, Attach Style Sheet
Utilities	Spelling, Thesaurus, Hyphenate, Renumber, Revision Marks, Line Draw, Sort

Getting Help with Commands

If you need help with a specific menu or command, first highlight the menu name or command (by using the direction keys), and then press the F1 key or click the <F1=Help> button in the status bar to get instant on-screen help. If you need assistance with a dialog box or a message, press the F1 key or click the <F1=Help> button while the dialog box or message is displayed.

After you call for help, Word opens the Help window to display information specific to the highlighted or displayed menu, command, dialog box, or message. The Help window is placed on top of your document, which is no longer visible.

You can also get help by choosing a command from the Help menu listed on the far right end of the menu bar:

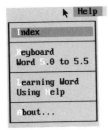

From the Help menu, choose the Index command to see a list of all Help topics. The Keyboard command displays an index of topics concerning how to use the keyboard with Word. The Word 5.0 to 5.5 command leads you to an index describing differences between Word 5.5 and earlier versions. Learning Word takes you to the Word Tutorial with step-by-step instructions and hands-on exercises. The Using Help command explains how to use Help. The About command displays the Word version number, the copyright, and the serial number of the Word package you are using.

If you don't have a hard disk, or if you haven't copied Learning Word to your hard disk with the Setup program, you are asked to insert the Learning Word disk when you request tutorial help. If you don't have enough memory to use tutorial help from within Word, you see the message *Insufficient memory*. In that case, you can exit Word and run the Learning Word program by itself. To start this program, type *learn* at the DOS prompt.

Moving around the Help window

Use the PgUp and PgDn keys to scroll through the Help window. With the mouse, click the <PgUp> or <PgDn> button or, if you see a vertical scroll bar, use the scroll bar to scroll up and down as you would in a document.

In the Help index, as well as in other Help text, certain topics or terms are enclosed in angle brackets, like this: <*scrap*>. You can get more information about any word or phrase in angle brackets by choosing it. Press the first letter of the topic or press the Tab key until the topic is highlighted, and then press the Enter key. (The Tab key takes you forward to the next topic; Shift-Tab takes you backward to the previous topic.) With the mouse, point to a topic and click to choose it.

The Help window also displays command buttons enclosed in angle brackets. The <Index> button is the same as the Index command on the Help menu: It takes you to the Help index. Choose the <Using Help> button if you want assistance in finding your way around Help screens. The <Back> button takes you to the previously displayed Help topic. The <Exit> button closes the Help window and takes you back to your document. To choose a command button, press the first letter of the command to highlight it, and then press Enter. With the mouse, point to the command button and click.

Trying out what you learn

If you want a related tutorial, with a chance to practice what you've learned, look for a lesson button (for example, <Lesson: How to Use Help>) at the bottom of a Help screen. Type *L* (for *lesson*) or tab to the button, and then press Enter to see the lesson. With the mouse, point to the lesson button and click.

Leaving the Help window

Choosing the <Exit> command button or pressing the Esc key usually closes the Help window and takes you back to your document. The Window Close command also does the trick. Some kinds of help appear in overlay boxes that are closed by choosing the <OK> button (pressing Enter).

If you want to leave the Help window open while you work on your document, choose the Window Arrange All command. Word splits the screen space so that you can see both your document and the Help window at the same time. (See Chapter 7 for information on using more than one window at a time.)

LEARNING COMMANDS

As you read through the remaining chapters of this book, take some time to try each command you read about. You can't be sure that you understand what a command does until you see for yourself the effect it has. Try the commands on any document—the sample letter you created in Chapter 2 of this book or a copy of a document you created on your own. It doesn't matter what you practice on. In most cases, you can use any text to experiment with. When you finish experimenting, you can quit without saving the changes so that the document you might have mangled appears untouched. (To quit without saving, choose the File Exit Word command and press N to confirm that you do not want to save the changes.)

If you're choosing commands with the keyboard, you'll be well prepared if you remember how to use the keys illustrated on the following page.

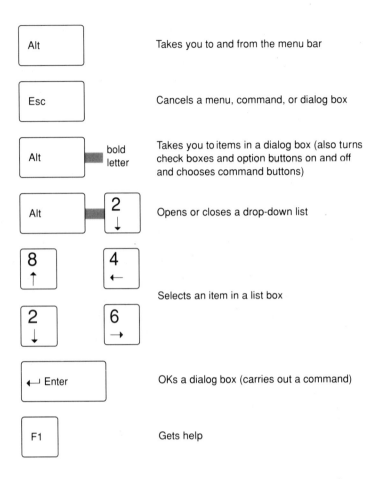

Alt — Takes you to and from the menu bar

Esc — Cancels a menu, command, or dialog box

Alt + bold letter — Takes you to items in a dialog box (also turns check boxes and option buttons on and off and chooses command buttons)

Alt + 2↓ — Opens or closes a drop-down list

8↑ 4←
2↓ 6→ — Selects an item in a list box

←┘ Enter — OKs a dialog box (carries out a command)

F1 — Gets help

If you're choosing commands with the mouse, you can do everything by pointing and clicking the mouse button except type a response in a text box. Point and click to do the following:

■ Choose a menu, command, item in a list box, option button, or command button (such as the <OK> button to carry out a command or the <Cancel> button to cancel a command)

■ Move the cursor to a text box so that you can type a response

■ Turn a check box on or off

What If You Don't Like Menus?

For those of you who don't like menus, Word offers alternatives. You can invoke many of the most commonly used menu commands by using shortcut keys. Shortcut keys are displayed next to command names on menus. A shortcut key is usually a function key, used alone or in combination with the Shift, Alternate, or Control key. For example, when you want to print a file, you can press Shift-F9 instead of using the Alt, F, P sequence to choose the File Print command.

You can invoke most formatting commands by using speed formatting keys. Speed formatting keys combine the Control key with various letter keys. For example, to underline characters, you can press Ctrl-U instead of using the Alt, T, C sequence to choose the Format Character command and then pressing additional keys to move to the check box that controls underlining. The summary of commands in Appendix C lists the preassigned shortcut keys and speed formatting keys.

Many of Word's key assignments have changed with version 5.5. If you know the key assignments from an earlier version of Word and don't want to retool, use the Utilities Customize command to turn on the Use Word 5.0 Function Keys check box. Turn off the Use INS for Overtype Key check box if you want to give the Insert key and the Delete key their old jobs, inserting text from and deleting text to the scrap. If you make this change, use Shift-Del to delete text without sending it to the scrap, and use Alt-F5 to toggle overtype on or off.

If you don't like Word's old or new key assignments, you can make up your own. You can create macros that reassign any of the function keys (F1 to F12), function-key combinations (such as Shift-F2), or Control-key combinations (such as Ctrl-PS). This capability means that if you're accustomed to another word processor that employed function keys or Control-key combinations to give commands, you don't need to start over: You can redesign Word to issue commands in the same way your former word-processing program did. See Chapter 16 to find out how to make your own key assignments by recording macros.

Chapter 6

Searching and Replacing

Instead of scrolling through a document to find text, let the computer do the searching for you. With commands from the Edit menu, you can find and select any text or location in a document. When you know where you want to go, the Edit Go To command or the Edit Search command can take you there in one leap. Think of these commands as tools for scrolling and moving the cursor quickly and precisely. They are often the fastest ways to move the cursor to an exact spot.

The Edit Go To command finds a location you specify, such as a numbered page. The Edit Search command finds a character, word, phrase, or any sequence of characters. A related command, Edit Replace, not only finds text quickly but also deletes it and inserts other text in its place. Using this command, you can replace every occurrence of a word in a document with another word.

The Edit Search and the Edit Replace dialog boxes have command buttons that let you find and replace formats instead of text. You can, for example, find all italicized characters and replace them with boldface characters. These two command buttons (<Search for Formatting Only> and <Replace Formatting Only>) are explained in Chapter 9, along with other formatting commands.

GOING PLACES

The Edit Go To command lets you find a specified page number, a bookmark, a footnote, or an annotation. A bookmark is a special place-marker inserted in a document. Footnotes and annotations are sideline notes added to the bottom of a page or the end of a document and referenced with numbers or symbols in the text. Using the Edit Go To command to find footnotes is explained in Chapter 10, where you learn how to create footnotes.

Finding Pages

To find a page in a document, first choose the Edit Go To command or, with the mouse, point to the status bar and double-click. After you choose the Edit Go To command, Word displays the Edit Go To dialog box:

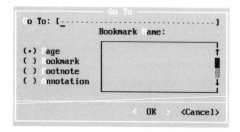

In the Go To text box, type the page number of the page you want to find. If the Page option button is not already on, turn it on, and then choose <OK> to go to the specified page. When typing page numbers, use Arabic numerals— 1, 2, 3, and so forth—regardless of the format you choose for printing page numbers in your document. (The <Page Numbers> command button of the Format Section command lets you choose Arabic numerals, Roman numerals, or letters for page numbering.)

If a document has been formatted into more than one section, it might use the same page number more than once, in different sections. In that case, include the section number with the page number. For example, type

3s2

to jump to page 3 in the second section. (See Chapter 9 for more information on sections and formatting.)

Word normally determines where pages break as you type or make changes. But you can turn off this feature by choosing the Utilities Customize command and turning off the Background Pagination check box. With background pagination turned off, the document isn't divided into pages until it's printed or until you use the Utilities Repaginate Now command. Some people like to turn off background pagination so that the page numbers of a document on the screen correspond to the page numbers of the most recently printed copy. For example, if you ask to go to page 5, the cursor moves to the first character of what was page 5 in the previous printout. This is helpful when you're making changes marked on a printed copy.

Making and Finding Bookmarks

Bookmarks mark places or text that you want to find later. To make a bookmark:

1. Move the cursor to the place you want to mark, or highlight the block of text you want to mark.

2. Choose the Insert Bookmark command (Alt, I, M).

3. When you see the Insert Bookmark dialog box, type a name for the bookmark in the Bookmark Name box, and choose <OK> (press Enter):

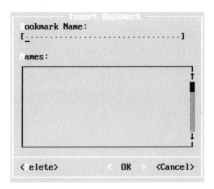

The name of the bookmark can contain as many as 31 characters and must begin and end with a letter or a number. It can include letters, numbers, underscores (_), periods (.), and hyphens (-).

If you type a name that's already been used or choose a name from the list of existing bookmarks in the Names box, that bookmark moves from its previous location to the new location or text. Before moving an existing bookmark, Word asks you to confirm that you want to do so. You can also delete a bookmark with the Insert Bookmark command: Choose the bookmark's name from the Names box, and choose the <Delete> command button at the bottom of the dialog box.

To find a bookmark, choose the Edit Go To command. The Bookmark Name box in the Edit Go To dialog box lists the names of the bookmarks you've created, as shown in Figure 6-1. Choose the name you want from the list, and then choose <OK> (press Enter). Or, with the mouse, double-click the bookmark name. (You can also type the bookmark name in the Go To box, but be sure the Bookmark button is turned on.) Word responds by moving the cursor to the bookmark. If you marked a block of text instead of a single cursor position, Word highlights that text.

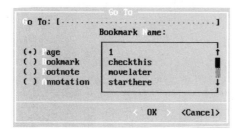

Figure 6-1. *The Edit Go To dialog box, with bookmark names listed in the Bookmark Name box.*

You can also use bookmarks to create cross-references that are automatically updated as the document is changed. For more information, see the manual *Using Microsoft Word* that comes with the Word package.

SEARCHING FOR TEXT

A search starts from the cursor location and continues in one direction until Word locates the first occurrence of the text you want to find. You can specify the direction of the search: up (backward to the beginning of the document) or down (forward to the end of the document). Because the cursor's location determines the starting point, you might want to move the cursor before you choose the Edit Search command. To confine the search to one section of a document, highlight that section. If any text is highlighted, Word searches only within the highlighted text.

After you choose the Edit Search command, the Edit Search dialog box appears on the screen:

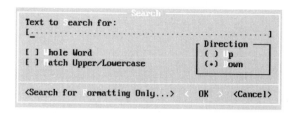

Most important, Word needs to know what text you want to find. The Whole Word, Match Upper/Lowercase, and Direction options give the command flexibility and help you pinpoint the target. Word assumes that the text you're looking for is not necessarily a whole word, that you want to ignore whether letters are uppercase or lowercase when looking for a match, and that you want to search forward. If these proposed responses fit your needs, choose <OK> (press Enter) after you type in the search text. Otherwise, change the options before you OK the dialog box.

The following sections explain the dialog box options. Familiarize yourself with them, but don't let them deter you from using either the Edit Search or the Edit Replace command. In most cases, you can find what you want without paying much attention to the options. And if you get unintended results, you can always undo them.

Telling Word What to Find

Type the text you want to find in the box labeled Text to Search For. You can search for a single character, a word, a phrase, a sentence, or any piece of text as long as 256 characters.

The symbols ? and ^ have special meanings when typed in the Text to Search For box. These symbols are used in codes to search for special characters such as tabs and paragraph marks or for unspecified characters. (More about search codes later.) To search for a question mark or a caret (^), precede the symbol with a caret. This signals Word that you're searching for the symbol itself, not using it as a code for something else. For example, to search for the phrase *Do you understand?*, type

Do you understand^?

To find the characters ^C, type

^^C

Searching Up or Down

The option buttons in the Direction box tell Word which way to look. Turn on the Up button to search backward if the cursor is at the end of the document or is located after the part of the document you want to search. Turn on the Down button to search forward if the cursor is at the beginning of the document or is located before the part of the document you want to search.

Looking for Whole Words

Word assumes that the text you're looking for is not necessarily a whole word. This lets you find a word by searching for part of it. For example, if you're searching for the word *telecommunications,* it's faster and easier to type *telecom* as the search text than to type the whole word. The shorter your search text, the less chance you have of making a mistake when typing it.

Typing part of a word with the Whole Word check box turned off also lets you find various forms of a word without searching for each form individually. For example, if you want to locate all the references in this book to deleting text, you can search for *delet* to find *delete, deletes, deleted, deleting, deletion,* and *deletions.*

Turn on the Whole Word check box to search for a word like *ear* without finding words in which it is embedded: *research, linear,* or *pear,* for instance. You can also avoid these unwanted words by searching for *(space)ear(space),* but you won't find *ear.* or *ear,* or *ear:* if you specify a space after the word. If you tell Word to search for whole words only, it looks for a match that has a space, tab, or punctuation mark before and after it.

Matching or Ignoring Case

A word's letter case is often determined by its position in a sentence. When you're searching for a word, you usually want to find it regardless of where it occurs in a sentence. For example, if you want to find the phrase *something scrumptious,* you probably don't care whether it occurs at the beginning of a sentence with an uppercase *S,* in the middle of a sentence with a lowercase *s,* or in a special block of all-caps text. As long as the Match Upper/Lowercase check box is turned off, you can find *something scrumptious, Something scrumptious, Something Scrumptious, SOMETHING SCRUMPTIOUS,* and other combinations.

If, however, you want to find only text with exactly the same uppercase and lowercase letters as the words you type in the Text to Search For box, turn on the Match Upper/Lowercase check box. Use this option when you are looking specifically for words that are in all caps or that have initial caps, such as acronyms, proper names, or the first word of a sentence. For example, turn on this option if you want to find *WAVES* in uniform rather than *waves* in the sea or *China* in the Far East rather than *china* on the shelf.

After the Search

If Word finds the text you specify, it brings the text into view and highlights it. You can immediately start to edit, format, or examine what you've found. If Word doesn't find the text, you hear a beep and see a message box that requires a response. If Word has searched the entire document, you see this message:

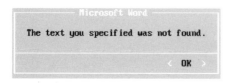

Press the Enter key or click the <OK> button to acknowledge the message. If Word searched highlighted text, a similar message reminds you that Word looked in the selection only:

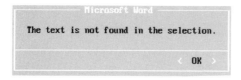

If the cursor is not at the beginning or end of the document when you start the search, Word searches only part of the document. If it doesn't find the search text, Word asks whether you want to continue searching through the other part. For example, if the cursor is in the middle of a document when you give the command to search down, Word displays the message shown on the following page if it doesn't find the text.

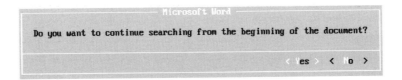

Repeating the Search with Shift-F4

The Edit Search command finds the first occurrence of the text you're looking for. To find the next occurrence, repeat the command. The easiest way to do that is to press Shift-F4.

Shift-F4 repeats the last search, with all the same options. (If the last search was done with the Edit Replace command, Shift-F4 searches for the text specified in that command.) Word remembers your previous responses in the dialog box until you change them (with either the Edit Search or the Edit Replace command), until you quit Word (with the File Exit Word command), or until you clear all memory (with the File Close All command).

Searching for Special Characters

Pressing the Tab key or the Enter key inserts a special character into your document. Special characters are not letters, numbers, or symbols. They are basically formatting tools and are usually either invisible or visible only as blank space. They can be deleted, copied, or moved like any other character. You can search for them, but you must use a special code to do so.

The table in Figure 6-2 lists the special characters, the keys pressed to generate them, and their search codes. You'll learn when and why these special characters are used when you look at formatting in Chapter 9.

All search codes (except ^w) have a one-to-one correspondence to a special character. For example, ^t embedded in search text tells Word to look for text with a single tab character embedded in it. If you search for

1^t2

you will find

1 2

if the space between 1 and 2 was made by pressing the Tab key once.

Special Character	*Keys Pressed*	*Search Code*
Nonbreaking space	Ctrl-Shift-Spacebar	^s
Tab character	Tab	^t
Paragraph mark	Enter	^p
Newline mark	Shift-Enter	^n
Section mark	Insert Break command	^d
Page break	Ctrl-Enter	^d
Nonrequired hyphen	Ctrl-hyphen key (or automatically inserted with the Utilities Hyphenate command)	^-
White space (any amount of blank space)	Any combination or number of these keys: Spacebar, Ctrl-Spacebar, Tab, Enter, Shift-Enter, Ctrl-Enter	^w

Figure 6-2. *Special-character search codes.*

Searching for white space

The search code ^w corresponds to any combination or number of characters that appear as white, or blank, space. This code helps you search for white space without requiring you to specify how the space was created. (This search code does not, however, find blank space created by formatting commands, such as indents and line spacing.)

You might, for example, want to look for text that has a block of space in it, although you're not sure whether the space was created by the Spacebar or the Tab key. Or, even if you know which key you pressed, you might not be sure how many times you pressed it. If you search for

1^w2

you will find

1   2

regardless of whether the space was created by pressing the Spacebar several times, the Tab key once, the Tab key twice, or some combination of both the Tab key and the Spacebar.

Searching for hyphenated words

The way to search for a hyphenated word depends on the kind of hyphen it contains. Word uses three kinds of hyphens: normal, nonbreaking, and non-required. *Normal hyphens* are used in compound words that can be broken at the end of a line. *Nonbreaking hyphens* are used in words that should *not* be broken at the hyphen. Both normal and nonbreaking hyphens are always visible. *Nonrequired hyphens* occur in words that can be broken, but these hyphens are visible only if needed for a line break. Examples of each and the keys pressed to type them are shown in Figure 6-3. (See Chapter 9 for a complete description.)

Type of Hyphen	Example	Keys Pressed
Normal	cross-country	Hyphen key
Nonbreaking	Cooper-Smith, -30°F	Ctrl-Shift-hyphen key
Nonrequired	mul-ti-tude	Ctrl-hyphen key

Figure 6-3. *The three kinds of hyphens.*

To search for a word with a normal hyphen, press the hyphen key to type the hyphen in the search text. To search for a word with a nonbreaking hyphen, press Ctrl-Shift-hyphen key to type the hyphen. When you're not sure whether a word contains a normal or a nonbreaking hyphen, type a question mark in place of the hyphen.

To search for a word that might have a nonrequired hyphen, type the word without a hyphen. The special search code ^- can be used for nonrequired hyphens, but it's not practical for most searches. For example, when the word *keyboard* is the search text, Word finds both *keyboard* and *key-board* (with a nonrequired hyphen). If *key^-board* is the search text, however, Word finds *key-board* (with a nonrequired hyphen) but not *keyboard*.

Searching for unspecified characters

You don't need to specify every character you're looking for. If you put a question mark in your search text, Word interprets the question mark to mean any single character.

You might use this option, for example, when you're not sure how to spell the word you want to find. Suppose you want to locate all mentions of Allan Reid in a document, but you can't remember how his name was spelled. You can search for *All?n R??d* to find *Allan Reed, Allen Reed, Allan Reid, Allen Reid, Allan Ried,* or *Allen Ried.* (This search would not find *Alan.*)

You can also use this feature to locate all the dates—or some other set of numbers of equal length—that fall into a certain range. For example, searching for *196?* finds *1960* through *1969.*

Searching for hidden text

If you want to search for text that has been hidden from view, you must first make the text visible. (Text can be formatted as hidden text by using Ctrl-H or the Format Character command; see Chapter 9 for more information.)

To make hidden text visible on the screen, choose the View Preferences command, turn on the Hidden Text check box, and choose <OK> (press Enter). Then choose the View menu, and check to see that the toggle command View Layout is turned off (not marked). If it is on, choose View Layout to turn it off.

REPLACING TEXT

The Edit Replace command finds text, deletes it, and inserts other text in its place. It looks for text the same way the Edit Search command does and offers the same options for letter case and whole words.

Unlike the Edit Search command, the Edit Replace command searches in one direction only—down from the cursor to the end of a document—until every occurrence has been found. If the cursor is under a single character, the text extending from (and including) that character to the end of the document is searched. But if the cursor is highlighting one or more characters, only the highlighted text—from the first character to the last character in the selection—is searched.

If you want to confine an Edit Replace command to a certain part of a document, highlight that part before you choose the command. If you want to replace throughout an entire document, move the cursor to the beginning of the document before you choose the command.

After you choose the Edit Replace command, you see the Edit Replace dialog box:

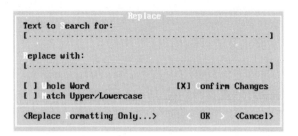

The Whole Word, the Match Upper/Lowercase, and the Confirm Changes check boxes provide options that help prevent unwanted replacements. Word assumes that the text you're looking for is not necessarily a whole word, that you want to ignore whether letters are uppercase or lowercase when looking for a match, and that you want to see the text Word finds before it's replaced. If these choices are acceptable, OK the command after you type in the replacement text. Otherwise, change the responses before you choose <OK>.

Telling Word What to Find and Replace

Type the text you want to find in the box labeled Text to Search For. The search text can be as long as 256 characters, including special characters and unspecified characters. Because the symbols ? and ^ are reserved for coding, you must type ^? to find ? and type ^^ to find ^.

Type the replacement text in the Replace With box. You can specify as many as 256 characters. You can include special characters such as tabs—but not unspecified characters such as ? and ^w. Because the caret is reserved for coding special characters, type ^^ if you want ^ to appear in the replacement text. Do not type any replacement text if you want to find and delete text without replacing it.

Asking for Confirmation

Turning on the Confirm Changes check box allows you to approve replacements before they take effect. By default, this check box is on. Leave it on to confirm replacements until you get a feel for what the computer finds when you ask it to search for something. (You might be surprised how exacting and literal a computer can be.) With the Confirm Changes check box on, Word stops to highlight each occurrence of the text it finds and displays this message box:

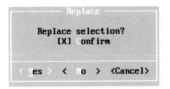

Choose <Yes> to replace the highlighted text and search for the next occurrence. Choose <No> to leave the highlighted text in place and search for the next occurrence. To stop the Edit Replace command from continuing, choose <Cancel>. To make the Edit Replace command continue without asking for further confirmations, press Alt-C to turn off the Confirm Changes check box, and then press the Enter key. If you're using the mouse, click the Confirm Changes check box, and then click <Yes>.

If you turn off the Confirm Changes check box, Word performs the replacements without asking for your approval. This speeds up the process but might cost you time later if you haven't defined your search text carefully.

Matching or Ignoring Case

When the Match Upper/Lowercase check box is off, you can replace all occurrences of the search text, regardless of letter case. When replacing text, Word retains the case of the text being replaced if it is all lowercase, all uppercase, or initial caps (first letter of each word capitalized). For example, if you ask Word to search for *chaos* and replace it with *order,* it will replace *chaos* with *order, Chaos* with *Order,* and *CHAOS* with *ORDER.* But if it finds *cHAos*, it will replace it with *order.*

Turn on the Match Upper/Lowercase check box when you want to find and replace only those occurrences of text that have the same uppercase and lowercase letters as the search text. That way, if you ask Word to replace *China* with *Hong Kong,* it will replace only *China*—not *china*—so you won't end up with something like *Our fine Hong Kong was damaged in transit.*

Replacing Whole Words

The Whole Word check box in the Edit Replace dialog box works as it does with the Edit Search command. Having the option to search for whole words only is especially important when replacing text. For example, if you try to change every *man* to *person* without specifying whole words only, you could end up with gibberish like *persony*, *personuscripts*, *personifest*, *hupersonistic*, and *personner*.

After the Search and Replace

After all replacements are made, the cursor returns to where it was when you chose the Edit Replace command. The message bar tells you how many replacements were made. When Word can't find the search text, a message box alerts you to any additional places to search, as it does with the Edit Search command. If the Edit Replace command makes some unexpected changes, remember that you can reverse them with the Edit Undo command.

Repeating the Replace Command

To repeat the last Edit Replace command, choose and OK it again. Except for the Confirm Changes check box, Word retains your previous responses in the Edit Replace dialog box until you change them (with either the Edit Search or the Edit Replace command), quit the program, or clear your entire work area. For safety, Word turns the Confirm Changes check box back on after carrying out an Edit Replace command.

Chapter 7

Windows and Viewing Options

The window you see when you start Word is only one of nine windows that can be open at one time. You can open more than one window on the same document, or you can open windows with different documents in each one. With more than one window open, you can compare documents or different parts of the same document. You can easily cut or copy text from one window and paste it into another.

Whether you have one or several windows open, you can control what you see on the screen. You can remove various parts of the Word screen to see additional text, and you can choose to display or hide nonprinting characters or line numbers. You can also see a list of display modes available for your monitor and choose one from the list.

WORKING WITH WINDOWS

Being able to have more than one window open at a time makes your computer screen more like a desktop, where you can have more than one file folder open or within easy reach. The windows can be stacked on top of one another or arranged so that all or some of them are visible at the same time. They can overlap or be arranged side by side. You can resize them and move them around. You can work in only one window at a time, but you can easily move from one window to another. The commands for working with windows and the titles of all open windows appear on the Window menu, which is shown on the following page.

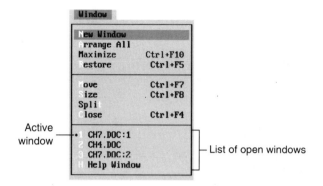

The mouse is especially handy for working with windows. Instead of using the Window commands, you can point to icons and special places on the screen to manipulate windows. Figure 7-1 shows where the "hot spots" for the mouse are located and how to use them.

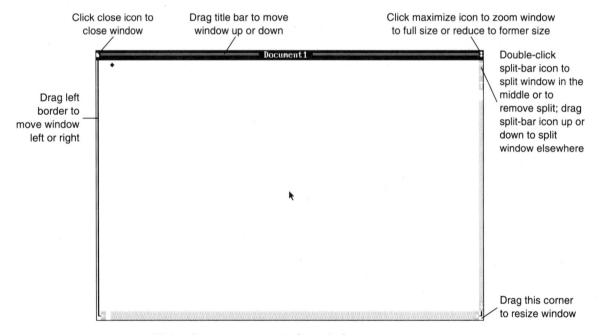

Figure 7-1. *Using the mouse to manipulate windows.*

Opening Windows

When you use the File New, File Open, or Window New Window command, Word opens a new window and stacks it on top of the current window. The newly opened window becomes the active window. A window opened with the File New command is blank, ready for you to create a new document. A window opened with the File Open command displays the file opened with that command, and a window opened with the Window New Window command displays another copy of the document you were working on when you chose the command. Each window containing the same document is assigned a number, which appears after the document name in the title bar.

Use the File New or the File Open command when you want to work with more than one document at a time. Use the Window New Window command when you want to see various parts or views of the same document.

In addition to nine document windows, you can open a Help window (using the Help menu or the F1 key). Unless you arrange multiple windows so that you can view more than one at a time, they remain layered one on top of the other.

Activating a Window

You can work in only one window at a time, the *active window.* The active window appears on top of the stack and contains the cursor and the scroll bars. All open windows are listed at the end of the Window menu. A dot marks the active window in the list.

To activate a window:

1. Choose the Window menu (Alt, W).

2. Choose the document or window name from the list at the bottom of the menu. With the keyboard, press the number shown next to the name. With the mouse, point to the name and click.

If the window you activate is hidden, Word moves it to the top of the stack so that you can see it and work on it.

Instead of using the Window menu, you can press Ctrl-F6 to skip to the next window listed on the Window menu or press Ctrl-Shift-F6 to skip back to the previous window on the list. You can continue pressing Ctrl-F6 until you find the window you want, because Word keeps cycling through the entire list of open windows.

If the window you want to activate is visible on the screen, the mouse can seek it out without any formalities: Simply point to it and click.

Rearranging Windows

To view more than one window at the same time, you must rearrange them on the screen. Word can do this for you, or you can rearrange them yourself by resizing and moving the windows.

Arranging windows automatically

The Window Arrange All command makes all open windows visible at the same time. Word divides the screen and arranges all open windows so that none of them overlap, as shown in Figure 7-2.

The Window Arrange All command works well with two or three windows, but when you have more than three open windows, the space available for each one is quite small. To see more text, you might decide to keep only a few of the open windows visible. Or you might want to see more of some windows and less of others. You can do this by adjusting the size or location of individual windows.

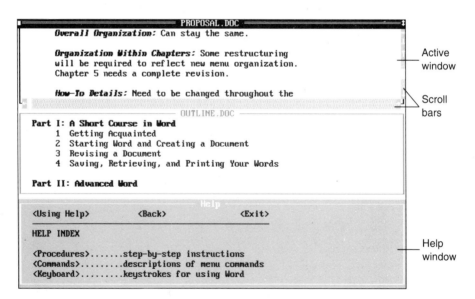

Figure 7-2. *Three windows arranged automatically with the Window Arrange All command.*

Resizing and moving windows

If you rearrange the open windows yourself, you usually need to move windows as well as adjust their sizes. When you change a window's size, with either the keyboard or the mouse, you can move only the right or the bottom window border. This limits how much you can resize a window unless you also move the window or its neighbors. When you don't need to view a window, you can cover it up by enlarging or moving another window over it.

With the keyboard, use the Window Size command to change the size of a window:

1. Activate the window you want to size.

2. Choose the Window Size command (Alt, W, S). The background of the window borders changes to black, and you see the word SIZE in the status bar. (You cannot edit the document or use the mouse while SIZE appears in the status bar; clicking the mouse button cancels the Window Size command.)

3. To change the width, move the right window border with the Left or Right direction key. To change the height, move the bottom border with the Up or Down direction key.

4. Press the Enter key to carry out the change, or press the Esc key to cancel it.

With the mouse, drag the lower right corner, which is the *size icon* (▯), to resize a window:

1. Point to the lower right corner.

2. Hold down the mouse button while you drag the corner to a new position. (The background of the window borders turns black as you drag the corner.)

3. Release the mouse button.

You can use the Window Move command to change the location of a window on the screen. If you move a window to a place already occupied by another window, the moved window overlaps the other one. To move a window with the keyboard:

1. Activate the window you want to move.

2. Choose the Window Move command (Alt, W, M). The background of the window borders changes to black, and you see the word MOVE in the status bar. (You cannot edit the document or use the mouse while MOVE appears in the status bar; clicking the mouse button cancels the Window Move command.)

3. Use the Left or Right direction key to move the window sideways. Use the Up or Down direction key to move the window up or down.

4. Press the Enter key to execute the move, or press the Esc key to cancel it.

With the mouse, you can drag the window to a new location:

1. Point to the left window border if you want to move the window sideways, or point to the title bar if you want to move it up or down.

2. Hold down the mouse button while you drag the left or top border to the new location. (The background of the window borders turns black as you drag the border.)

3. Release the mouse button.

Enlarging a window to full size

If you feel cramped working in a window that has been reduced in size or moved partially off the screen, you can instantly enlarge it to fill the screen. With the keyboard, use the Window Maximize command to zoom a window to full size:

1. Activate the window.

2. Choose the Window Maximize command (Alt, W, X). The abbreviation MX appears in the status bar.

The other open windows remain open behind the enlarged window. To see any one of the other open windows, you can choose the name of the window you want to see from the Window menu, or you can cycle through the open windows using Ctrl-F6. As long as MX appears in the status bar, the window you activate becomes the maximized window.

The MX abbreviation stays in the status bar until you resize or move the active window or until you choose the Window Arrange All or the Window Restore command. To see all the open windows at one time, choose the

Window Arrange All command. To see all the windows that were visible before you maximized one of them, and to reduce the maximized window to its former size, use the Window Restore command.

With the mouse, you can maximize and restore a window by using the *maximize icon*. The maximize icon is a double-headed arrow (◪) in the upper right corner of the active window. To enlarge a window to full size with the maximize icon, first activate the window and then click the icon.

You can also click the maximize icon when you want to reduce a maximized window to its former size. (You know that a window has been maximized when you see MX in the status bar.)

Closing a Window

When you finish working with a window, you can close it to remove it from the screen and to remove the contents of the window from memory. Use either the Window Close or the File Close command to close the active window. If you want to close all the open windows, use the File Close All command. Before you close a window, you can activate it and choose the File Save command to save its contents, or you can wait until you are prompted to save. Each of these commands prompts you to save if you have not saved all your changes. If you close all the open windows, your work area on the screen becomes blank, and fewer menus and commands are available. When you open a file, the screen comes back to life, and all menus are restored.

To quickly close a window with the mouse, activate the window, and simply click the *close icon* (◻) in the upper left corner of the window.

Splitting a Window

Splitting a window is a fast way to get two views of the same document. A split window is divided horizontally into two *window panes,* as shown in Figure 7-3 on the following page. Each pane scrolls vertically, independent of the other, so you can see one part of a document in one pane and another part in the other pane. Using View commands, you can get two different views of the same document. For example, you can view the outline of a document in one pane and the entire text in the other. Or you can make hidden text visible in one pane and hide it in the other. Changes made by all other commands affect the text in both windows.

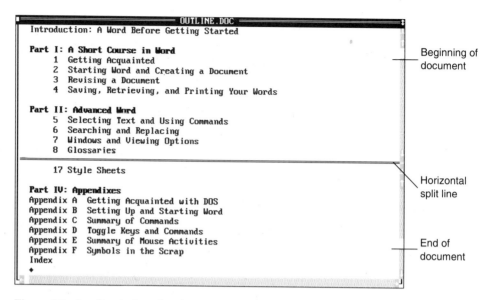

Figure 7-3. *A split window showing two parts of the same document.*

You cannot split a window vertically. If you want to view two parts of the same document side by side, use the Window New Window command to open a second window on the same document, and then arrange the windows as needed.

With the keyboard, use the Window Split command to split a window into panes:

1. Activate the window.

2. Choose the Window Split command (Alt, W, T). A double line called the *horizontal split line* is drawn across the top of the window. (You cannot use the mouse or edit the document until you complete the command.)

3. Press the Up or Down direction key to move the horizontal split line to the place where you want to split the window.

4. Press the Enter key to split the window. If you decide to cancel the command, press the Esc key.

To remove a split using the Window Split command, move the split line up to the top of the scroll bar and press the Enter key.

With the mouse, you can quickly split a window into two equal parts. Just double-click the *split-bar icon* (=) in the right window border. Or you can drag the split-bar icon up or down the scroll bar to the place where you want the window split. To remove a split, drag the icon to the top of the scroll bar or, easier still, double-click the split-bar icon.

Moving from one pane to another

To move the cursor from one pane to another, press the F6 key. With the mouse, point to the pane you want and click.

CUTTING AND PASTING WITH WINDOWS

You can use the same cut-and-paste techniques that you use within a window to move and copy text between windows or between window panes. Let's look at the procedure for using window panes to cut and paste between two parts of the same document. Then we'll try opening a second window to cut and paste between two different documents.

Using Window Panes to Cut and Paste

To cut and paste between two parts of the same document:

1. Use the File Open command to open the document you want to work with.

2. Choose the Window Split command. Use the Up or Down direction key to position the horizontal split line, and press Enter to split the window into two parts. With the mouse, double-click the split-bar icon or drag the icon to the location where you want to split the window.

3. When necessary, use the F6 key to move from one pane to another. With the mouse, click the pane you want to move to.

4. If necessary, scroll through each window pane until you see both the text you want to move or copy in one window and its destination in the other window.

5. Select the text to be moved or copied, and then delete it (using Shift-Del or the Edit Cut command) or copy it to the scrap (using Ctrl-Ins or the Edit Copy command).

6. Move the cursor to the destination in the second window pane, and insert the text from the scrap (using Shift-Ins or the Edit Paste command).

7. Remove the window split when you have no more use for it. Choose the Window Split command, press the Up direction key until the split line is at the top of the window, and press Enter. With the mouse, double-click the split-bar icon.

You don't need to save before removing the split. Any changes made in one window pane can be viewed and saved through the other pane.

Using Windows to Cut and Paste

To cut and paste between two documents:

1. Use the File Open command to open one of the documents.

2. Use the File Open command to open the second document.

3. Choose the Window Arrange All command to make both windows visible. (You can instead size and move the windows with the Window Size and the Window Move commands.)

4. When necessary, use Ctrl-F6 to move from one window to another. With the mouse, click the window you want to move to.

5. Scroll through each window until the text you want to move or copy appears in one window and its destination appears in the other window.

6. Select the text to be moved or copied, and then delete it (using Shift-Del or the Edit Cut command) or copy it to the scrap (using Ctrl-Ins or the Edit Copy command).

7. Move the cursor to the destination in the other window, and then insert the text from the scrap (using Shift-Ins or the Edit Paste command).

8. Before closing either window, save the changes.

Instead of opening a second document, you can open a second window on the same document with the Window New Window command. Or you can use the File New command to open a blank window in which you can create a new document or perhaps take notes. You can then cut and paste between your new document or note pad and a document in another window.

Undoing Window Work

You can undo any cutting and pasting done between windows, exactly as you can within a single window. But the Edit Undo command has no effect on opening, closing, sizing, moving, arranging, or splitting windows.

VIEWING OPTIONS

The View commands let you control what you see on the screen. The viewing options introduced here are those most useful for editing; later chapters discuss other options as the need for them becomes apparent. (For a complete list of options that let you control what you see or how Word operates, see "Customizing Word" in Appendix C.)

You can remove various parts of the Word screen to allow more room for text display. To turn off the status bar, choose the View Status Bar command. (To turn the status bar back on, simply choose the same command again—View Status Bar is a toggle command.) To turn off the menu bar, the window borders, the message bar, or the scroll bars, use the View Preferences command and turn off the appropriate check box:

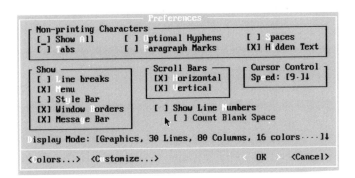

 NOTE: If you turn off the menu bar, you can restore it temporarily whenever you need it by pressing the Alt key. If you turn off the two scroll bars or the window borders, you will not be able to size, move, or scroll through windows with the mouse. If more than one window is open and visible, the borders of those windows cannot be removed.

Nonprinting characters such as spaces, tabs, newline marks, and paragraph marks are usually indistinguishable on the screen because they all look like blank space. To make them visible, choose the View Preferences command and turn on the check box for each type of character you want to see.

You can even adjust the speed of the cursor. Choose the View Preferences command, and enter a number from 0 to 9 in the Cursor Control Speed box to indicate how fast you want the cursor to move. (The fastest speed is 9.) The cursor speed is most noticeable when you hold down a cursor-moving key for continuous movement.

If you want to keep track of which line the cursor is in, you can add the line number to the page and column display in the status bar. Line numbers begin with 1 on each new page. To turn on the line number display, turn on the Show Line Numbers check box after you choose the View Preferences command.

The Display Mode box of the View Preferences command drops down to list the display modes available for your monitor. As explained in Chapter 1, the two main display modes are text mode and graphics mode. (Recall that you must have a graphics monitor and adapter to be able to operate in graphics mode.) Graphics mode displays actual character formats (such as italics and boldface) on the screen; text mode indicates special character formats by changing color or intensity. The mouse pointer is an arrow in graphics mode and a box in text mode. When you are scrolling through text, text mode can be noticeably faster than graphics mode.

Within both text and graphics modes, you might have a choice of how many lines of text and columns of characters are displayed. With the View Preferences command, you can try out all of the display modes available for your monitor to see what they look like. Drop down the list for the Display Mode box, choose the mode you want to try, and choose <OK> (press Enter). Word remembers the last two modes chosen and lets you switch between them by pressing Alt-F9.

Chapter 8

Glossaries

Glossaries let you create your own shorthand for words, phrases, or any amount of text that you use over and over again. They provide a convenient way to copy anything you would otherwise type repeatedly. Copying text instead of retyping it speeds up document preparation, reduces your chances of making errors, and enables you to easily match the exact wording, spelling, capitalization, and often the format of recurring items that require consistent treatment and precise wording.

You can also use a glossary instead of the scrap to copy or move text when you don't want to take the time to find the new location right away. Text can be stored only temporarily in the scrap, but it can be stored in a glossary for as long as you want.

WHAT IS A GLOSSARY?

A glossary is a storage place for pieces of text. After you store text in a glossary, you can retrieve a copy of it at any time to insert anywhere in a document—or in any number of documents any number of times. (You can also store sequences of commands, or macros, in a glossary. Macros are discussed in Chapter 16.)

You can store many pieces of text in a glossary, giving each glossary entry a unique name. You can also have more than one glossary, saving each with a unique filename. You might, for example, create one glossary for business correspondence, one for scientific terms, and one to help you prepare legal contracts. The only limit to the length of your glossaries and the number of glossaries you create is your available disk space.

Samples of the kinds of text you might include in a glossary are shown in Figure 8-1 below.

Usage	Entry Name	Text
Parts of a Letter		
Often-used mailing addresses	*return*	National Health Organization Department of Nutrition 1500 Holgrain Lane Washington, D.C. 20107
Closings	*close*	Yours in Good Health, Evelyn Eatwell, Ph.D. Chair, Department of Nutrition
Stock paragraphs	*sorry*	Thank you for your order. Unfortunately, we cannot send you any merchandise without advance payment until you clear your account with us.
Stock sentences	*help*	If I can be of further help to you, please don't hesitate to call me.
Legal Phrasing		
Copyright notices	*copyright*	Copyright 1990 by Metaphors Unlimited. All rights reserved.
Trademark notices	*ibmtrade*	IBM is a registered trademark of International Business Machines Corporation.
Miscellaneous Words and Phrases		
Company names	*ns*	National Semiconductor Corporation
Organization names	*ioof*	Independent Order of Odd Fellows
Product names	*mw*	Microsoft Word
Phrases	*rda*	Recommended Daily Allowance
Words	*hip*	hippopotamus

Figure 8-1. *Sample glossary entries.*

BUILDING YOUR MAIN GLOSSARY

NORMAL.GLY is the glossary you're likely to use most often—and for many of you, it will be the only glossary you need. In this section, you'll learn how to add entries to NORMAL.GLY, retrieve text from it, and save it.

Adding Entries to NORMAL.GLY

You can start building your main glossary by adding a few useful items to NORMAL.GLY. If you used the Setup program described in Appendix B, this glossary is found on your working copy of one of the Word Program disks (or in the same directory as Word on your hard disk) and is loaded into memory each time you start Word. NORMAL.GLY already contains glossary entries supplied by Word (described later in this chapter).

To create your own glossary entries, you must have a window on the screen (with or without a document in it). Begin by storing in the glossary the closing you most frequently use in letters:

1. Type the closing, exactly as you would in a letter. (You can type it anywhere on the screen because you can delete it right away.) For example, you could type this closing:

   Yours in Good Health,

   Evelyn Eatwell, Ph.D.
   Chair, Department of Nutrition

2. Highlight the entire closing, and then choose the Edit Glossary command (Alt, E, O). Word displays the Edit Glossary dialog box:

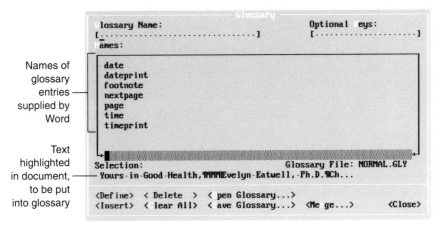

Names of glossary entries supplied by Word —

Text highlighted in document, to be put into glossary —

3. Make up a name for the text, and type the name in the Glossary Name box. This *entry name* identifies the piece of text being put into the glossary. In this case, you might type *close*.

4. Choose the <Define> command button.

A copy of the highlighted text is placed in the glossary, filed under the entry name. The dialog box disappears, and the text is still highlighted in the document. To delete it, press the Del key or choose the Edit Cut command.

Add a few more entries to the glossary—items that you type often, such as your company name, a frequently used address, or a distribution list for memos. Give each a short entry name using only letters and numbers—no spaces or symbols. (More options for naming glossary entries are described later in the chapter.)

Using NORMAL.GLY

Let's say you just finished typing the body of a letter, and you're ready to add the closing. Move the cursor to where you want the closing to appear, and type *close*. Then press the F3 key. The closing you stored in the glossary immediately replaces the entry name *close*.

Saving NORMAL.GLY

Now save the entries you added to NORMAL.GLY so that they don't disappear when you quit. To save NORMAL.GLY:

1. Choose the Edit Glossary command (Alt, E, O).

2. Choose the <Save Glossary> command button.

3. The Save Glossary dialog box appears:

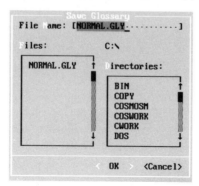

The proposed response in the File Name box is the current glossary, which initially is NORMAL.GLY.

4. Choose <OK> (press Enter) to accept the proposed response and carry out the command.

NORMAL.GLY, containing the entries you've saved and the entries supplied by Word, is opened and ready to use each time you start Word.

WORKING WITH GLOSSARIES

While working with NORMAL.GLY in the previous sections, you learned how to store text in a glossary and retrieve text from it. The following sections tell you more about naming glossary entries, show you alternative ways to retrieve glossary text, and explain what the supplied glossary entries do. You also learn how to edit and delete glossary entries and how to use glossaries for cut-and-paste work.

All of this work with glossaries can be done with the Edit Glossary command. Figure 8-2 shows the Edit Glossary dialog box and points out the information and tools you need to work with glossaries.

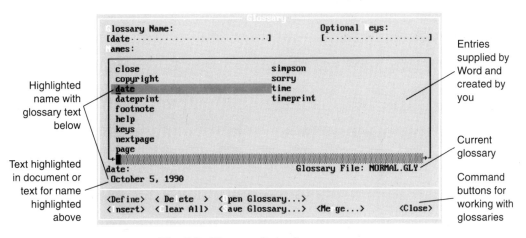

Figure 8-2. *The Edit Glossary dialog box.*

Storing Text in a Glossary

Recall that to store text in a glossary you must first type the text in a document or a blank window and highlight it. When you choose the Edit Glossary command, the selected text appears below the Names box. After you type the glossary entry name in the Glossary Name box, choosing the <Define> command button copies the highlighted text to the glossary file in memory.

Naming glossary entries

Word gives you a lot of flexibility in choosing glossary entry names. They can be as long as 31 characters and can include any letters or numbers but no spaces. You can use uppercase letters, underscores, periods, and hyphens to help make multiple-word names more readable. For example, the entry name *Property_Lease_Refund_Terms* is preferable to *propertyleaserefundterms*.

 NOTE: Although you can use underscores, periods, and hyphens within a glossary entry name, you cannot begin or end an entry name with these characters.

A name should be short enough to be remembered and typed easily, yet long enough to clearly indicate what it stands for. If you try to give the same name to two different glossary entries in the same glossary, Word displays this message:

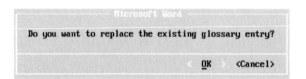

Choose <Cancel> (press Esc) to avoid replacing the existing glossary entry. You can then assign a different name to the new entry. If you choose <OK> in the message box (press Enter), Word replaces the existing entry with the new one. For example, if you use the name *pc* to stand for *IBM Personal Computer* and then later assign *pc* to *peanut clusters*, Word replaces *IBM Personal Computer* with *peanut clusters*.

Retrieving Text from a Glossary

You can retrieve copies of glossary entries to insert in any document that's visible on the screen. A glossary file must be open before you can retrieve text stored in it. To see which glossary file is open (if you have more than one), choose the Edit Glossary command and look at the glossary filename shown below the Names box.

Use either the F3 key or the Edit Glossary command to retrieve glossary text. Before you press the F3 key, recall that you must first type the glossary entry name where you want the glossary text inserted. If the entry name has already been typed in the document, either move the cursor to the right of the name or highlight the name before you press F3.

If the cursor is an underscore when you press the F3 key, Word looks immediately to the left of the cursor for an entry name. (A space, symbol, or punctuation mark must precede the name to mark its beginning.) If the cursor is highlighting more than one character, Word expects the highlighted text to be the entry name. If Word doesn't find an entry name when you press F3, a message box tells you that the glossary entry does not exist. Choose <OK> to dismiss the message, and try again after making sure that your cursor is positioned properly.

If you don't remember the name of a glossary entry, use the Edit Glossary command instead of the F3 key. This command lets you choose the entry name from a list and shows you the glossary text before you insert it in the document. To retrieve a glossary entry with the Edit Glossary command:

1. Position the cursor where you want to insert the glossary text.

2. Choose the Edit Glossary command (Alt, E, O).

3. With the keyboard, press Alt-N to move to the Names box, and use the direction keys to highlight the glossary entry name. If you are using the mouse, point to the entry name and click. After you highlight the name, you can see the text represented by that name below the Names box, as shown in Figure 8-2.

4. Choose the <Insert> command button to insert the text in your document.

Instead of choosing from the list, you can type the entry name in the Glossary Name box and then choose the <Insert> button. If you type a name that isn't in the current glossary, a message box tells you that the glossary entry does not exist. Press the Enter key or click the <OK> button to make the message disappear, and then retype the name or choose one from the list in the Names box.

Speeding up glossary retrieval

You can assign an optional key code to your most frequently used glossary entries. Then, instead of using the Edit Glossary command or the F3 key to insert glossary text, you can type the key code. Key codes can be a combination of the Control key plus one or, preferably, two characters, such as Ctrl-GL. To avoid conflicts with speed formatting keys, it's a good idea to use two-character key codes whose first character is a letter or number not used for speed formatting.

Instead of using a Control-key combination, you can assign a function key (such as F5) or a function-key combination (such as Shift-F5 or Ctrl-F5) as a key code. Keep in mind, however, that Word has already assigned tasks to all function keys and most function-key combinations.

When a function key, a function-key combination, or a speed formatting key is assigned a new task, you must first press Ctrl-A before you can use the function key or speed formatting key for its original purpose. For example, if you assign F5 to a glossary entry, you must press Ctrl-A and then F5 to choose the Edit Go To command. Although Ctrl-A gives you access to original key assignments, it's best not to assign a function key or a speed formatting key to a glossary entry unless you don't use the key often.

You can assign a key code when you create or change a glossary entry. In the Edit Glossary dialog box, type the entry name as usual in the Glossary Name box. Then move to the Optional Keys box (Alt-K), and press the keys you want to use in the code. For example, to assign the key code Ctrl-FA to a glossary entry, hold down Ctrl while you press F, and then *either* hold down or release Ctrl while you press the second character, A. Then choose the <Define> command button to complete the command.

Using Supplied Glossary Entries

Word supplies some glossary entries that are always available (and that cannot be changed or deleted), no matter what glossary file is in memory: *page*, *nextpage*, *date*, *dateprint*, *time*, *timeprint*, *footnote*, and—if you are using Microsoft Windows—*clipboard*.

With *page,* you can include page numbers in headers and footers. (See discussion of the Format Header/Footer command in Chapter 10.) The entry *nextpage* is used to include the page number of the following page in headers or footers. (In some countries, the number of the next page is customarily included at the bottom of each page of a legal document.)

The *date* and *dateprint* entries are handy for instantly inserting the current date in a document. Try it out: Type *date* and then press the F3 key. Today's date appears. Word uses the date format *January 18, 1990.* You can change the format so that the day precedes the month: *18 January, 1990.* To do this, choose the Utilities Customize command and choose DMY in the Date box.

Use *dateprint* instead of *date* if you want the current date printed each time you print the document. This entry is useful for form letters and other dated documents that are prepared ahead of time and sent out more than once. Using *dateprint* also helps you keep track of various versions of documents that go through several revisions. After you type *dateprint* and press the F3 key, Word displays *(dateprint)* on the screen and substitutes the current date at printing time.

The *time* and *timeprint* entries work like *date* and *dateprint,* but they allow you to insert the current time (in the form *8:10 AM*) in a document. You can change to a 24-hour clock format—to have 8:05 PM appear as *20:05,* for instance—by choosing the Utilities Customize command and choosing 24 hour in the Time box.

Because Word gets the current date and time from DOS, the date and time it inserts in place of glossary entries are only as accurate as the information DOS has. DOS reads the date and time from a built-in calendar/clock, if your computer has one. If it doesn't, DOS relies on the answers you provide to the date and time questions when you start DOS.

The *footnote* glossary entry is used by Word primarily for automatic footnote numbering. (Footnotes are discussed in Chapter 10.)

The *clipboard* entry is used only if you run Word under the Microsoft Windows program. In a way that resembles the workings of the scrap, *clipboard* allows you to pass text or data between Word and other application programs run with Microsoft Windows. Instead of sending text to or retrieving text from the scrap, you send text to or retrieve text from the entry name *clipboard.* (Word can receive—but cannot send—graphics via *clipboard.*)

Editing a Glossary

You can make changes to an open glossary by adding new entries, changing existing entries, and deleting entries. Remember that when you edit a glossary, you change only the copy in memory. To replace the original glossary on disk with the new edited version, you must save the edited glossary, using the original filename.

Changing entries

You've already learned how to add new entries to an existing glossary. But suppose, for example, that you want to change the text of an existing glossary entry named *pc* from *IBM Personal Computer* to *IBM PC*. Type the new text, *IBM PC*, in your document, highlight it, and choose the Edit Glossary command. Then type the old entry name, *pc*, in the Glossary Name box, and choose the <Define> command button. Before it replaces the existing text, Word prompts you to confirm that you want the text replaced. Choose <OK> (press Enter) to do this.

Instead of retyping the entire text, you might find it easier to retrieve the old text and edit it. For example, suppose you typed the wrong zip code in an address stored in the glossary. Use either the F3 key or the <Insert> command button of the Edit Glossary command to retrieve the address and put it on the screen. Then correct the zip code, highlight the entire corrected address, and choose the Edit Glossary command. Type the original entry name in the Glossary Name box, and choose the <Define> button. After you confirm that you want to overwrite the existing glossary text, Word replaces the incorrect address with the new, corrected address.

Deleting entries

To delete an entry from a glossary, choose the Edit Glossary command. Move to the Names box, and highlight the entry name you want to delete. Check the glossary text displayed under the Names box to be sure you've selected the right name. When you choose the <Delete> command button, the name disappears from the list.

You can continue deleting other entries by selecting each entry name and then choosing the <Delete> button. When you finish, choose the <Close> button (press Esc) to leave the Edit Glossary dialog box.

If you want to erase *all* glossary entries, choose the <Clear All> command button. Word asks for confirmation:

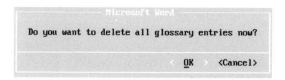

If you choose <OK> (press Enter), all glossary entries except the ones supplied by Word are deleted from memory. Choose <Cancel> (press Esc) to cancel the command if you don't want to do this.

 NOTE: If you accidentally delete the wrong glossary entries, don't save your glossary. Changes in a glossary aren't permanent until you save it using the previous glossary filename.

Using a Glossary to Cut and Paste

You can use a glossary instead of the scrap to temporarily hold pieces of text that you want to copy or move. A glossary is a less volatile storage place than the scrap. Unlike the scrap, a glossary can hold more than one piece of text at a time. Text put in a glossary stays there until you quit Word (with the File Exit Word command) or clear the memory (with the File Close All command). You thus have more time to find the new location for text you want to move or copy. And you're free to do other editing without worrying about losing your scrap of text.

You can permanently save your scraps by saving the glossary to a file on disk, but you don't usually need to save glossary entries used for cut-and-paste work. In fact, it's better not to clutter your disks with scraps of text if you don't have a frequent or long-term use for them.

HANDLING GLOSSARY FILES

If you work with more than one glossary, you need to know how to create separate glossary files, clear glossary entries and files from memory, save and open glossary files, and perhaps combine glossary files. In addition, you can print glossary files to help you keep track of what's in them.

Creating a New Glossary File

If you want to create a new glossary that includes some entries from the glossary in memory, you can delete those entries you don't want, add any new entries, and then save the glossary under a new name. If, instead, you want to create a new glossary from scratch, you must first clear the glossary memory.

Clearing the glossary memory

If you don't clear the glossary memory before building a new, separate glossary, the new glossary will include everything that's currently in glossary memory. (Always save the contents of memory before clearing it if you want to keep any recent changes.)

To clear glossary memory:

1. Choose the Edit Glossary command (Alt, E, O).

2. Choose the <Clear All> command button.

3. When Word asks you to confirm that you want to delete all glossary entries, choose <OK> (press Enter).

Word asks for a confirmation even if the contents of memory have been saved. Choosing <OK> erases all glossary entries in memory except the ones supplied by Word. Choosing <Cancel> (pressing Esc) cancels the command to clear the glossary memory.

Saving a Glossary File

Although you should discard a glossary that has only short-term value to you, in most cases you'll want to save a glossary to be used again. Word warns you whenever a newly created or edited glossary is about to be discarded and gives you a chance to save it. For example, if you have not saved changes to NORMAL.GLY before you try to quit Word, you see this message:

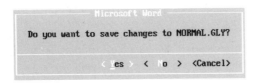

Choose <Yes> to save the glossary (under the name shown in the message). Choose <No> to discard it. Choose <Cancel> to cancel the command to quit Word or the command to close all files.

To save a glossary:

1. Choose the Edit Glossary command (Alt, E, O).

2. Choose the <Save Glossary> command button.

3. The Save Glossary dialog box appears:

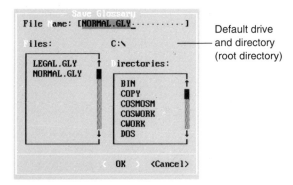

Default drive and directory (root directory)

The proposed response in the File Name box is the name of the glossary file currently in memory. If you're updating the current glossary, leave the proposed filename as is. If, instead, you're creating a new glossary file, type the new filename in the File Name box. Include (or choose from the Directories list box) the drive and directory in which the new glossary should be stored if you don't want to use the default path, which is shown below the File Name box.

4. Choose <OK> (press Enter).

Choosing a filename

Choose the filename NORMAL.GLY for the glossary you use most frequently. If you're saving an additional, special-purpose glossary, give it a name of as many as eight characters. (The same rules that apply to document filenames apply to glossary filenames; see Appendix A for details.)

You need not type a filename extension: Word assigns the extension .GLY to glossary files unless you type in a different extension. If you give the file a different extension, you must type both the filename and the extension each time you open it.

If you type a filename that has already been given to a glossary file, Word displays this message:

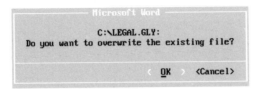

The message warns you that the glossary being saved will replace an existing glossary that has the same name. If you don't want this to happen, choose <Cancel> (press Esc) to cancel the command, and start over again, using a new name.

Because a copy of the glossary stays in memory after it's saved, you still have access to it until you quit Word, close all files, or open another glossary.

Opening a Glossary File

A glossary must be open before you can use it. (NORMAL.GLY is automatically opened when you start Word.) When you open a glossary, you transfer a copy of it from the disk to glossary memory, where it can be used and edited.

To open a glossary:

1. Choose the Edit Glossary command (Alt, E, O).

2. Choose the <Open Glossary> command button.

3. Word displays the Open Glossary dialog box:

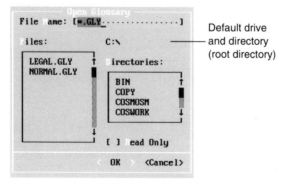

4. Type the filename of the glossary you want to open in the File Name box, or choose one from the list in the Files box. (Word lists only filenames with the extension *.GLY;* if the glossary you're opening has a different extension, you must type both the filename and its extension.) If the glossary you want to open is not in the default path shown under the File Name box, either include the path when you type the filename or choose a drive and directory from the Directories box.

5. Choose <OK> (press Enter).

If a different glossary is already in memory, it is removed after you're given the chance to save any changes you've made to it. If Word can't find the file you want to open, a message tells you that the file or directory does not exist. Choose <OK> to make the message disappear. Check to be sure you gave the correct filename and included the correct drive and directory.

Merging Glossary Files

Temporarily merging glossaries allows you to retrieve text from more than one glossary at a time. As long as you don't save what is merged in memory, the glossaries remain separate and distinct files on the disk.

To temporarily merge two glossaries:

1. If one of the glossaries is not already open, choose the Edit Glossary command and then use the <Open Glossary> command button to open it.

2. Choose the Edit Glossary command, and then choose the <Merge> command button.

3. The Merge Glossary dialog box appears:

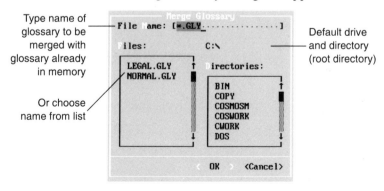

Type name of glossary to be merged with glossary already in memory

Or choose name from list

Default drive and directory (root directory)

4. Type the filename of the second glossary in the File Name box, or choose the name from the list in the Files box. If the glossary you want to merge is not in the default path, either include the path when you type the filename or choose a drive and directory from the Directories box.

5. Choose <OK> (press Enter).

You can merge a series of glossary files by repeatedly adding files with the <Merge> button in the Edit Glossary dialog box. To permanently join merged glossaries, use the <Save Glossary> button in this dialog box.

 CAUTION: If the glossary file you are adding to memory contains a glossary entry with the same name as a glossary entry already in memory, the entry that is already in memory is replaced without warning.

Printing a Glossary File

To print a glossary:

1. Open the glossary you want to print.

2. Choose the File Print command (Alt, F, P).

3. When you see the File Print dialog box, move the cursor to the Print box, and choose Glossary from the drop-down list:

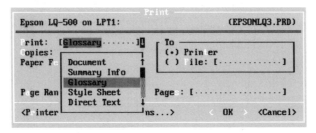

4. Choose <OK> (press Enter).

Chapter 9

Formatting

Formatting is packaging. It's the visual presentation of words. To make a document look more appealing, you can break the monotony of line after line of text by varying the amount of white space surrounding and between blocks of text. To make some words stand out more than others, you can vary the size, thickness, and shape of the letters.

THE ELEMENTS OF DESIGN

Three basic elements make up the visual design of a printed document: page format, line format, and typeface. To help you format a document in a systematic way, Word asks you to view the document as consisting of three kinds of units: sections, paragraphs, and characters. Word ties the elements of design to these three units, linking *sections* to page format, *paragraphs* to line format, and *characters* to typeface.

Sections and Page Format

Page format determines how text is laid out on the printed page. A *section* is the smallest unit in a document to which you can assign a particular page format. Most documents need only one page format and only one section. If you need more than one page format in a document, Word lets you divide the document into sections and assign a different page format to each section. A section can be any length, from one paragraph to the entire document.

Word starts you out with a conventional page format suitable for many documents. The margins form a border of white space around the text on each page, with 1 inch at the top and the bottom and 1¼ inches on each side. The default page size is 8½ by 11 inches, leaving 6 inches as the maximum length of each line of text, a comfortable reading length. Page numbers are not printed. That suits most business correspondence because most business letters are only one page long. This default page format is shown in Figure 9-1; text is printed in the shaded area.

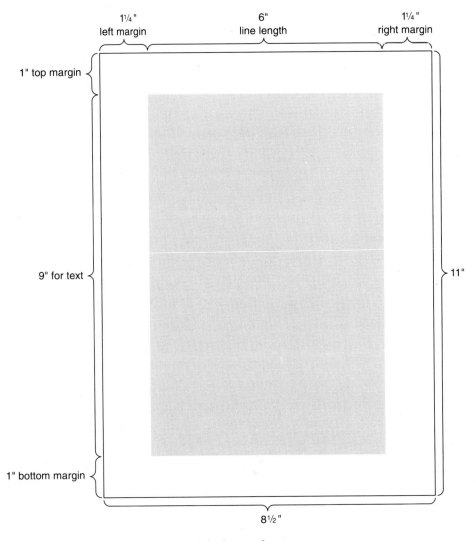

Figure 9-1. *Word's default page format.*

Most changes in page format can be made with the Format Section command. In this chapter, you learn how to use this command to

■ Change the margins

■ Change the page size

■ Add special margins for bound documents

■ Add page numbers

■ Add line numbers

For convenience, Word offers separate commands for changing the margins and adding page numbers: the Format Margins command and the Insert Page Numbers command.

Paragraphs and Line Format

Line format determines the placement of individual lines within the boundaries set by the page format. You can assign a particular line format to an entire document, to any group of paragraphs in a document (even if they are not in the same section), or to a single paragraph. A *paragraph* is the smallest unit to which you can assign a line format.

Documents prepared with Word's default line format are single-spaced with no indents at the beginning or end of any line. Each line in a paragraph starts at the left margin (unless you press the Tab key) so that the left edge of the text forms a straight line. If a line doesn't fill the space allowed by the margins, the extra space appears at the end of the line, which makes the right edge of the paragraph uneven. When the left edge of the text is straight and the right edge is ragged, we describe the text as aligned *flush left*.

To change this initial line format, you can use the Format Paragraph command, the speed formatting keys, or the ruler. The speed formatting keys are a combination of the Control key and a letter or number key. They let you format text quickly but do not allow the precise control over measurements that the Format Paragraph command provides. When you use the ruler, you can quickly change tabs and paragraph indents by clicking and dragging symbols along the ruler with the mouse. In this chapter, you learn how to use these tools to

■ Position lines flush left or flush right, justify lines, or center lines

■ Indent the first line of a paragraph

- Indent an entire paragraph
- Change the line spacing
- Add blank lines between paragraphs
- Prevent a page break from occurring within a specific paragraph or between two specific paragraphs

Characters and Typeface

Typeface controls the appearance of individual characters. A *character* is the smallest unit to which you can assign a typeface. You'll usually want to assign a typeface to an entire document or to whole words or phrases rather than to single characters.

If you don't tamper with character format, all characters will be 10-pitch (10 characters per inch) and will have a uniform appearance. But you can change the appearance of characters to emphasize certain words or certain parts of the text.

You can use the Format Character command, the formatting ribbon, or speed formatting keys to format characters. This chapter shows you how to use these tools to

- Change the font (type style) and the font size
- Change the font color, if you have a color printer
- Apply special printing effects such as boldface, italics, and underscoring
- Change the vertical position of characters to create subscripts and superscripts

Measurements

Word initially uses *lines* to measure the space above or below lines of text and uses *inches* to measure other attributes such as page size, margins, and indents. Instead of using inches or lines, however, you can specify measurements in *centimeters, points, p10s* (tenths of an inch), or *p12s* (twelfths of an inch).

Points are a special unit of measure used in the printing industry; 72 points equal 1 inch. They let you pinpoint the size of characters or other measurements with great accuracy. The *p10* and *p12* (*p* for *pitch*) units of measure let you think in terms of a number of characters or columns. If you're printing with a 10-pitch font (10 characters per inch), 1 p10 equals the width of 1 character. If you're printing with a 12-pitch font (12 characters per inch), 1 p12 equals the width of 1 character.

For many documents, inches and lines, the default units of measure, are sufficient. But you should use the unit of measure you're most familiar and comfortable with. If you want to use a different unit, include its abbreviation when typing a measurement. To indicate fractions of a unit, use decimals; for example, type *1.5cm* to represent 1½ centimeters. You must use the following abbreviations for units of measure:

in *or* "	for inches
cm	for centimeters
p10	for ¹⁄₁₀ inch, or for the width of 1 character when using a 10-pitch font
p12	for ¹⁄₁₂ inch, or for the width of 1 character when using a 12-pitch font
pt	for points (1 inch = 72 points; 1 line = 12 points)
li	for lines (1 line = ⅙ inch, or 12 points)

If you prefer to use a measure other than inches for most of your work, you can set a new default unit of measure to avoid repeatedly typing abbreviations. To do this, choose the Utilities Customize command, and choose a default unit of measure in the Measure text box. (For line spacing options, you can't change the default unit of measure—which is lines—but you can specify another unit for an individual measurement by including the unit abbreviation with the measurement.)

FORMATTING SECTIONS: CHANGING PAGE FORMAT

The Format Section, Format Margins, and Insert Page Numbers commands apply to entire sections. If a document has only one section, these commands affect the entire document, regardless of where the cursor is located when you choose the command. If a document has more than one section, these commands affect the section in which the cursor is located or the sections in which some text is highlighted when the command is chosen. If you want a page format—for example, increased margins or printed page numbers—to apply to all sections, select the entire document (press Ctrl-5) before you choose and carry out the command.

If you want to format text as you type, choose the appropriate command before you start typing. The formats you choose are applied to the section you're typing and to any subsequent sections you type unless you choose new page formats for them.

Starting a New Section

You need to start a new section only if you want to use a different layout for part of your document—for example, if you want part of the document to be formatted into more than one column.

When you begin a new section, Word starts a new paragraph. By default, Word starts printing a new section on a new page—the next page. But you can specify a different kind of section break if necessary.

To end one section and start a new one:

1. Choose the Insert Break command (Alt, I, B).

2. When Word displays the Insert Break dialog box, choose the Section button:

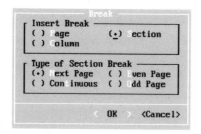

3. If you do not want the new section to start printing on the next page, choose one of the other option buttons in the Type of Section Break box. Choose Continuous if you want to start printing the new section on the same page as the previous section. Choose Even Page to start printing the new section on the next even-numbered page, or choose Odd Page to start printing the new section on the next odd-numbered page.

4. Choose <OK> (press Enter).

After you carry out the command, Word inserts a *section mark,* a special nonprinting character, to the left of the cursor. If you later decide to change the type of section break, you can do so with the Section Start box of the Format Section command:

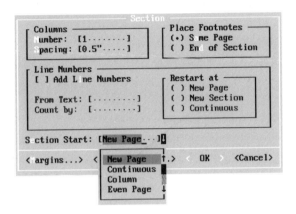

The Section Start box contains a drop-down list of all the break options that appear in the Type of Section Break box, plus an additional one, Column. Choose the Column option for documents with more than one column on a page if you want the new section to start in a new column. (Formatting sections into multiple columns is explained in Chapter 10.)

The section mark

A section mark appears on the screen as two dotted lines (a row of colons):

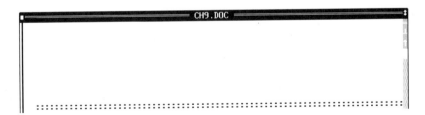

A section mark can be selected, deleted, copied, or moved like any other character. The section mark at the end of a section stores all the instructions for that section's page format. If you delete the section mark at the end of a section, you delete the formatting specifications for page layout in that section. The section then takes on the formatting stored in the next section mark that occurs in the document. If you copy or move a section mark, the formatting that is stored with it is also copied or moved and is applied to the preceding text.

The page formatting for the last section in a document (or for the entire document if you have only one section) is stored with the section mark that appears above the endmark (♦). This final (or only) section mark appears in a document only after you change or check the page format with the Format Section, the Format Margins, or the Format Apply Style command.

Once a section mark is visible, it becomes an icon for the mouse: You can double-click a section mark to choose the Format Section command.

Changing Page Size or Margins

To change the page size or the margins, use the Format Margins command or choose the <Margins> command button in the Format Section dialog box. Both commands lead to the Section Margins dialog box:

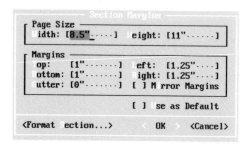

Word lets you print on paper as large as 22 inches wide and 22 inches long. If you're not using 8½-by-11-inch paper, type new measurements in the Width and Height boxes. You can use any unit of measure except lines for page width. (When measuring the width of your paper, don't include the tear-off strips that are used to feed continuous paper through a printer.)

A printed page of text has four margins: top, bottom, left, and right. The top and bottom margins are initially set to 1" (1 inch). The left and right margins are set to 1.25" (1¼ inches). The margins, together with the page size and the gutter margin (if any), determine how much space is available for text on a page. To change any of the margins, type a new measurement in the appropriate box.

A *gutter* is an extra margin of space used for binding a document that has been printed or duplicated on both sides of the paper. Gutter margins are added to the right margin of even-numbered pages and to the left margin of odd-numbered pages, as shown in Figure 9-2. If you're printing or duplicating on only one side of the paper, don't make a gutter. Instead, make the left margin bigger because, in this case, the extra binding space is needed on the left side of all pages.

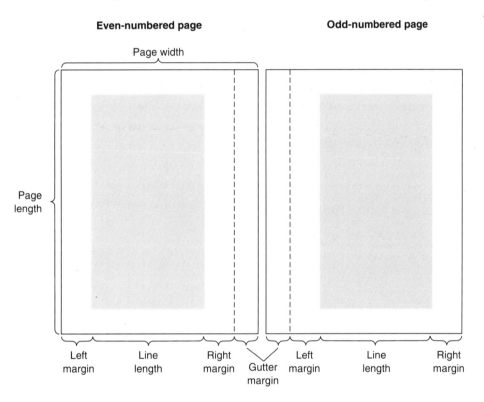

Figure 9-2. *Gutters on even-numbered and odd-numbered pages.*

You can *mirror* the margins on opposite pages of your document by turning on the Mirror Margins check box in the Section Margins dialog box. Word then interchanges the left and right margins on even-numbered pages. If, for example, you want to leave a large space for notes along the outside edge of every page, you could set the right margin to 3 inches. With Mirror Margins turned on, the 3-inch margin appears on the right side of every odd-numbered page and on the left side of every even-numbered page. This gives facing pages in a bound document a symmetrical look.

If you regularly use margins different from those Word initially sets, you can set your preferred margins and turn on the Use as Default check box. Word then adopts your margins as its defaults whenever you begin a new document.

Notice that the <Format Section> command button at the bottom of the Section Margins dialog box lets you tunnel back to the Format Section command, where you can make other changes in page format.

Adding Page Numbers

Word does not print page numbers in a document unless you tell it to. You can use either the Insert Page Numbers command or the <Page Numbers> command button of the Format Section command. Either route takes you to the Page Numbers dialog box:

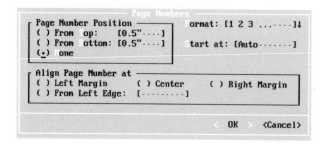

To print page numbers, choose either the From Top or the From Bottom button in the Page Number Position box. If you choose From Top, Word prints the page numbers 0.5 inches from the top of the paper and 7.25 inches from the left edge of the paper. If you choose From Bottom, page numbers are printed 0.5 inches from the bottom of the paper and 7.25 inches from the left edge of the paper.

To change the page numbers' vertical position, type a new measurement in the From Top or From Bottom box. This measurement must be at least ⅙ inch (1 line) less than the top margin measurement so that the page numbers will not print on the text. To change the page numbers' horizontal position, type a new measurement in the From Left Edge box. Or, instead, specify that you want the page numbers to be centered, aligned with the left margin, or aligned with the right margin by turning on the appropriate button in the Align Page Number At box.

Word numbers pages with Arabic numerals. To change to Roman or alphabetic numbering, choose the style you want from the drop-down list in the Format box:

1 2 3	for Arabic
a b c	for alphabetic lowercase
A B C	for alphabetic uppercase
i ii iii	for Roman lowercase
I II III	for Roman uppercase

Page numbers usually start with 1 for the first page of a document and continue in sequence to the end of the document. To start numbering the pages of a document or a section with another number, type the starting number in the Start At box.

Another way to print page numbers is to incorporate them into headers or footers. If you do put page numbers in headers or footers, be sure the None button in the Page Number Position box is turned on; otherwise, the page number prints twice. (See Chapter 10 for more information on headers and footers.)

Adding Line Numbers

For legal documents such as contracts, printed line numbers make it easy to refer to specific parts of the document. To print line numbers in the left margin of a document, choose the Format Section command and turn on the Add Line Numbers check box:

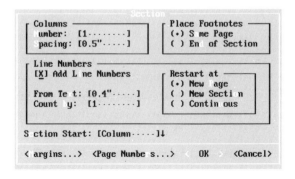

The From Text box indicates how far from the left margin the line number will be placed; the default is 0.4 inches. If you type in a measurement larger than the left margin, the line numbers won't print. If you type in a measurement that doesn't allow enough room for the longest line number, line numbers that don't fit are truncated from the left.

Word normally prints every line number, but you can specify that line numbers be printed only at particular intervals. For example, you can tell Word to print every fifth line number (5, 10, 15, and so on) by typing 5 in the Count By box.

Word restarts line numbering with 1 at the beginning of each page unless you specify New Section or Continuous in the Restart At box. If you turn on the New Section button, line numbering starts with 1 at the beginning of the currently selected section. (If you have highlighted more than one section, line numbering restarts at 1 at the beginning of each section.) To guarantee consecutive line numbering throughout the entire document, highlight the entire document before you choose the Format Section command, and turn on the Continuous button.

Viewing line numbers

To get a glimpse of line numbers on the screen, choose the File Print Preview command. If you then turn on the View 1-Page toggle command, you might be able to read the very small text next to the very small line numbers. Press the Esc key when you're ready to leave the Print Preview screen. (See Chapter 12 for more details on Print Preview.)

The status bar can keep you posted as to what line the cursor is in. To include line numbers in the status bar and to ensure that they match printed line numbers:

1. Choose the View Preferences command (Alt, V, E).

2. Turn on the Show Line Numbers check box.

3. If the Count Blank Space check box is on, turn it off. (Turning off this check box tells Word not to count line spacing added by the Format Paragraph command before or after paragraphs or between lines. When Word prints line numbers, it doesn't count those kinds of blank lines.)

4. Turn on the Line Breaks check box. (This ensures that the line breaks that are shown and counted on the screen correspond to the line breaks shown and counted on the printed copy.)

5. Choose <OK> (press Enter).

FORMATTING PARAGRAPHS: CHANGING LINE FORMAT

To format paragraphs as you type, use the Format Paragraph command and choose the desired options in the dialog box. For some changes, you can use speed formatting keys or the ruler. The formats you choose are immediately applied to the paragraph you're typing and to any succeeding paragraphs you type until you choose a new paragraph format.

To format a paragraph after it's been typed, move the cursor to any place in the paragraph before you choose the Format Paragraph command, press the appropriate speed formatting keys, or use the ruler. To format more than one paragraph at the same time, highlight some text in each paragraph. To apply a particular format to all paragraphs in a document, press Ctrl-5 to quickly select the entire document.

Starting a New Paragraph

To end one paragraph and start a new one, press the Enter key. Pressing the Enter key inserts a *paragraph mark* to the left of the cursor. A paragraph mark indicates the end of one paragraph and the beginning of the next paragraph. Although paragraph marks are nonprinting characters and are normally invisible on the screen, you can make them appear on the screen by choosing the View Preferences command and turning on the Paragraph Marks check box. When visible, a paragraph mark looks like this: ¶

A paragraph mark can be selected, deleted, copied, moved, or searched for like any other character. The mark at the end of a paragraph stores all the instructions for formatting lines in that paragraph. If you delete the paragraph mark at the end of a paragraph, you delete the specifications for line formatting in that paragraph. The paragraph is then joined to the next paragraph and takes on the formatting stored there. You can copy the formatting of one paragraph and apply it to another paragraph by copying the paragraph mark.

Starting a New Line

As you would expect, Word starts each new paragraph on a new line. Within a paragraph, Word automatically starts a new line when it reaches the right margin. You can, however, tell Word to end a line and begin a new one at a specific place, regardless of how far that place is from the right margin or from the end of a paragraph.

To end one line and start another without starting a new paragraph, press Shift-Enter. Pressing Shift-Enter inserts a *newline mark* to the left of the cursor. This special nonprinting character indicates the end of one line and the beginning of the next line. Newline marks are normally invisible; they look like spaces. But you can select, delete, copy, move, or search for them. To make newline marks visible, choose the View Preferences command and turn on the Show All check box. When visible, a newline mark looks like this: ↓

Use Shift-Enter instead of the Enter key to end each line in a block of closely related text such as an address, a poem, or a table. This way, the entire address, poem, or table is treated as one paragraph and can easily be formatted as one unit. If you use Enter rather than Shift-Enter to separate the lines in a table, for example, and later carry out a command that puts extra space between paragraphs in the document, you'll end up with unwanted space between the lines in the table.

Aligning Paragraphs

Paragraph alignment is the horizontal placement of lines within margins or indents. Word normally aligns paragraphs flush left. But you can also align them flush right, center them, or justify them, as illustrated in Figure 9-3.

When paragraphs are set *flush left,* the left edge of the text looks straight, and the right edge looks ragged. Any extra space in a line is put at the end of the line. Flush-left (left-aligned) text is the easiest to read.

In paragraphs set *flush right,* the right edge of the text looks straight, and the left edge looks ragged. Any extra space in a line is put at the beginning of the line instead of the end. Right-aligned text is rarely used. It works well as a device to capture your attention, but it can be difficult to read at length.

In *centered* paragraphs, neither edge of the paragraph looks straight. Extra space in a line is divided between the beginning of the line and the end of the line. Centering is often used for special announcements, invitations, poems, and single lines such as headings.

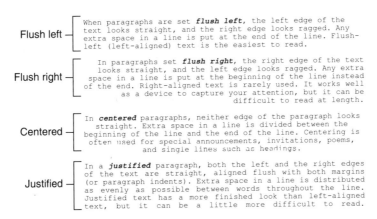

Flush left — When paragraphs are set ***flush left***, the left edge of the text looks straight, and the right edge looks ragged. Any extra space in a line is put at the end of the line. Flush-left (left-aligned) text is the easiest to read.

Flush right — In paragraphs set ***flush right***, the right edge of the text looks straight, and the left edge looks ragged. Any extra space in a line is put at the beginning of the line instead of the end. Right-aligned text is rarely used. It works well as a device to capture your attention, but it can be difficult to read at length.

Centered — In ***centered*** paragraphs, neither edge of the paragraph looks straight. Extra space in a line is divided between the beginning of the line and the end of the line. Centering is often used for special announcements, invitations, poems, and single lines such as headings.

Justified — In a ***justified*** paragraph, both the left and the right edges of the text are straight, aligned flush with both margins (or paragraph indents). Extra space in a line is distributed as evenly as possible between words throughout the line. Justified text has a more finished look than left-aligned text, but it can be a little more difficult to read.

Figure 9-3. *The four types of text alignment.*

In a *justified* paragraph, both the left and the right edges of the text are straight, aligned flush with both margins (or paragraph indents). Extra space in a line is distributed as evenly as possible between words throughout the line. Justified text has a more finished look than left-aligned text, but it can be a little more difficult to read. If you justify text, be sure to use Word's automatic hyphenation feature (explained in Chapter 14). Hyphenating words at the ends of lines fills each line with as many characters as possible and prevents big gaps of space between words in justified text.

The Format Paragraph command displays the alignment options in the first line of its dialog box:

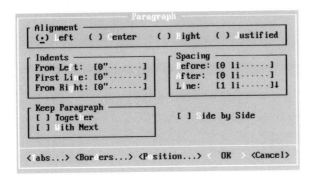

You can use speed formatting keys instead of the Format Paragraph command to change the alignment of paragraphs:

Ctrl-L	Aligns text flush left
Ctrl-R	Aligns text flush right
Ctrl-C	Centers text
Ctrl-J	Justifies text

Indenting

The second group of options in the Format Paragraph dialog box lets you indent text without changing the margins or repeatedly pressing the Tab key:

Indents make lines shorter than the length allowed by the margins. You can indent an entire paragraph, the first line of a paragraph, or all lines except the first. Use indents to emphasize blocks of text or to set them apart from surrounding text. When you want to temporarily increase margins, use indents rather than starting a new section and using the Format Margins command.

Indenting entire paragraphs

If you indent a paragraph from the left, the left margin for that paragraph is increased by the amount of the indent. For example, if your left margin is set to 1¼ inches and you type *1"* in the From Left box, the left margin becomes, in effect, 2¼ inches. Lines start 2¼ inches from the left edge of the paper.

Indenting a paragraph from the right increases the right margin for that paragraph by the amount of the indent. If your right margin is 1 inch and you type *1"* in the From Right box, the right margin becomes, in effect, 2 inches. Lines end 2 inches from the right edge of the paper. See Figure 9-4 for an example of a paragraph set off from the surrounding text with indents.

Instead of using the Format Paragraph command to indent paragraphs, you can use these speed formatting keys:

Ctrl-N	Increases left indent to next tab stop
Ctrl-M	Decreases left indent by one tab stop
Ctrl-Q	Increases left and right indents by one tab stop

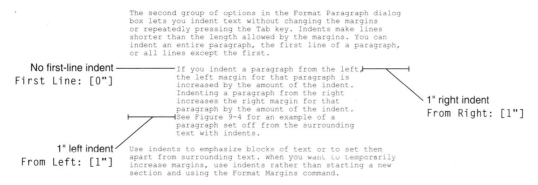

Figure 9-4. *Whole paragraph indents, with settings used in the Format Paragraph dialog box.*

Indents created by Ctrl-N are cumulative: Each time you press Ctrl-N, the paragraph is indented to the next tab stop. If your tab stops are set at ½-inch intervals, press Ctrl-N twice to indent a paragraph 1 inch. You can reduce the left indents assigned by Ctrl-N (or by the Format Paragraph command) by pressing Ctrl-M. Each time you press Ctrl-M, the left indent for the selected paragraphs is reduced by one tab stop.

Using Ctrl-M and Ctrl-N, you can easily nest paragraphs underneath each other in outline fashion by increasing or decreasing the left indent, as shown in Figure 9-5.

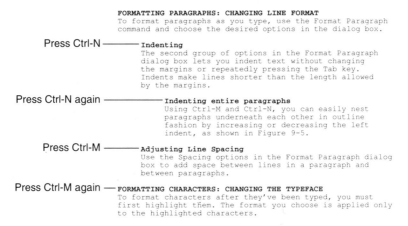

Figure 9-5. *Indenting and "outdenting" using Ctrl-N and Ctrl-M.*

Indenting the first lines of paragraphs

Word lets you indent the first lines of paragraphs without pressing the Tab key at the beginning of each paragraph. To automatically indent the first line of each paragraph as you type, choose the Format Paragraph command before you start typing and then enter a measurement in the First Line box. For example, if you want to indent first lines ½ inch, type *0.5"* in the First Line box. The first line of each paragraph you type from then on will start ½ inch from the left edge of the rest of the paragraph, as shown in Figure 9-6.

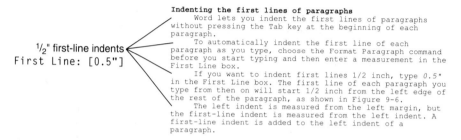

Figure 9-6. *First-line indents, with setting used in the Format Paragraph dialog box.*

The left indent is measured from the left margin, but the first-line indent is measured from the left indent. A first-line indent is *added* to the left indent of a paragraph. If a paragraph's left indent is 1 inch and the first line is indented ½ inch, the text on the first line is indented a total of 1½ inches from the left margin.

Creating hanging indents

Instead of indenting the first line of each paragraph, you can "outdent" it to make a *hanging indent*. When you "outdent" the first line of a paragraph, you must *indent* the entire paragraph, because you can't print outside the margins. To create a hanging indent, type a positive measurement in the From Left box, and then type a negative measurement in the First Line box. The number in the First Line box must be equal to or smaller than the number in the From Left box.

For example, type *0.5"* in the From Left box, and type *-0.5"* in the First Line box to make the first line stick out ½ inch from the rest of the paragraph text. The first line starts at the left margin, and the remainder of the paragraph is indented ½ inch from the left margin, as shown in Figure 9-7.

Bibliography

¹/₂" hanging indent ⎯
From Left: [0.5"]
First Line: [-0.5"]

Andrews, Nancy. <u>Microsoft Word, Command Performance Series</u>.
    Redmond, WA: Microsoft Press, 1987.

Rampa, Janet Marian. <u>Learn Word Now</u>. Redmond, WA: Microsoft
    Press, 1989.

Rinearson, Peter. <u>Word Processing Power with Microsoft
    Word</u>. 3d ed. Redmond, WA: Microsoft Press, 1989.

Rinearson, Peter, and Woodcock, JoAnne. <u>Microsoft Word Style
    Sheets</u>. Redmond, WA: Microsoft Press, 1987.

Figure 9-7. *Hanging indents in a bibliography, with settings used in the Format Paragraph dialog box.*

Using Ctrl-T is an easier and quicker way to create hanging indents:

Ctrl-T   Sets left indent to next tab stop and first-line indent
                to left margin

Ctrl-M   Reduces hanging indent by decreasing left indent by
                one tab stop

Hanging indents can be used to format numbered or bulleted lists in which the item number or marker (sometimes called a bullet) stands alone, to the left of the list text. To type a numbered or bulleted list, press Ctrl-T and type the first number or bullet. Then press the Tab key to align the text that immediately follows with the text in the remaining lines. (See Figure 9-8 for an example.) Continue typing the next items in the list, remembering to press the Tab key after each number or bullet. Ctrl-T and Ctrl-M are cumulative: Each time you press either combination, it increases or decreases the hanging indent by increasing or decreasing the left indent.

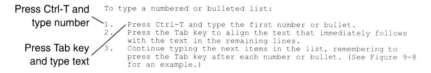

Press Ctrl-T and
type number

Press Tab key
and type text

To type a numbered or bulleted list:

1. Press Ctrl-T and type the first number or bullet.
2. Press the Tab key to align the text that immediately follows
   with the text in the remaining lines.
3. Continue typing the next items in the list, remembering to
   press the Tab key after each number or bullet. (See Figure 9-8
   for an example.)

Figure 9-8. *Using Ctrl-T to create a hanging indent in a numbered list.*

Using the ruler to set indents

If you have a two-button mouse, you can set indents by turning on the ruler and dragging indent symbols along the ruler. To turn the ruler on or off, choose the View Ruler command, or click the ruler icon (⊥) in the upper right corner of the right window border. The ruler appears below the title bar. As illustrated on the next page, it shows the positions of the left, right, and first-line indents for the selected paragraphs.

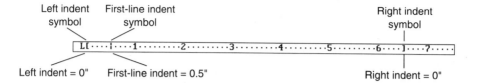

Left indent symbol First-line indent symbol Right indent symbol

Left indent = 0" First-line indent = 0.5" Right indent = 0"

To change an indent, drag (using the right mouse button) the symbol for the indent to the desired setting. The first-line indent symbol is hidden by the left indent symbol if a first-line indent hasn't been set. To change the first-line indent when its symbol is hidden, first move the left indent symbol out of the way. After you set the first-line indent, reset the left indent.

Adjusting Line Spacing

Use the Spacing options in the Format Paragraph dialog box to add space between lines in a paragraph and between paragraphs:

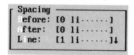

The Line box controls spacing between lines. It is initially set to 1 li (1 line, which is ⅙ inch, or 12 points). This gives you single-spaced text for standard 12-point characters. To get double-spaced text, type *2* in the Line box. With double spacing, a blank line appears above each line in a paragraph, as shown in Figure 9-9. You can also set the line spacing to a fraction of a line. For example, to set the line spacing to 1½ lines, type *1.5* in the Line box.

Single-spaced text
Line: [1 li]

Use the Spacing options in the Format Paragraph dialog box to add space between lines in a paragraph and between paragraphs. The Line box controls spacing between lines. It is initially set to 1 li, which gives you single-spaced text for standard 12-point characters.

Double-spaced text
Line: [2 li]

To get double-spaced text, type 2 in the Line box. With double spacing, a blank line appears above each line in a paragraph, as shown in Figure 9-9. You can also set the line spacing to a fraction of a line.

Figure 9-9. *Single-spaced and double-spaced text, with settings used in the Format Paragraph dialog box.*

If you're using fonts smaller than 12 points (⅙ inch) and if you want more than 6 lines per inch, type a measurement smaller than 1 line in the Line box. For example, to use 8 lines per inch, type *9 pt* (72 points divided by 8) or

0.125" (1 inch divided by 8). (Your printer might not cooperate if it requires a minimum amount of space between lines.) If you're using fonts larger than 12 points, you can type or choose *auto* in the Line box to make Word automatically adjust line spacing to accommodate the font.

The Before and After boxes refer to the space above and below a paragraph. They let you put additional space between paragraphs, as shown in Figures 9-10 and 9-11. The total amount of space between two paragraphs is the sum of the line spacing, the space after the first paragraph, and the space before the second paragraph. To avoid confusion, use only the Before box to put extra space between normal paragraphs. (Word deletes extra space before a paragraph that starts a page.)

If you want to add extra space before or after a special paragraph (such as a heading, list, or indented quotation), attach the extra space to the special

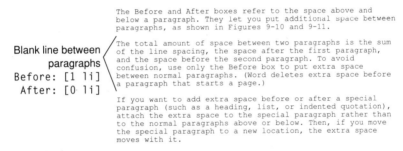

Figure 9-10. *Adding a blank line between paragraphs, with settings used in the Format Paragraph dialog box.*

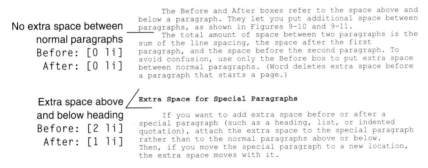

Figure 9-11. *Adding extra space above and below a heading, with settings used in the Format Paragraph dialog box.*

paragraph rather than to the normal paragraphs above or below. Then, if you move the special paragraph to a new location, the extra space moves with it.

Three speed formatting keys let you adjust the line or paragraph spacing without using the Format Paragraph command:

Ctrl-2	Double-spaces text
Ctrl-1	Single-spaces text
Ctrl-O (the letter O)	Inserts one extra line before each paragraph (open spacing)

Keeping Paragraphs Together: Controlling Page Breaks

The Keep Paragraph options, Together and With Next, in the Format Paragraph dialog box are tools for controlling where page breaks occur. Use them to prevent special paragraphs from being split between two pages or to prevent a heading from being separated from the text it identifies.

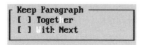

Turn on the Together check box to prevent a page break from occurring within a selected paragraph. Then, if that paragraph falls at the bottom of a page (or column) but won't quite fit, Word moves the entire paragraph to the next page (or column). With the Together check box turned off (the default setting), Word prints part of the paragraph on one page and the rest on the next page.

If only the first line of a paragraph fits at the bottom of a page, Word ordinarily moves that line to the next page so that it won't be isolated from the rest of the paragraph. If all but the last line of a paragraph fits at the bottom of a page, Word moves the last two lines of the paragraph to the next page. (Single lines left alone at the top or bottom of a page are called *widows* or *orphans* and are traditionally avoided. If you want to minimize the number of pages printed, however, you can tell Word to abandon this tradition: Choose the Utilities Customize command and turn off the Widow/Orphan Control check box.)

The With Next option prevents a heading that accompanies a section of text or a table from appearing at the bottom of a page without any text below it. The last two lines of the selected paragraph (or heading) are kept on (or moved to) the same page as the beginning of the paragraph that follows it. The second paragraph can be broken after its second line (unless you've used the Together option to keep it together), but a page break can't occur between the two paragraphs.

Keeping Words Together: Controlling Line Breaks

If you don't start a new line by pressing Shift-Enter, Word starts one for you when your text reaches the right margin. Word breaks a line after the nearest space or hyphen only—not in the middle of a word or number.

When you want to avoid breaking a line after a particular space or hyphen, you can insert a *nonbreaking space* instead of a normal space, or a *nonbreaking hyphen* or minus sign instead of a normal hyphen or minus sign:

Ctrl-Shift-Spacebar	Inserts a nonbreaking space
Ctrl-Shift-hyphen key	Inserts a nonbreaking hyphen or minus sign

These keys produce spaces, hyphens, and minus signs that look like normal characters, but these characters are treated differently if they fall at the end of a line. Use them in names, phrases, numbers, and expressions such as the following, which are best kept on one line:

Chapter 1	Rand-McNally
A. M. Rinaldi, Jr.	$a^2 - b^2 = c^2$
1024 bytes	$-23°F$

In addition to nonbreaking hyphens, two other kinds of hyphens—*normal* and *nonrequired*—are available:

Hyphen key	Inserts a normal hyphen
Ctrl-hyphen key	Inserts a nonrequired hyphen

Use normal hyphens for compound words such as *cross-country* or *lickety-split* that can be broken if they occur at the end of a line. You want normal hyphens to print whether the word needs to be split between two lines or not.

Use a nonrequired hyphen when you want it to appear in a word only if the word needs to be split between two lines. For example, the words *communication* and *keyboard* can be hyphenated if they fall at the end of a line and don't quite fit; otherwise, they shouldn't be hyphenated. Nonrequired hyphens don't show up on either the screen or the printed copy unless they are needed. To make nonrequired hyphens visible so you can easily delete or move them, turn on the Optional Hyphens check box of the View Preferences dialog box.

You can automatically hyphenate words in a document with the Utilities Hyphenate command. This command, which inserts nonrequired hyphens where needed, is described in Chapter 14.

FORMATTING CHARACTERS: CHANGING THE TYPEFACE

If you choose character formats before you start typing or when the cursor is an underscore, the formats are applied to any characters you type from then on (starting at the cursor location).

To format characters after they've been typed, you must first highlight them. The format you choose is applied only to the highlighted characters. You cannot select a single character to format by moving the cursor under it; the character must be highlighted. If the cursor is underscoring rather than highlighting a single character, Word formats the text you type from then on rather than the character above the cursor. To highlight a single character, move the cursor to it and press Shift-Right direction key. With the mouse, drag the pointer over the character.

Changing Fonts and Colors

Laser printers and many dot-matrix printers are able to reproduce the alphabet in a variety of shapes (fonts) and sizes. Some even print in more than one color. If Word has access to the printer description file for your printer, you can see and choose from a list of the font names, font sizes, and colors that are available with your printer. After you choose the Format Character command, Word displays the Format Character dialog box (shown on the next page). The Font, Point Size, and Color boxes each have a drop-down list. If you drop down the Font list, you see a list of fonts for the printer currently specified in the File Printer Setup dialog box (discussed in Chapter 12).

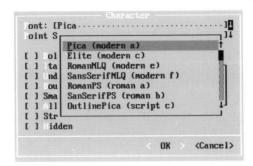

In Word, font size is a measure of the character height and must be specified in points. Don't try to measure characters to determine their size. Instead, choose a size from the drop-down list in the Point Size box. The most commonly used sizes are 10 points and 12 points; 12 points is the default.

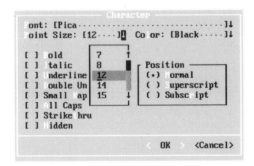

If you choose another font size, you might want to use the View Layout command to get a better picture of what your printed document will look like. With View Layout turned on, you don't see the actual font size, but you do see where lines will break when printed.

With impact printers such as daisy-wheel or thimble printers, different fonts are generated by different printing elements. You must manually change the daisy wheel or thimble when you want to change fonts. When Word encounters a change of fonts for impact printers, it stops printing, reminds you to change printing elements, and waits for you to tell it to resume printing.

Character size on printing elements is usually specified by *pitch,* which is the number of characters per inch. To convert pitch sizes to font sizes in points, use the table on the following page.

Pitch Size	Point Size
10	12
12	10
15	8

Proportionally spaced printing elements, which do not have a fixed number of characters per inch, usually correspond to 12-point type.

If your printer can print in more than one color, you can choose the color from the drop-down list for the Color box in the Format Character dialog box. If the printer prints only one color, the Color box lists Black only.

Although you can't use speed formatting keys to change the font or font size, you can press Ctrl-Spacebar to restore selected text to the default font and size.

Using the ribbon to change fonts

The formatting ribbon is another tool that allows you to change fonts and font sizes. To toggle the formatting ribbon on or off, choose the View Ribbon command. With the mouse, point to the ruler icon (⌐) in the upper right corner, and click the right mouse button. When the ribbon is turned on, it appears below the menu bar:

```
Style:[Paragraph 7* (PP)·]↓  Font:[Pica·········]↓  Pts:[12·]↓  Bld Ital Ul
```

To choose a font from the ribbon, press Ctrl-F to move the cursor to the Font box on the ribbon. Then press Alt-Down direction key to see the list of available fonts. Use the Up or Down direction key to highlight the font you want, and press the Enter key to choose it. With the mouse, click the arrow to the right of the Font box to see the list of available fonts, and click the font you want to use.

Use the same techniques to choose a font size (in points) from the Pts box on the ribbon. If you're using the keyboard, press Ctrl-P to move the cursor to the box.

You can also use the formatting ribbon with the mouse to choose the Format Character command: Point to Font or Pts on the ribbon and double-click the mouse button to see the Format Character dialog box.

Adding Special Printing Effects

The check boxes of the Format Character dialog box offer a variety of special printing effects that can enhance your documents. To assign a special printing effect, turn on the appropriate check box:

Check box turned on

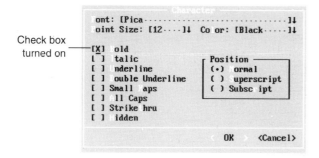

In a sea of letters and words that all look the same, a heading or a word printed in **boldface** or *italics* draws attention to itself. Underlining is another way to emphasize text. You can also double underline for added emphasis. A double underline is the conventional way to set off the totals in an accounting or financial statement.

SMALL KAPS are capital letters printed in a smaller, or condensed size. Small capital letters are often used in acronyms or in combination with standard capital letters in titles or headings. Text must be typed in lowercase letters to be formatted in small caps; using the small caps format does not change uppercase letters.

The All Caps check box lets you change lowercase letters to UPPERCASE without retyping them. If you change your mind, you can switch back to lowercase letters by turning off the All Caps check box.

If you're preparing a legal document, you might want to ~~cross out~~ text instead of simply deleting it, so that interested parties know what was removed from the original document. The Strikethru feature prints a dash through ~~selected characters~~. (You can also use the Utilities Revision Marks command to automatically mark text that you add, move, copy, and replace, as well as text that you delete.)

The following speed formatting keys allow you to turn most of the special printing effects on or off:

Ctrl-B	Boldface
Ctrl-I	Italics
Ctrl-U	Underline
Ctrl-D	Double underline
Ctrl-K	Small caps

With a mouse, you can use the formatting ribbon to quickly turn boldface (Bld), italics (Ital), or underlining (Ul) on or off. Just click the format you want to turn on or off. The format abbreviation brightens when it is turned on.

```
Style:[Normal··········]↓  Font:[Pica··········]↓  Pts:[12·]↓ Bld Ital Ul
```

Whether you use the Format Character command, speed formatting keys, or the formatting ribbon, you can assign more than one special printing effect to a character or group of characters. Here are some possible combinations:

boldface italics

boldface italics underlined

boldface double-underlined

italics underlined

BOLDFACE SMALL CAPS DOUBLE-UNDERLINED

ITALIC CAPS UNDERLINED

You can combine speed formatting keys to apply more than one character format. For example, press Ctrl-BI if you want to make characters **_boldface italic_**.

A character attribute that has been assigned to text must be turned off to remove it from the text. For instance, if you make a word boldface and then assign it italics, the word becomes _both_ boldface and italic. If instead you want to _change_ from boldface to italics, you must toggle boldface off by pressing Ctrl-B, clicking Bld on the ribbon, or turning off the Bold check box in the Format Character dialog box.

Changing Character Case

Word makes it extremely easy to change capitalization. Simply highlight the word or words you want to change, and press Shift-F3 to cycle through the possibilities: all lowercase, all uppercase, or initial capital letters.

Hiding Characters

You can hide comments, questions, notes, or instructions in a document so that they don't appear in the printed copy. But you have the option of printing them as well as the option of making them invisible on the screen.

To apply the hidden-text format to selected characters, turn on the Hidden check box of the Format Character dialog box or use Ctrl-H. Word normally displays hidden text on the screen but does not print it. Word marks hidden text on the screen with a solid underline, a dotted underline, or a different color, depending on your system.

To make all text formatted as hidden text invisible on the screen, choose the View Preferences command and turn off the Hidden Text check box. To print all hidden text on paper, turn on the Hidden Text check box in the Print Options dialog box before you start printing. (To display this dialog box, choose the File Print command and then the <Options> command button.)

Subscripts and Superscripts

When you're typing footnote references, mathematical equations, or chemical formulas, you can raise characters to produce superscripts, as here:

Cakes are round, but πr^2

Or you can lower characters to produce subscripts, as here:

$$\frac{bridge}{troubled\ H_2O}$$

The Position box of the Format Character dialog box contains option buttons for raising or lowering characters:

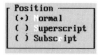

On some printers, choosing the Superscript or Subscript button changes only the vertical position of a character; other printers also reduce the size of the character. If your printer doesn't automatically reduce the size of subscripts and superscripts but is able to print more than one size, you can reduce the size in the Point Size box.

Use these speed formatting keys to turn superscript and subscript position on and off:

Ctrl-plus sign key	Superscript
Ctrl-equal sign key	Subscript

REMOVING AND COPYING FORMATS

With the following speed formatting keys, you can quickly remove all or most paragraph and character formatting to restore text to the default formats:

Ctrl-X	Resets paragraph formats to defaults
Ctrl-Spacebar	Resets character formats to defaults
Ctrl-Z	Resets all character formats to defaults except font and point size

These keys come in handy when you've applied several formats that you want to remove. Ctrl-X restores flush-left alignment, removes all indents and extra line spacing, and turns off the Keep Paragraph options. Ctrl-Spacebar removes all special printing effects such as boldface and italics, and it restores selected characters to the normal position and to the default font and size. Ctrl-Z removes all special printing effects and restores characters to the normal position but does not change the font or size.

Copying character and paragraph formats with the mouse is a simple matter. First select the characters or paragraphs you want to format, and then point to the character or paragraph that has the format you want to copy. (If you're copying paragraph formats, move the mouse pointer to the selection bar, and point to the paragraph from there.) Then hold down the Ctrl-Shift keys while you click the mouse button.

SEARCHING FOR AND REPLACING FORMATS

Word provides a way to find and change most formatting instructions. You can search for and replace both character and paragraph formatting with the Edit Search and the Edit Replace commands. (You cannot search for or replace section or tab formats unless these formats have been assigned by a style sheet.)

The Edit Search and Edit Replace dialog boxes have command buttons for finding and replacing formats instead of text: the <Search for Formatting Only> button and the <Replace Formatting Only> button. After you choose one of these buttons, a dialog box lets you choose which kind of formatting you want to find or replace: Character, Paragraph, or Style. Choose Character or Paragraph to search for or replace a format assigned with the Format Character command, the Format Paragraph command, speed formatting keys, the ribbon, or the ruler. Choose Style to search for or replace any format assigned by a style sheet.

If, for example, you want to substitute underlining for a boldface-italic format, choose the Edit Replace command. When you see the Edit Replace dialog box, choose the <Replace Formatting Only> button, which leads to the Replace Formatting dialog box:

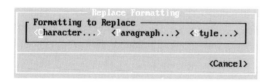

Because you're replacing character formatting, choose the <Character> command button. The Replace Character Formatting dialog box, which resembles the Format Character dialog box, appears. Use it to specify the format you're looking for, as well as formats you specifically don't want to find. For example, to search for and replace a boldface-italic format, turn on the Bold check box and the Italic check box. If you don't want to find text that is bold, italic, *and* underlined, turn off the Underline check box.

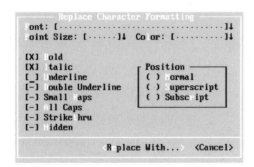

An X in the check box indicates that it's turned on, a space indicates that it's turned off, and a dash indicates that it's neither on nor off. Word looks for words with character formats that are turned on, specifically rejects words with character formats that are turned off, and ignores character formats that are neither on nor off.

After you specify what formats to find, press Enter or choose the <Replace With> command button. When you see the Replace With Character Formatting dialog box, specify the format you want to substitute. You must also specify that the searched-for format be turned off. For example, to substitute an underline format for boldface italics, turn on the Underline check box and turn off the Bold and the Italic check boxes. Then choose <OK> (press Enter) to carry out the command.

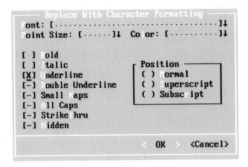

Where Word searches depends on where the cursor is located when you choose the Edit Replace command. If the cursor underscores a single character, Word searches forward from the cursor to the end of the document until every occurrence is found. If the cursor is highlighting one or more characters, Word searches only within the selected text.

When you search for and replace paragraph formats, you choose formats from dialog boxes that resemble the Format Paragraph dialog box. When you search for and replace styles, you must specify formats by typing in the two-character code assigned to the style you want to find or substitute. (Styles and style sheets are explained in Chapter 17.)

STRATEGY FOR FORMATTING

With Word, you can format a document at any time: before you begin typing, during the typing session, or after you've typed the entire document. You might prefer to take advantage of Word's on-screen formatting capabilities and see the final format as you type. Or you might want to type the document without interruption and then format it.

I recommend a strategy that minimizes interruptions and lets you see as much formatting as possible while typing. With this strategy, you use fewer formatting commands, and it's easier to keep track of what formatting instructions are being applied to what text.

Format Most of the Document as You Type

Before you start typing, define the formats that apply to most of the document. Usually, most of a document has the same section, paragraph, and character formats. To define these formats:

1. Choose the Format Margins command, and check to see that the page size and margins are set the way you want.

2. If you want page numbers printed, use the Insert Page Numbers command.

3. If you want to set up multiple columns, place footnotes at the end of the document, or add line numbers, use the Format Section command.

4. Choose the Format Paragraph command. Check to see that the alignment options, the first-line indent, the spacing before paragraphs, and the line spacing options are set to give you the format you want. (The other options in the Format Paragraph dialog box are typically for special paragraphs, not for overall formatting.)

5. If you want to change the font, point size, or color for most of the characters in the document, choose the Format Character command (or choose a font from the formatting ribbon).

When you assign the line format that applies to most of the document, remember to take advantage of Word's ability to automatically indent the first line of each paragraph and to put extra space between paragraphs. Set the first-line indent to something like 0.5 inches, or set the space before each paragraph to 1 li (1 line). This way, you can save yourself some typing time, and the document will be easier to read as you type and edit it.

If you change your mind about any of the formatting instructions you've given, press Ctrl-5 to highlight the entire document, and use the formatting command that lets you make the desired change. The new formatting instructions will be applied to the existing document and to any subsequent typing.

Format the Rest of the Document After You Type It

If some paragraphs or characters require special treatment, go back and change them after you finish typing. If one section of a document needs a special page format, move the cursor to any place in that section, and use the Format Section or the Format Margins command. The new formatting instructions are applied only to that section, assuming that the beginning and end of the section are properly marked with section breaks.

If a single paragraph needs a special line format, move the cursor to any place in that paragraph. If you want to change two or more paragraphs in sequence, highlight some text in each paragraph. Then use the Format Paragraph command (or speed formatting keys) to reformat the selected text.

If you want to assign a special typeface to any sequence of characters in the document, highlight those characters and use the Format Character command (or speed formatting keys or the ribbon).

You can review the formatting instructions that are in effect at a specific location in your document by moving the cursor there and choosing the appropriate Format command.

THERE'S MORE

In this chapter, we looked at four ways to format text *directly:* using the Format commands, using speed formatting keys, using the ruler, and using the formatting ribbon. You can also format text *indirectly* by creating and applying style sheets.

Similar to glossaries, which store frequently used words, style sheets are separate files that store frequently used formatting instructions. When you want to use text stored in a glossary, you type a code assigned to the text instead of retyping the text itself. Similarly, when you want to use formatting instructions stored in a style sheet, you type a code assigned to the instructions instead of redefining them.

If you find yourself repeatedly defining the same formats for a number of different documents, style sheets can save you a lot of time. They let you reuse formatting instructions without re-creating them. You can also make formatting changes throughout several documents without having to open the documents and find the text that needs reformatting. Simply change the style sheet—and the documents linked to the style sheet automatically change. Chapter 17 will introduce you to the power of style sheets, showing you how to use the ready-made style sheets provided by Word and how to change style sheets to suit your needs.

Chapter 10

Formatting Special Text

With typewriters or conventional word processors, formatting special text can take more time than it's worth. Typing a document in multiple columns, placing footnotes at the bottom of the page where they are referenced, centering headings over columns in a table, and aligning the decimal points of numbers in a column are painstaking tasks that require skill and patience. Adding running heads on each page is easy but time-consuming.

When you use Word, you don't have to be a skilled or patient typist to do special formatting and to make your documents look professionally prepared. Word does the formatting for you. In this chapter, you learn how to instruct Word to format special text such as tables, multiple columns, footnotes, and running heads.

FORMATTING TABLES

When you want to arrange facts or figures in columns, you can use the Tab key as you do on a typewriter. Word initially sets tab stops at ½-inch intervals across the page. You can change the default tab stops with the Utilities Customize command by typing a new measurement for the distance between tab stops in the Default Tab box, or you can reset the tab stops with the ruler or the Format Tabs command. You can also draw vertical lines between columns of a table with the Format Tabs command.

Tab stops are part of paragraph formatting and can be changed from paragraph to paragraph. Word remembers the tab stops for each paragraph from one editing session to the next.

Tips for Typing Tables

Because tabs are a part of paragraph formatting, treat a table as one paragraph when you type it. End each line in the table (except for the last line) by pressing Shift-Enter to start a new line rather than a new paragraph. At the end of the last line, press the Enter key to mark the end of the table paragraph. If you want the column headings centered over the columns, treat the heading line(s) as a separate paragraph so that you can set different tabs for the column headings.

It's often easier to set tab stops after you type the text for a table. As you type, press the Tab key once between column entries. After you finish, you can determine where to set the tab stops. Although the column entries won't be aligned as you type, they instantly fall into place after the tab stops are set to accommodate the longest entry in each column. After the text is typed and the tab stops are set, it's simple to insert vertical lines between columns of the table.

About Tab Stops

Tab stops have three attributes: position, alignment, and leader characters. The *position* of a tab stop is the distance from the left margin to the tab stop. The *alignment* determines how text in a column is positioned in relation to the tab stop. *Leaders* are strings of characters that lead your eyes from one column to the next.

Position

Tab stop positions are measured from the left margin in inches, unless you specify a different measurement with the Format Tabs command or change the default unit of measure in the Measure box of the Utilities Customize command.

Although you can type a measurement if you use the Format Tabs command, it's easier to pick a position on the ruler. With the ruler, you can forget about measurements and simply point to the spot where you want to set a tab or draw a vertical line.

Alignment

When you set a tab stop, you specify how text will be aligned in relation to the tab stop. The alignment options are left, center, right, decimal, and vertical. The default is left alignment, in which the text aligns flush left with the tab stop. Center alignment centers the text on the tab stop. With right alignment, the text aligns flush right with the tab stop. Decimal alignment aligns the decimal points of a column of numbers with the tab stop. (If the text has no decimal point, it aligns flush right with the tab stop.)

The vertical alignment option actually has nothing to do with aligning text. When vertical alignment is chosen, Word draws a vertical line at the position specified for the tab stop, rather than setting a tab. Vertical lines are an attractive way to separate columns of a table. Figure 10-1 illustrates these vertical lines and the various kinds of tab alignment.

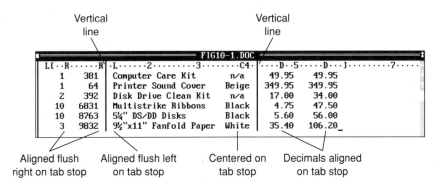

Figure 10-1. *Various tab alignments.*

Leaders

You have the option of assigning a leader character to a tab stop. Leaders are strings of characters that fill up tabbed space. They lead your eyes from column to column, helping you keep track of which line you're on. Dot leaders, for example, are sometimes used in a table of contents to connect chapter or section names with the corresponding page numbers, as shown in Figure 10-2 on the following page.

Instead of dots, you can choose hyphens (-) or underscores (_) as the leader characters. (Hyphens form a broken line across the page; underscores create a solid line.) Vertical lines drawn with tabs cannot have leaders.

Table of Contents

Right-justified tab
with dot leaders

Figure 10-2. *Table of contents with dot leaders.*

Using the Ruler

The easiest way to set, clear, or move tab stops is to use the ruler. To turn the ruler on or off using the keyboard, choose the View Ruler command. To turn the ruler on or off with the mouse, click the ruler icon (↓) at the top of the vertical scroll bar.

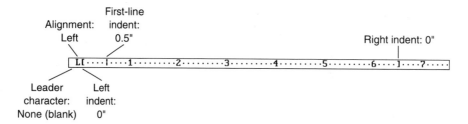

The ruler starts at the left margin and continues across the width of the window. It initially displays only the indents for the selected paragraphs, not the default tabs. The two characters between the left window border and the beginning of the ruler indicate the current leader character and the type of alignment. With the mouse, you can point to these characters and click until the symbol for the desired alignment or leader option appears.

After you set tab stops or draw vertical lines, the ruler shows the positions of the tab stops and the vertical lines and indicates the alignment and leader option chosen for each tab stop. If a leader character is assigned to a tab stop, it appears to the left of the tab stop:

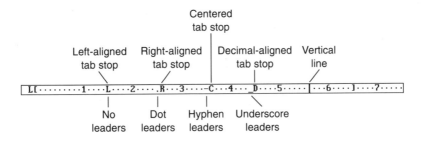

The following symbols mark tab stops on the ruler and indicate alignment and leader characters:

L   Left-aligned tab stop
R   Right-aligned tab stop
C   Centered tab stop
D   Decimal tab stop
            No leaders (blank)
.   Dot leaders
-           Hyphen leaders (broken line)
_   Underscore leaders (solid line)
| Vertical line position

To set, clear, or move tab stops, move the highlight or the mouse pointer along the ruler. If you're using the keyboard, press Ctrl-Shift-F10 to activate the ruler and its highlight. The direction keys move the highlight along the ruler. The Enter key enters changes made with the keyboard and deactivates the ruler; the Escape key cancels the changes and deactivates the ruler. With the mouse, the ruler is always active when it is visible.

Setting tabs and drawing vertical lines

When you set a tab stop, any default tab stops to the left of it are removed. For example, if you set a tab at 1.8 inches, the preset tabs at 0.5, 1.0, and 1.5 inches are cleared, making the first tab stop 1.8 inches from the left margin. If you want to use any of those preset tab stops, you must reset them. This feature can be useful: For instance, if you want your first tab stop at 3 inches, set a tab stop at 3 inches even though a preset tab already exists at that position. By setting the 3-inch tab stop, you clear all preceding preset tab stops with one quick move.

To set a tab stop or draw a vertical line with the keyboard:

1. Move the cursor to the paragraph (or highlight text in each of several paragraphs) where you want to set tabs or draw vertical lines.

2. Press Ctrl-Shift-F10, and use the Left and Right direction keys to move the highlight on the ruler to the position where you want to set the tab or draw the line.

3. Type one of the following letters to both set a tab stop and assign an alignment option:

L	Sets a left-aligned tab
C	Sets a centered tab
R	Sets a right-aligned tab
D	Sets a decimal-aligned tab
V	Draws a vertical line

4. To assign or change the leader character for the tab stop, type one of the following while the highlight is still on the tab stop:

Period	Adds dot leaders (…)
Hyphen	Adds broken-line leaders (---)
Underscore	Adds solid-line leaders (__)
Spacebar	Removes leaders (None)

5. Press the Enter key to carry out the command.

The Home and End keys move the highlight all the way to the left or right end of the ruler (but not beyond the indents). After you set your own tabs, you can use the Up and Down direction keys to quickly move the highlight from one tab stop to another.

To set a tab stop or draw a vertical line with the mouse:

1. Move the cursor to the paragraph (or highlight text in each of several paragraphs) where you want to set tabs or draw vertical lines.

2. Click the alignment character to the left of the ruler until the first letter of the alignment you want appears.

3. Click the leader character to the left of the ruler until the leader character you want appears.

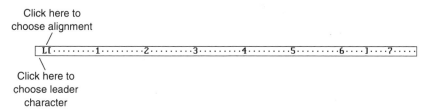

Click here to
choose alignment

Click here to
choose leader
character

4. Point to the position on the ruler where you want to set the tab or draw the line, and click the mouse button.

Removing tabs and vertical lines

To remove a tab stop or a vertical line with the keyboard, first press Ctrl-Shift-F10 to activate the ruler. Then use the direction keys to highlight the tab or vertical line you want to remove, and press the Del key.

To remove a tab stop or a vertical line with the mouse, point to the marker for the tab or the vertical line you want to remove, and drag it below the ruler.

If you want to remove all the tab stops that you've set and restore the default tab stops, use the Format Tabs command. Choose the <Clear All> command button and OK the command. All tab stops are cleared and reset to their initial positions at ½-inch intervals across the page (or to the positions defined by the Default Tab box of the Utilities Customize command).

Moving tabs and vertical lines

You can use the ruler to move tab stops or vertical lines that you've set and that appear on the ruler. Moving a tab stop allows you to change its position without redefining its alignment or leader character.

To move a tab stop or a vertical line with the keyboard, press Ctrl-Shift-F10 to activate the ruler. Use the direction keys to highlight the tab or vertical line you want to move. Then press Ctrl-Left direction key or Ctrl-Right direction key to move the highlight to the new position.

To move a tab stop or a vertical line with the mouse, point to the tab or vertical line you want to move, and drag it to the new position on the ruler.

Using the Format Tabs Command

You can set, clear, and move tab stops using the Format Tabs command. To set a tab stop or draw a vertical line:

1. Move the cursor to the paragraph (or highlight text in each of several paragraphs) where you want to set tabs or draw vertical lines.

2. Choose the Format Tabs command (Alt, T, T) to display the Format Tabs dialog box:

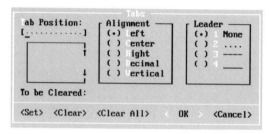

3. Type a measurement for the position of the tab or the vertical line in the Tab Position text box.

4. Turn on the desired Alignment and Leader options. If you don't want leaders, turn on the None option button in the Leader box. If you want to draw a line, turn on the Vertical option button in the Alignment box.

5. Choose the <Set> command button.

The dialog box stays on the screen so that you can continue to set tab stops. The tab stops or vertical lines you insert are listed in the Tab Position list box and become fixed when you choose <OK> in the dialog box. But before you carry out the command, you might want to change, remove, or move some tabs or vertical lines.

To change the alignment or leader character for a tab stop, first type the position of the tab stop in the Tab Position text box, or, if it appears in the Tab Position list box, simply highlight it. Then turn on the desired alignment or leader option, and choose the <Set> button. To remove a tab stop or vertical line, first type its position in the Tab Position text box or highlight it in the Tab Position list box. Then choose the <Clear> button. To move a tab stop, you must first delete it using the <Clear> button and then reset it in the desired location using the <Set> button. To remove all tab stops and restore the default tab stops, choose <Clear All>. Choose <OK> when you finish setting, changing, moving, or removing tab stops and vertical lines.

ADDING BORDERS AND BACKGROUND SHADING

Adding borders and background shading is a very easy and attractive way to enhance and emphasize special paragraphs or tables. You can completely enclose such text in boxes, or you can add borders to the sides or to the top and bottom only. Borders and boxes can be used with the vertical lines drawn by tab stops to create charts, tables, and forms. If you edit a bordered or shaded paragraph, the border or shading shrinks or stretches to fit the text. To move, copy, or delete such a paragraph, include the paragraph mark at the end when you select the paragraph, because the format is stored there. You can apply borders and shading separately or together. Figure 10-3 shows a table with background shading, framed by a double-line border.

Qty	Order #	Product Description	Color	Unit Price	Net Expansion
1	381	Computer Care Kit	n/a	49.95	49.95
1	64	Printer Sound Cover	Beige	349.95	349.95
2	392	Disk Drive Clean Kit	n/a	17.00	34.00
10	6831	Multistrike Ribbons	Black	4.75	47.50
10	8763	5¼" DS/DD Disks	Black	5.60	56.00
3	9832	9½"x11" Fanfold Paper	White	35.40	106.20

Figure 10-3. *Borders and background shading.*

Although not all printers can print these variations, Word offers a choice of line styles for borders: normal (I), bold (I), double (II), and thick (I). You can choose a percentage of shading to control the darkness of the shading: For example, type or choose 10% for light shading, 40% for medium shading, and 70% for dark shading. If you have a color printer, you can choose colors for both lines and shading. The quality of the lines and shading depends on the capabilities of your printer. The best way to find out what it can do is to experiment.

To add a border or shading to a paragraph:

1. Move the cursor to the paragraph you want to border or shade.

2. Choose the Format Borders command (Alt, T, B) to display the Format Paragraph Borders dialog box:

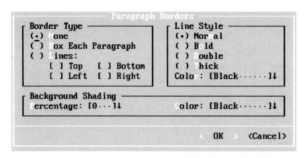

3. To add borders, choose either the Box Each Paragraph option or the Lines option. If you choose the Lines option, indicate where you want the lines by turning on the appropriate check boxes.

4. Choose a line style by turning on one of the option buttons in the Line Style box. If you have a color printer, choose a color for the lines in the Color box.

5. To add background shading, choose or type a number in the Percentage box to indicate how dark the shading should be. If you have a color printer (or one that prints shades of gray), choose a color for the shading in the Color box.

6. Choose <OK> (press Enter).

If you have selected more than one paragraph when you give the command to box each paragraph, Word puts a horizontal line between paragraphs. To avoid inserting these lines in boxed text, select all the paragraphs and add left and right lines using the Lines option rather than the Box Each Paragraph option. Then select the first paragraph and add a top line, and select the last paragraph and add a bottom line.

FORMATTING MULTIPLE COLUMNS

Word normally prints a document in one column that extends from the left margin to the right margin. You can, however, tell Word to print more than one column on a page by changing the page layout with the Format Section command. A multiple-column format (such as that shown in Figure 10-4) lets you put more text on each page. Because the length of each line is shorter, you can use a smaller font without detracting from readability. Newspapers,

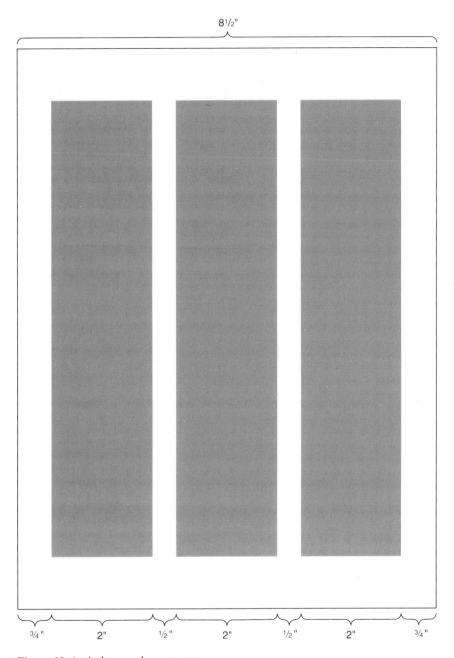

Figure 10-4. *A three-column page.*

magazines and some books use a multiple-column format not only to keep print-ing costs down but also to produce attractive, easy-to-read pages. If you prepare newsletters, brochures, or manuals, or if you want to give a professional touch to any document that lends itself to multiple columns, try this feature.

Word does not restrict the number of columns per page, but the width of your paper imposes some practical limits. It is difficult to print more than three columns on 8½-by-11-inch paper because you must allow space between columns as well as space for the left and right margins.

When you divide a page into multiple columns, decide how wide the col-umns will be, how much space will be needed between columns, and how wide the margins will be. In most cases, you should reduce the left and right margins to allow more space for text. The total width of the columns, the space between the columns, and the left and right margins should equal the page width. For example, a readable three-column format on 8½-by-11-inch paper would have three 2-inch columns of text with a ½-inch space between columns and with left and right margins of ¾ inches, as shown in Figure 10-4.

Creating Multiple Columns

To format a document into multiple columns:

1. Choose the Format Section command (Alt, T, S).

2. In the Format Section dialog box, type the number of columns you want on each page in the Number box (under Columns):

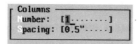

3. If necessary, change the amount of space between columns in the Spacing box.

4. Choose <OK> (press Enter).

If you also want to change the left and right margins, use the Format Margins command.

If you divide a page into multiple columns, it's usually not practical to justify the lines of text unless you use a small font size. The shorter lines make it difficult to avoid the unsightly gaps of space that are inserted between words to fill the lines of justified text.

Column breaks

When Word lays out text in multiple columns, it fills each column before putting text in the next column. If you want the next column to start at a particular place in the text, move the cursor to that place and press Ctrl-Shift-Enter (or choose the Insert Break command and the Column option button). This inserts a column break mark, which appears on the screen as a row of dots across the column. The first line of text after a column break mark is printed at the top of the next column.

Viewing and Editing Multiple Columns

On the normal editing screen, you don't see multiple columns. Instead, the text appears in one long column the width of a single printed column. To view multiple columns, use the View Layout command. With View Layout turned on, Word displays the columns side by side and lets you edit them. You can move from one column to another with the keyboard by first pressing Alt-5 and then using the Right or Left direction key. With the mouse, it's simply a matter of pointing and clicking. Because Word must do more work to display the actual layout, editing in layout view is considerably slower than editing in a standard window.

To get an idea of what the pages will look like when printed, use the File Print Preview command described in Chapter 12. You might not be able to read the text displayed by Print Preview, and you can't edit the text, but you can clearly see the column layout for whole pages on the screen.

FORMATTING FOOTNOTES

Word makes it easy to create and format footnotes. You can insert them as you type, or you can add them later. Word can number the footnotes for you and renumber them if you delete or insert footnotes or change their order.

A footnote consists of the *footnote reference mark* and the *footnote text*. The footnote reference mark is usually a number, but it can also be a symbol (such as *) or a letter. It appears in two places: embedded in the document where the footnote is referenced and next to the footnote text. The footnote text is stored at the end of the document but can be printed on the page where it is referenced.

Creating Footnotes

Use the Insert Footnote command to create footnotes:

1. Move the cursor to the place in the document where you want the reference mark to appear. (The reference mark is inserted to the left of the cursor.)

2. Choose the Insert Footnote command (Alt, I, N). The Insert Footnote dialog box appears:

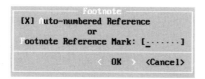

3. If you want Word to number the footnotes for you, be sure the Auto-numbered Reference check box is turned on. If you prefer to choose your own reference mark, type a symbol, a letter, or a word such as *Note* in the Footnote Reference Mark box. The reference mark can contain as many as 28 characters.

4. Choose <OK> (press Enter). Word inserts the reference mark and jumps to the end of the document (or to the footnote pane if you've opened one—see the next section).

5. Type the text of the footnote, which can be any length.

Word uses the default font and size for the reference mark. To make the reference mark a superscript and smaller than the rest of the text, use the Edit Go To command to go back to the reference mark embedded in the document and format it with the Format Character command.

Opening a Footnote Pane

A *footnote pane* resembles an ordinary window pane. When a footnote pane is open, you can see the part of the document where the footnote reference mark appears and the footnote text simultaneously. As you scroll through the document, Word scrolls the footnote pane to display any footnotes referenced in the window.

After you have created at least one footnote, Word makes the View Footnotes/Annotations command available, which allows you to open or close a footnote pane. When you choose View Footnotes/Annotations, the footnote pane appears at the bottom of the screen. A window that has been split to make a footnote pane cannot be split again until you close the footnote pane (by choosing View Footnotes/Annotations again). You can resize the footnote pane with the Window Split command or the split-bar icon, using the techniques for sizing window panes that you learned in Chapter 7.

If you have an open footnote pane and no mouse, you must use the Edit Go To command or the F6 key to get in and out of the footnote pane.

Going to Footnotes

Instead of scrolling through the document to find footnote reference marks or footnote text, use the Edit Go To command.

To find a footnote reference mark embedded in a document:

1. If the cursor is already on a reference mark, move it off.

2. Choose the Edit Go To command (Alt, E, G). The Edit Go To dialog box appears:

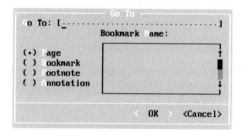

3. In the Go To box, type the letter *f* to go to the next footnote reference mark, or type *f* followed by the number of the reference mark you want to find. For example, to find the fourth footnote reference mark, type *f4* in the Go To box.

4. Choose <OK> (press Enter).

To find footnote text:

1. Highlight the reference mark for the footnote text.

2. Choose the Edit Go To command.

3. Choose <OK> (press Enter).

If the cursor is not on a reference mark or in the footnote text, the Edit Go To command finds the next reference mark (if any) in the document. If the cursor is on a reference mark, Edit Go To finds the footnote text for that reference mark. And if the cursor is in the footnote text, Edit Go To locates the reference mark in the document for that footnote.

Editing Footnotes

After you create a footnote, you can go back and change either the reference mark or the footnote text. You can also delete or move footnotes. If you let Word number footnotes for you, the program renumbers them after you delete, move, or insert footnotes.

To change a footnote reference mark, first highlight it. Then choose the Insert Footnote command, and type the new reference mark in the Footnote Reference Mark box. If you want automatically numbered footnotes, turn on the Auto-numbered Reference check box. After you choose <OK>, Word changes both occurrences of the reference mark—the one embedded in the document and the one next to the footnote text.

To change the footnote text, first highlight the reference mark for the footnote you want to edit. Then choose the Edit Go To command, and choose <OK> to move to the footnote text. Edit the footnote text as you would any other text in the document. If you accidentally delete an automatic footnote reference number adjacent to footnote text, move the cursor to where the number should be, type the glossary name *footnote*, and press the F3 key. After editing footnote text, use the Edit Go To command to move back to the footnote's reference mark.

To delete a footnote, delete the reference mark embedded in the document as you would delete any other character. Word deletes both the reference mark and the footnote text associated with it.

To move a footnote, move the reference mark in the document the same way you would move any other text. Word moves the footnote text for you.

Printing and Positioning Footnotes

Use the dialog box of the Format Section command to specify where you want footnotes printed. As mentioned earlier, Word stores the text for footnotes at the end of a document (or at the end of each section). But you can print each footnote on the same page as its reference mark by choosing the Same Page option in the Place Footnotes box:

If you choose the End of Section option, all footnotes for a section will print together at the end of the section (or at the end of the document if it has only one section).

FORMATTING RUNNING HEADS

A running head appears in the top or bottom margin of a page, separate from the main body of text. A reader can glance at running heads to find out, for example, the subject matter of the work as a whole or of individual chapters or major sections. Look at the running heads in this book: Those at the top tell you the part and chapter titles, and those at the bottom (which in this case are page numbers) tell you which page you're on.

The Format Header/Footer Command

Running heads are typed as regular text in a document and then formatted with the Format Header/Footer command. You only need to type a running head once and tell Word which pages to print it on.

After you type the text of the running head, choose the Format Header/ Footer command. You see this dialog box:

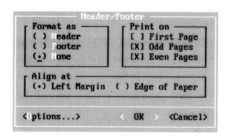

First specify whether the text is a header (to be placed at the top of a page) or a footer (to be placed at the bottom of a page). Then, in the Print On box, specify the pages on which the header or footer should be printed. Headers and footers are usually printed on every page except the first, but you have other options. For example, if you're printing or duplicating the document on both sides of the paper and fastening the pages together book

199

style, you might put one header on left (even-numbered) pages and a different header on right (odd-numbered) pages. The Align At box in the Format Header/Footer dialog box controls the horizontal placement of headers and footers, and the <Options> button lets you adjust the vertical placement.

Horizontal positioning of running heads

Running heads are usually printed within the same margins as the section in which they appear. If you want them to extend beyond the margins, turn on the Edge of Paper option in the Align At box:

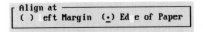

If you align a running head with the edge of the paper, use the Format Paragraph command to set left and right indents for the running head. These indents are measured from the *edges* of the paper—not from the margins, as is usually the case. You can also use the Format Paragraph command to format running heads flush left, flush right, centered, or justified. If you're printing on both sides of the paper, you might want to format the running heads of even-numbered pages flush left and those on odd-numbered pages flush right. This way, the running heads always appear on the outer corners of a page, as they do in this book.

Vertical positioning of running heads

By default, Word prints headers ½ inch from the top of the page and footers ½ inch from the bottom of the page. To change these measurements, choose the <Options> command button in the Format Header/Footer dialog box, which produces the Header/Footer Options dialog box:

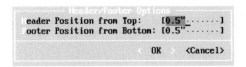

To vertically adjust a header position, type a new measurement that's less than the top margin in the Header Position from Top box. To vertically adjust a footer position, type a new measurement that's less than the bottom margin in the Footer Position from Bottom box. Consider the number of lines in the running head, and allow some space (at least 1 line, or ⅙ inch) between the header or footer and the main body of text.

Creating Running Heads

Type running heads at the beginning of the document, at the beginning of the section to which they apply, or just before the page break for the first page on which you want them to appear.

To create a running head:

1. Type the running head as a paragraph or a series of paragraphs. (Running heads can be any length.)

2. Move the cursor to the running-head paragraph. If the running head contains more than one paragraph, highlight some text in each paragraph.

3. Choose the Format Header/Footer command (Alt, T, H). (This command is not available when View Layout is turned on. If the Format Header/Footer command appears dimmed on the screen, choose the View Layout command to turn View Layout off.)

4. In the Format As box, choose Header to print the running-head text at the top of the page, or choose Footer to print it at the bottom of the page.

5. In the Print On box, indicate whether you want the header or footer to appear on the first page, on odd pages, or on even pages by turning the appropriate check boxes on or off.

6. If you want the header or footer to extend beyond the margins, turn on the Edge of Paper option.

7. To adjust the vertical placement of the header or footer, choose the <Options> command button and type a new measurement in the appropriate box.

8. Choose <OK> (press Enter) to carry out the command.

A paragraph formatted as a header or footer is printed at the position assigned in the Format Header/Footer command, not at the position where it is typed and appears on the screen. Word marks any paragraph formatted as a header or footer with a caret (^) to the left of the first line of the paragraph. A running head remains in effect from the point in the document where it is typed to the end of the section or until it is replaced by a new running head assigned to the same position.

After creating a running head with the Format Header/Footer command, you can use the Format Paragraph command to further define the horizontal placement, as described earlier in the chapter.

Putting page numbers in running heads

Although you can number pages without creating headers or footers, putting page numbers in running heads is the best way to coordinate the position of the page number with the running head. Even if you have no other running heads, you might want to create a header or footer for page numbers so that you have more control over the format of the numbers. You can format a page number in a running head the same way you format any other text.

To include a page number in a running head:

1. Type

    page

    in the running head at the place where you want the page number to appear. (A space must precede the word *page*.)

2. Press the F3 key when the cursor is immediately to the right of the word *page*. (Word puts parentheses around *page* after you press F3.)

You can include any other text with the page number. For example, if you want the word *Page* to precede the number, type

    Page page

instead of *page*. You can also include the section or chapter number (such as 1-1, 1-2, 1-3), or you can specify a number style such as -1-.

The word *page* is a glossary name. When you press the F3 key, you replace the glossary name with the special glossary entry *(page)*. During printing, Word inserts the correct page number on each page where the running head appears. If you include page numbers in running heads, be sure that the response in the Page Number Position box of the Insert Page Numbers command is None. Otherwise, each page number will print twice. You can use the Insert Page Number command to choose a number format and starting number for page numbers printed in running heads.

When you're printing on one side of the paper

Because most word-processed documents are printed on only one side of the page, you usually don't need to make the headers or footers for odd-numbered pages different from those for even-numbered pages. If you're printing on one side of the page, you need to consider headers and footers for the first page and for subsequent pages (both odd-numbered and even-numbered).

Suppose you're typing a document with a title page. The title tells you the subject of the document, so you don't need to identify the title page with a header or a footer. For subsequent pages, let's say you want to identify each page with a header that tells what the document is about and a footer that shows the page number. Type the text for the header as a paragraph in your document, and then choose the Format Header/Footer command to format it. Choose Header in the Format As box, and use the default settings in the Print On box: the First Page check box turned off and both Odd Pages and Even Pages turned on. Choose <OK> (press Enter) to carry out the command.

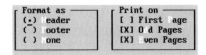

Type the text for the footer as a separate paragraph (including the glossary name *page*), and choose the Format Header/Footer command. Choose Footer in the Format As box, and OK the command, using the same default settings in the Print On box.

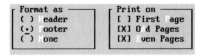

To have headers and footers appear on all pages, turn on all three check boxes in the Print On box when you format the headers and footers.

When you're printing on both sides of the paper

If you plan to print or duplicate a document on both sides of the paper, you might want to take advantage of Word's ability to print different headers and footers on odd-numbered and even-numbered pages. This feature is especially useful if you bind the document—whether you attach the pages with staples, fix the pages in a three-ring binder, or use a more permanent sort of binding. Bound documents often have page numbers and headers or footers located on the left side of left (even-numbered) pages and on the right side of right (odd-numbered) pages.

To plan which running heads go where, visualize or sketch the first three pages of the document (or section), and decide how you want headers, footers, and page numbers to appear on those pages. The sketch of the second page represents left or even-numbered pages, and the sketch of the third page represents right or odd-numbered pages. Use this sketch as a guide when you create headers and footers.

Suppose you want a report title to appear at the top of left pages and a section title to appear at the top of right pages (except the first page), with page numbers at the bottom of each page (except the first). Further suppose that you want the page numbers to appear in the outer corners of the pages, where they can be easily spotted (on the left side of left pages and the right side of right pages). Type two separate headers and two separate footers, as listed below. Make each header or footer a separate paragraph, and format each one using the Format Header/Footer command. Use the settings shown in parentheses for the Format As and Print On options:

- *Even-page header* for the report title on left pages (Header on, First Page off, Odd Pages off, Even Pages on)

- *Odd-page header* for the section title on right pages (Header on, First Page off, Odd Pages on, Even Pages off)

- *Even-page footer* for left-aligned page numbers on left pages (Footer on, First Page off, Odd Pages off, Even Pages on)

- *Odd-page footer* for right-aligned page numbers on right pages (Footer on, First Page off, Odd Pages on, Even Pages off)

Use the Format Paragraph command to assign left or right alignment to each header and footer. (Choose left alignment for left pages and right alignment for right pages).

Editing and Deleting Running Heads

You can edit and delete running heads using the same techniques you use to edit any other paragraph in a document. You can also change running heads back to normal paragraphs that are printed exactly where they are typed in the document: Choose the Format Header/Footer command while the cursor is in the running head, turn on the None option button in the Format As box, and OK the command.

Chapter 11

Filing

To understand what takes place when you handle electronic files, think of your computer's memory as a desktop where you work on documents, and think of directories and disks as file drawers where you store documents you're not working on. Saving a document on a disk is like placing the document in a file folder, sticking a label on the file, and putting it in a file cabinet. Opening a document is like pulling a file out of the filing cabinet, placing it on your desktop, and opening it so that you can read and work on it.

With a manual filing system, filing and retrieving a document involve removing it from one place and putting it in another. With an electronic filing system, you move *copies* of documents back and forth without removing the documents from either place. Saving a document on a disk does not remove it from memory; to remove a document from memory, you must close it. Opening a document does not remove it from the disk; to remove a document from a disk, you must delete it.

The back-and-forth transfer of copies of documents between memory and disks is done with commands on the File menu. You've already worked with the two most important file-handling commands: File Save, to store documents on a disk, and File Open, to retrieve documents. Safe storage and easy retrieval of files are the most important filing concerns. Word excels in both areas: Its file-handling commands have so many built-in safeguards that you should never accidentally lose a file.

An important part of Word's filing capabilities is its document-retrieval feature. Document retrieval, based on summary information you provide, lets you search across directories for documents. You can conduct a search on the basis of a document's title, the name of the author or preparer, the creation or revision date, or text in the file. You'll learn about Word's document-retrieval commands in Chapter 15.

In this chapter, you learn what kinds of files are used with Word and how they are named, how to save and open files (with various options), how to change the default path for saving and opening files, how to save everything in one step, how to save a file under a new name or in a new location, what to do if you run out of memory or disk space, and how to temporarily leave Word in order to run other programs.

TYPES OF FILES AND FILENAMES

The two main types of files are data files and program files. Data files are files you create; program files help you create them.

Data Files

The *data files* you create with Word are document files that store documents, glossary files that help you create and edit documents, and style sheet files that help you format documents. Word's recommended filename extensions indicate the types of data files. Unless you specify a different filename extension, Word assigns these:

> *.DOC to document files*
> *.GLY to glossary files*
> *.STY to style sheet files*

Word automatically makes a backup copy of any file you create: It saves the previous version of a document, glossary, or style sheet file each time you save a new version, giving the previous version the filename extension .BAK.

Program Files

A number of *program files* store the Word program, accessory programs, and information that Word needs to process your words. These files include the spelling dictionary, the thesaurus, the hyphenation file, and the Help file.

As you work, Word creates temporary files called *scratch files,* with the extension .TMP, to record the editing changes made to documents. These scratch files are erased after you save your work or end an editing session.

Word also creates a file called MW.INI (Microsoft Word Initialization) to record the name of the document you last worked on and many of the options you last chose so that they are remembered from one editing session to the next. For example, Word records in the MW.INI file all options chosen with the View Preferences command.

If you have two floppy-disk drives, it's usually more convenient to store program files on a disk in drive A and data files on a separate disk in drive B. If you have a hard disk, you can store both program and data files on the hard disk. For both hard disks and higher-capacity floppy disks, it's best to organize disk space into subdirectories, with separate subdirectories for various categories of files. (See Appendix A.)

SAVING FILES

When Word saves a file, it transfers a copy of the file in the active window from memory to a disk. The File Save and the File Save As commands save only the active document or style sheet. The File Save All command saves everything: all open documents and style sheets as well as the active glossary. (To save glossary files only, use the <Save Glossary> command button in the Edit Glossary dialog box.)

How to Use the File Save As Dialog Box

If you're saving a document or style sheet for the first time, the File Save, File Save All, and File Save As commands behave alike by displaying the File Save As dialog box:

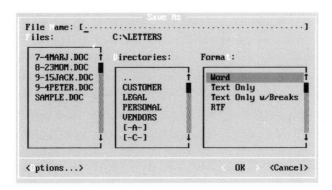

The File Save As command always displays this dialog box, but the File Save and the File Save All commands display it only the first time you save a document or style sheet, to allow you to assign a filename and location. The next time you save a file with either the File Save or the File Save All command, you do not see the dialog box, because Word assumes that you want to save the file under the same name and in the same location as before.

The File Name box

In the File Save As dialog box, the File Name box lets you specify the name you want to give to the document (or style sheet) you're saving. If you type a name that has already been given to another file in the same location, Word asks you to confirm that you want to overwrite (replace) that file.

The default path and how to change it

Word displays the default path under the File Name box. The default path is the drive and directory where Word stores and looks for data files. On a floppy-disk system, the default path is initially the root directory of drive B; on a hard-disk system, the default path is the drive and directory from which you started Word.

If you don't want to save a file in the default path shown under the File Name box, you can override the default path for the file you're saving, or you can change the default path for a single work session or for all work sessions.

To override the default path for a single file, type a different drive and directory in the File Name box, or highlight a directory in the Directories box. With the keyboard, move to the Directories box, and use the Up and Down direction keys. With the mouse, click the directory you want. The directory you highlight appears in the File Name box.

To change the default path for all files opened or saved during the current work session, choose a drive and directory from the Directories box of the File Save As or the File Open dialog box, and press the Enter key. With the mouse, point to the directory and double-click. Word remembers your new default path until you exit the program, unless you use the <Options> command button to designate a new default path for all work sessions.

To change the default path for all files opened or saved every time you use Word:

1. Choose the <Options> command button in the File Save As (or the File Open) dialog box. The <Options> button displays the File Options dialog box:

2. Type a drive and directory in the Default Path box, or choose a path from the Directories box. (Highlight your choice and press Enter, or point to it and double-click the mouse button.)

3. Turn on the Always Use as Default check box. (If this check box is off, the path you choose becomes the default for the current work session only and can be overridden by later choosing a path from the Directories box in the File Save As or the File Open dialog box as the default for the current work session.)

4. Choose <OK> (press Enter).

The Format box

For most files, the proposed response (Word) in the Format box of the File Save As dialog box need not be changed. You'll usually want to save files as Word files with all formatting. However, another option in the Format box, Text Only, lets you save a document as a standard ASCII file in which only the text (without formatting) is saved. The Text Only w/Breaks option saves a document as a standard ASCII file including the text and the line breaks. You are also given the option of converting the format to what is called *Rich Text Format* (RTF).

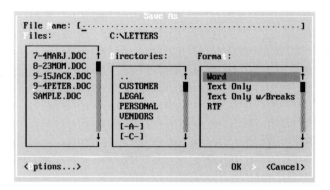

Saving a document without Word's formatting is sometimes necessary if you want to use the file with other software or to transmit the file to other equipment, such as typesetting equipment or non-IBM computers. Most other programs do not understand Word's unique formatting instructions. An ASCII file, however, contains characters encoded in a way that is standard throughout most of the computer industry. (Pronounced *as-kee*, ASCII stands for American Standard Code for Information Interchange.) ASCII files include printable characters such as letters, numbers, punctuation marks, and symbols, as well as nonprintable characters such as spaces, tabs, carriage returns, linefeeds, and formfeeds. A standard ASCII file does not include any special characters or instructions that control either the formatting or printing of a document.

A Text Only file is a standard ASCII file that includes a carriage return at the end of each paragraph. If you want to use a Word file with another program, such as a word-processing or database program that does not need a carriage return at the end of each line, save the file as a Text Only file. If you use Word to write computer programs or to create DOS command files such as CONFIG.SYS and AUTOEXEC.BAT, save them as Text Only files.

Choose Text Only w/Breaks to create a partially formatted ASCII file that is more suitable for telecommunications and that can be printed without being reformatted. When you choose this option, Word replaces many formatting instructions with standard ASCII characters that produce the same results. For example, it replaces instructions about left indents and tabs with spaces. And it maintains the same line breaks by inserting a carriage return and linefeed at the end of each line.

Rich Text Format was developed by Microsoft to allow documents to be transferred from one Microsoft application to another without losing any formatting. With RTF, all formatting is converted into ASCII codes, which many, but not all, programs can interpret.

If you choose Text Only, Text Only w/Breaks, or RTF in the File Save As dialog box, Word reminds you that formatting will be lost and asks you to confirm your choice, as shown in this example:

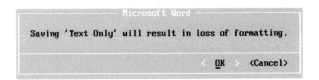

When you want to save a file in Text Only, Text Only w/Breaks, or RTF format, it's a good idea to save it first with Word's usual formatting and then save it again without Word's formatting, using another filename extension. Changing the filename extension from the usual .DOC is an easy way to identify and separate copies of a file that have a nonstandard format. For example, use .TXT (for Text Only format), .TLB (for Text Only w/Breaks format), or .RTF (for Rich Text Format).

How to Save Files

If you want to save everything in one step, choose the File Save All command. This command saves all open documents, the active glossary, and any active style sheets.

To save a single document or style sheet:

1. Move the cursor to the document or style sheet if it isn't already located there.

2. If you're saving the document or style sheet for the first time, you can choose either the File Save command (Alt, F, S) or the File Save As command (Alt, F, A). If you've saved the file before, choose File Save.

3. If you're saving the file for the first time, the File Save As dialog box appears. Type the name you want to give to the file in the File Name box. Include the pathname if you don't want to store the file in the default path shown under the File Name box.

4. Change the response in the Format box only if you don't want to save Word's usual formatting instructions.

5. Choose <OK> (press Enter).

After you save the document, Word renames the previous version of the file with the filename extension .BAK to indicate that it's a backup copy. If a backup copy for the file already exists, the old .BAK file is deleted. (Should anything happen to the current version of the file, you can open the backup copy and rename it, using the .DOC filename extension or any other extension you choose.)

The first time you save a document or style sheet, Word displays a dialog box titled Summary before completing the save. Your answers to the questions in this box provide information for the File Management command on the File menu. (See Chapter 15 for more information on finding and managing files and providing summary information.) To bypass the summary, press the Esc key. By choosing the Utilities Customize command and turning off the Prompt for Summary Info check box, you can tell Word not to display summary questions when you save new documents or style sheets.

If, when you're saving a file, you assign it a filename that has already been given to another document (or style sheet) on the same floppy disk or in the same directory, a message box asks if you want to overwrite that file:

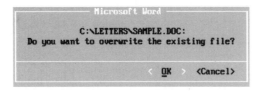

If you choose <OK> (press Enter), the file you're saving replaces the existing file. You can cancel the command at this point by choosing <Cancel> or by pressing the Esc key.

Saving files with new names, locations, or formats

The File Save As command lets you save a file under a new name, in a new location, or with a new format. If you save a file under a new name or in a new location, you actually create a new file; the previous version of the file remains unchanged, as a separate file. (If you want to rename or move a file without keeping a copy under the old name or in the old location, it's best to use the File Management command on the File menu, which is explained in Chapter 15.)

After you choose the File Save As command, you see the same dialog box that appears when you save a file for the first time:

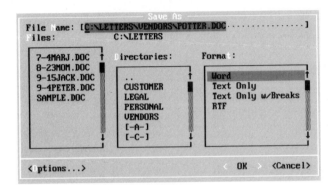

The pathname and filename shown in the File Name box are the existing location and filename.

If you have multiple directories, be careful that you don't inadvertently give a file a new location when you merely want to rename it. If you type a new filename without including a path, Word assumes that you want the file stored in the default path shown under the File Name box, regardless of where the file is now stored.

You can type a new directory location for a file in the File Name box—with or without changing the file's name—or you can choose a new location from the Directories box.

If you save the file under a new name, the new name appears in the title bar. If you type the name of a file that already exists in the path specified, Word lets you know you're about to overwrite an existing file and gives you a chance to cancel the command.

When to Save Files

It's a good practice to save your work every 15 minutes or so. Then, if the power or your equipment fails, your loss is minimized. Saving at frequent intervals also helps you avoid running out of working space in memory and on your disk. As you work, Word uses memory and disk space to keep track of the changes you make. Each time you save your work, temporary scratch files are erased from your Word Program disk, and some working space in memory is cleared.

When the word SAVE appears in the status bar, Word is telling you that it is running out of working space in memory. If saving all documents, glossaries, and style sheets with the File Save All command doesn't restore the available memory space and turn off the SAVE indicator, choose the File Close All command. If you continue working while the SAVE indicator is on, it starts blinking to warn you that the Word program might fail and the computer might lock up. If this happens, you'll lose everything you did since you last saved, and you'll need to restart the computer and Word.

If Word runs out of space for temporary scratch files on your Word Program disk, it does not allow any more editing, and a message tells you that the Word disk or the scratch file is full. If your computer seems to lock up while you're working, immediately save any open documents, glossaries, and style sheets with the File Save All command. If the message doesn't disappear, use the File Close All command to clear all memory and erase all scratch files. You can then reopen the document you were working on.

Automatic saving

With the *autosave* feature turned on, Word saves changes made to your files as you work. At an interval you specify (and whenever the SAVE indicator appears), Word stops for a moment and saves—in temporary files—changes made to the documents, style sheets, and glossary you are using. Although you must still save these as permanent files when you finish editing them, autosave can free you from worry about losing work because of power failures or running out of working space in memory or on your Word Program disk.

To turn on autosave, choose the Utilities Customize command. Type the number of minutes you want between automatic saves in the Frequency box under Autosave. If you want to OK each save, turn on the Confirm check box:

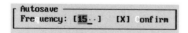

To disable the autosave feature after it has been turned on, type *0* (zero) in the Frequency box.

Word uses special filename extensions when it autosaves files: .SVD for documents, .SVS for style sheets, and .SVG for glossaries. You do not usually see these temporary files because Word deletes them when you save with the File Save or the File Save All command. But if something happens to your computer while you are working in Word—for example, you accidentally turn the power off—the autosave files remain on your disk. When you start Word again, it looks for autosave files. If it finds any, it asks if you want to recover them. Choose <Yes> to have Word recover the autosave files and save the changes stored in them under the original filenames.

When Your Document Disk Is Full

When you save a file, Word needs enough space on the document disk or directory for both the latest version of the file and the previous version (the .BAK file). If Word can't find enough space, it cancels the File Save command and displays a message telling you that your document disk is full.

You can make room for the file you want to save by deleting .BAK files or other files you don't need anymore. To delete files, you can temporarily suspend the Word program by choosing DOS Commands from the File menu. Then use the DOS command DEL to delete unnecessary files. (See "Running Other Programs" later in this chapter.) You can also use the File Management command from the File menu within Word to delete files (Chapter 15). After you delete any unneeded files, try the File Save command again.

If that doesn't do the trick, you can save the file on another formatted floppy disk. (If necessary, you can format a new disk without exiting Word by using the File DOS Commands command and the DOS FORMAT program, as explained later in this chapter.) When Word saves a file on a new floppy disk, it needs access to both the old and the new disks, as well as to the Word Program disk. Word prompts you to switch floppy disks when necessary.

To save a file on a new floppy disk:

1. Remove your current document disk, and insert the new, formatted disk.

2. Choose the File Save command, and OK the dialog box as usual.

3. Switch disks when prompted. If you see a message that requests access to a .DOC or .BAK file, insert the original disk. If you see a message requesting access to .TMP files, insert the new disk.

You might need to switch disks several times before the save is complete. But do not switch them unless you are prompted.

OPENING FILES

When Word opens a file, it transfers a copy of the file from a disk to memory. After you choose the File Open command, you see the File Open dialog box:

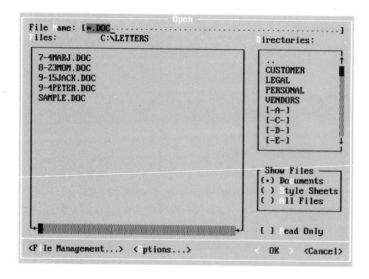

Although you can type a filename in the File Name box, it's usually easier to choose one from the list in the Files box. The list initially shows only those files with the .DOC extension stored in the default path.

In addition to .DOC files, you can open .BAK files and document files with filename extensions other than .DOC. To see a complete list of all files in the default path, including .BAK files, turn on the All Files button in the Show Files box. Or type

.

in the File Name box and press the Enter key. The asterisk (*) is called a wildcard: It replaces any number of unspecified characters. You can use it, for example, to request a list of only those files that have a particular filename extension. Suppose you assign the extension .LET to files that store letters. You can then type

.let

and press Enter to see a list of all .LET files. To see a list of style sheets only, turn on the Style Sheets button in the Show Files box.

To see a list of files in another drive or directory, type the path in the File Name box and press the Enter key. Or, instead of typing the path, you can highlight it in the Directories box and press Enter. (Choosing a path from the Directories box changes the default path for your work session unless you have designated a default path to be remembered for all work sessions.)

If you type the filename instead of choosing it from the list, you don't need to type the filename extension .DOC. If the filename has no extension, type a period after the name so Word won't assume that the extension is .DOC. You don't need to type the pathname unless the file isn't in the default path shown under the File Name box.

In most cases, you can leave the Read Only check box turned off. When the Read Only box is on, you can view the file, but you cannot revise it unless you save the revised version under a different name (with the File Save As command). This option protects a file from accidental changes.

To open a file:

1. Choose the File Open command (Alt, F, O).

2. When you see the File Open dialog box, type the name of the file you want to open in the File Name box, or choose a name from the list in the Names box. Include the path if the file is not in the default path shown under the File Name box.

3. Turn on the Read Only box only if you don't want to make changes to the file.

4. Choose <OK> (press Enter).

Word opens a new window to display the file. If another file is already open, Word puts it in the background.

If Word cannot find the filename you requested, a message box asks if you want to create the file:

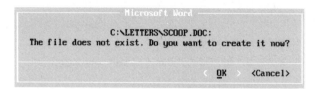

Choose <OK> (press Enter) only if you want to create a new file. If you don't want to create a new file, choose <Cancel> (press Esc), and choose the File Open command again. This time, check the list of files for the filename you want. You might have typed the wrong filename or the wrong path, inserted the wrong document disk, or forgotten to specify the path for a file not in the default directory.

CLOSING FILES

You can close a single document or style sheet with the File Close command, or you can close all files in memory with the File Close All command. Closing files clears them from Word's memory and frees that memory for other work. Closing files also frees disk space by eliminating any temporary files that Word created. Closing files does not affect anything already saved on disk. Before closing files, Word notifies you if work hasn't been saved and gives you the chance to save it.

Closing a Single File

Closing a file removes the file and the style sheet attached to it, if any, from memory. Using the File Close command does not affect the contents of glossary memory. To clear only the glossary from memory, use the <Clear All> button in the Edit Glossary dialog box, as described in Chapter 8.

To close a file:

1. Move the cursor to the document or style sheet you want to close, if it isn't already there.

2. Choose the File Close command (Alt, F, C). You can also use the Window Close command. Or, if you have a mouse, click the close icon (◻) in the upper left corner of the window.

After you choose the command, Word immediately closes the window in which the file was displayed. If you have not saved all changes to the file, a message box gives you the chance to save them:

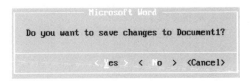

Choose <Yes> (press Y or Enter) to save the file before closing it. Choose <No> (press N) to close it without saving. Choose <Cancel> (press Esc) to cancel the command without saving or closing the file.

If you have not saved all changes to the style sheet attached to the document, a similar message offers you the option of saving the style sheet before closing it.

Closing All Files

Using the File Close All command is almost like exiting and restarting Word. It cleans up everything, closing all windows and erasing from memory all documents, glossaries, style sheets, and the contents of the scrap as well as the temporary files Word creates. The File Close All command is a quick way to close all windows without quitting Word. After using it, you can create a new document (with the File New command) or open a document stored on a disk (with the File Open command).

If unsaved changes to any documents, glossaries, or style sheets remain in memory, Word displays messages that identify each unsaved file and that give you the opportunity to save each file or to cancel the File Close All command.

RUNNING OTHER PROGRAMS

The File DOS Commands command is your key to running other programs without exiting the Word program. As discussed in Appendix A, DOS has a number of commands and programs that help you manage files, such as COPY, DIR, FORMAT, DEL, and REN. To run these or other programs without quitting Word, choose DOS Commands from the File menu. You see the File DOS Commands dialog box:

If you want to run a single program, type the DOS command that starts the program in the Command box and press the Enter key. For example, to format a blank floppy disk in drive B so that you can save files on the disk, you can type

format b:

and press Enter. The FORMAT program takes over, prompting you to insert the disk to be formatted. After the FORMAT program finishes, Word displays this message:

Press a key to resume Word

If the program you try to run or the file specified in your command cannot be found, Word displays this message:

Bad command or file name. Press a key to resume Word

If this message appears, press any key and try again. Include the path for the program and for any files mentioned in the command if they are not located in the default path.

If you plan to use more than one DOS command before returning to Word, type

command

in the File DOS Commands dialog box, or press the Enter key if the word *COMMAND* already appears there. This allows you to stay in DOS, where you can run a series of programs or give a series of commands. When you're ready to return to Word, type

exit

at the system prompt and press the Enter key. You are then prompted to press any key.

Chapter 12

Printing

Word offers an assortment of printing commands and options. You can, for example, print multiple copies of a document, print only part of a document, or print on both sides of a page. Whether you need to change printers, speed up printing, edit while printing, or preview a printed document, Word's capabilities give you a wide range of alternatives.

STARTING AND STOPPING

You can start printing a document at any time—even before you save it—if the document is open and visible in a window. If you have more than one open window, move the cursor to the document you want to print. You can usually start printing by turning on your printer, choosing the File Print command, and choosing <OK> (pressing Enter) in the File Print dialog box.

After printing starts, you can temporarily interrupt it, or you can cancel it altogether. To interrupt or stop printing, press the Esc key. Word stops printing and displays this message:

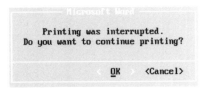

When you're ready to restart printing, continuing from where you left off, choose <OK> (press Enter). If you decide to cease printing, choose <Cancel> or press the Esc key.

If you experience difficulties, see the section "Setting Up Your Printer" later in this chapter. You can also refer to the manual *Printer Information for Microsoft Word* that comes with the Word package; it details exhaustive printing information, including troubleshooting tips.

USING THE PRINTING OPTIONS

Before you OK the File Print command, you might want to examine the options shown in the File Print dialog box:

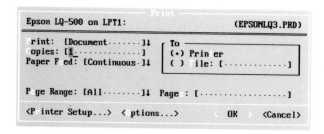

With the alternatives offered in this dialog box, you can

- Print a glossary, a style sheet, or a summary sheet instead of a document

- Use your computer as a typewriter

- Print more than one copy of a document

- Change the paper source

- Print only part of a document

- Print to a file instead of to a printer

Choose the <Options> command button in the File Print dialog box before you start printing if you want to

- Speed up printing

- Print on both sides of the paper

- Print summary information with your document

- Print hidden text

After you choose <Options>, the Print Options dialog box overlays the File Print dialog box:

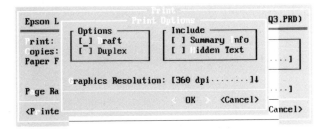

If you change any options in the Print Options dialog box, choose <OK> (press Enter) to carry out those changes and to return to the File Print dialog box, where you can then choose <OK> to start printing.

Printing a Glossary, Style Sheet, or Summary Sheet

To print the glossary, style sheet, or summary sheet attached to a document instead of the document itself, first choose the File Print command. Then choose Glossary, Style Sheet, or Summary Info from the drop-down list in the Print box:

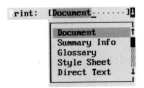

You can use the <Options> button in the File Print dialog box to print a document *and* its summary information, as described later in this chapter.

Using Your Computer as a Typewriter

No matter how well versed you are in Word or in any other word-processing program, you might sometimes prefer to use a typewriter. Creating, formatting, and printing a file can seem like a long route to take when you merely want to type a short note or an address on an envelope. Using the Direct Text option makes your printer and keyboard behave more like a typewriter.

Printing starts at the far left edge of the paper, unless you space over to another printing position, and continues to the right edge of the paper. You can type as many as 255 characters before printing, although it's best to print after each line. Before the lines are printed, you can correct mistakes by using the Backspace key or by moving the cursor and using the Delete key. You can also insert characters at the cursor position.

To use your computer as a typewriter:

1. Choose the File Print command (Alt, F, P).

2. Choose Direct Text from the drop-down list in the Print box, and choose <OK> to display the Print Direct Text dialog box:

3. If you don't want to start printing at the left edge of the paper, space over to where you want printing to begin.

4. Type the text and press Enter (or choose the <Print Text> button) after each line. Press Enter twice to skip lines.

5. When you finish typing, choose <Cancel> (press Esc) to close the dialog box.

Printing Multiple Copies

To print more than one copy of a document, type the number of copies you want in the Copies box of the File Print dialog box. This method is faster and easier than repeatedly choosing the File Print command to generate multiple copies. Word remembers your response to the Copies box, so be sure to reset it the next time you print if you want a different number of copies.

Changing the Paper Source for Your Printer

The Paper Feed box in the File Print dialog box (and also in the File Printer Setup dialog box) tells Word where to find the paper used for printing. When the list drops down, Word displays the types of paper feeders available for your printer, as shown in the example on the next page:

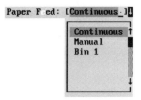

With the default setting (Continuous), Word expects paper to be fed to the printer continuously by either an automatic sheet feeder or a tractor feed for continuous paper. When you choose Manual feed, Word stops after printing each page and waits for you to insert another sheet. After you press Y to continue, it prints the next page.

The Bin 1, Bin 2, and Bin 3 responses tell Word that you have an automatic sheet feeder. The number (1, 2, or 3) tells Word which bin of paper to use. When you choose Mixed, Word takes a sheet of paper from bin 1 of a multiple-bin feeder to print the first page and takes paper from bin 2 to print subsequent pages. Choose Mixed for a document that requires letterhead stationery for its first page and blank sheets or a different letterhead for other pages. If your printer has an envelope feeder, choose Envelope if you want to print envelopes.

Printing Part of a Document

To print only part of a document, highlight the part you want to print before you choose the File Print command. Then choose Selection from the drop-down list in the Page Range box:

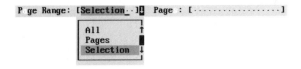

Instead of printing a highlighted section of the document, you can print specified pages by typing those page numbers in the Pages box. To print a range of pages, type the starting page number and the ending page number, separated by either a hyphen (-) or a colon (:). For example, type

4-7

to print pages 4, 5, 6, and 7.

If you want to print the last part of a document but don't know the last page number, type a large number after the hyphen or colon. For example, to print text from page 20 to the end of a 52-page document, you could type

20-100

If the pages you want to print are not consecutive, separate the page numbers with commas instead of hyphens or colons. For example, type

4,7,9

to print pages 4, 7, and 9. You can specify both consecutive and nonconsecutive page numbers at the same time. Type the numbers

2-4,22,24

to print pages 2, 3, 4, 22, and 24.

Because page numbering can restart at page 1 for each section, you might have duplicate page numbers in a document. In that case, type the section number after the page number to specify the page you want to print. For example, type

8s2

to print page 8 in the second section.

Word remembers your responses to the Page Range and Pages boxes, so be sure to reset them the next time you print.

Printing to a File

With the To box in the File Print dialog box, you can send the printer version of a document to a permanent file on disk rather than to a printer. After you quit Word, you can print this file using the DOS command COPY or PRINT (or any equivalent copy or print utility). You cannot print it using Word, but you get almost the same results by using DOS commands. This feature comes in handy when you want to create a file that can be printed by someone who has the same disk operating system (or an equivalent) but does not have the Word program.

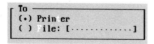

To print a document to a file, type a name for the new file in the File box. Give it a filename extension that distinguishes it from ordinary document files—.PRN, for instance. If you don't specify an extension, Word does not add one. As soon as you start typing in the File box, the File button is turned on. When you OK the dialog box, Word creates the print file.

Printing at Top Speed

If you're more interested in reviewing the content of a document than in seeing its formatting, you can speed up printing by choosing the <Options> command button in the File Print dialog box and then turning on the Draft check box in the Print Options dialog box:

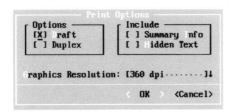

When Word prints a draft, it saves time by ignoring special formats such as boldface and italics, microspace justification for dot-matrix printers, and font changes for impact printers. (It also omits any graphics that have been inserted.)

Printing on Both Sides of the Paper

If your printer allows it, you can print on both sides of a sheet of paper: Simply choose the <Options> button, and turn on the Duplex check box. (If your printer cannot print on both sides, the Duplex option is dimmed.)

Printing Summary Sheets with Documents

To print a summary sheet along with a document, choose the <Options> button, and turn on the Summary Info check box in the Print Options dialog box:

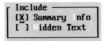

When Summary Info is turned on, Word prints the summary sheet on a separate page before printing the document. To print only the summary sheet, choose Summary Info in the Print box of the File Print dialog box.

Printing Hidden Text

Text marked as hidden with the Format Character command (or Ctrl-H) is usually not printed. If you want to print hidden text, whether it is visible on the screen or not, choose the <Options> button, and turn on the Hidden Text check box in the Print Options dialog box:

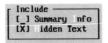

SETTING UP YOUR PRINTER

To take advantage of the features your printer offers, Word needs to know what kind of printer it is and how it is connected to your computer. Using the Setup program gives Word this information. (See Appendix B.) If you tried printing and had difficulty, choose the File Printer Setup command, and check to see if Word has the correct information about your printer.

You can use the File Printer Setup command to

- Change printers or printer hookup

- Change the graphics resolution for printing images

- Suppress the prompt to download fonts (applicable only if your printer has downloadable fonts)

- Set up queued printing

File Printer Setup also lets you specify the paper source for printing (although this option is more accessible with the File Print command).

After you choose the File Printer Setup command, you see a dialog box similar to this one:

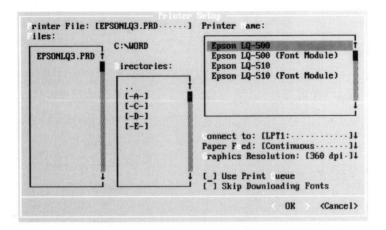

If you change any responses in the File Printer Setup dialog box, don't forget to choose <OK> to carry out your changes. Word records your responses and remembers them until you change them.

Changing Printers or Printer Hookup

When you choose the File Printer Setup command, the Printer File box should show the name of the .PRD file that matches your printer. If it doesn't, choose a .PRD from the list of printer description files in the Files box. If the printer description file for your printer is not in the path shown under the Printer File box, type the path in the Printer File box and press Enter, or choose a path from the Directories box. If you can't find a .PRD file that matches your printer, run the Setup program again, as described in Appendix B, to add the correct printer description file to your copy of Word.

NOTE: If you have a system with two 360-KB floppy-disk drives, you won't be able to print unless a copy of the .PRD file for your printer is on the document disk in drive B. The Setup program puts a copy on one document disk; you must copy it to other disks you use as document disks. Use the DOS command COPY to copy the .PRD file from the document disk Word sets up to other document disks.

The Printer Name box further describes your particular printer. Choose from the list the model name that matches your printer. (The models listed depend on the file chosen in the Printer File box.)

The Connect To box tells Word where to send the printer signals by providing the DOS device name that describes the printer hookup. Valid responses shown in the drop-down list are LPT1:, LPT2:, LPT3:, or LPT4: for parallel printers connected to parallel-printer adapters and COM1:, COM2:, COM3:, or COM4: for serial printers connected to asynchronous communications adapters.

The easiest way to find the correct device name for your printer is to try the various names until you find the one that works. If only one printer is connected to your computer, the name is either LPT1: (for a parallel printer) or COM1: (for a serial printer). If you're not sure whether you have a parallel printer or a serial printer, first try LPT1: and then COM1: as the device name. The other device names are used only if you have more than one printer of the same type connected to your computer at the same time (or have other communication devices such as a modem or serial mouse).

Changing Graphics Resolution

To change the graphics resolution, use either the File Printer Setup command or the <Options> command button of the File Print command. The response in the Graphics Resolution box determines the quality of printed graphics. The more dots per inch (*dpi*) printed, the clearer the graphic, the longer it takes to print, and the more memory your printer requires.

Suppressing the Prompt to Download Fonts

Some printers are able to use special fonts that are not stored in the printer's memory. These special fonts are stored as files on your disk system and must be sent to the printer with the document files that include them. If you're using a printer with such *downloadable* fonts, Word prompts you to download each time you use the printer.

If, however, you decide to download the fonts ahead of time using special software, you can save time by telling Word to omit this prompt. To do this, turn on the Skip Downloading Fonts check box in the File Printer Setup dialog box. This option is dimmed if the printer model chosen does not support downloadable fonts. (See your printer manual for additional information.)

Printing While Editing

Normally, you cannot create and edit documents while Word is printing. If you want to continue working on documents while you print, turn on the Use Print Queue check box in the File Printer Setup dialog box. Word can then print in the background, leaving the screen free for you to continue working. Once queued printing is set up, the File Print and the File Print Queue commands control the starting and stopping of printing.

Word manages your computer's resources so that editing while printing is not so slow as to be impractical—as it is with many other word processors. The dual tasks do slow down editing, however, and also require space on your document disk for an extra copy of the file being printed. (Before it starts printing a queued file, Word stores the printer version of the file on your document disk, freeing most of the computer's memory for other tasks. This temporary printer file is deleted after it's printed.)

To print while editing:

1. Open the document you want to print.

2. Choose the File Printer Setup command (Alt, F, R), and turn on the Use Print Queue check box.

3. Choose <OK> (press Enter).

4. With the cursor in the document you want to print, choose the File Print command to start printing.

Wait for Word to write the printer file on the disk. When Word starts printing, you can begin editing the document that's being printed or any other document. You can even close the document being printed.

To interrupt queued printing, choose the File Print Queue command. (This command is accessible only when the Use Print Queue check box is turned on.) The File Print Queue dialog box indicates the status of printing and contains command buttons for stopping and starting queued printing:

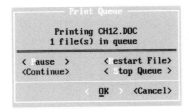

Choosing the <Pause> button stops printing temporarily. When you're ready to continue printing from where you left off, choose <Continue>. If you want to restart printing from the beginning of the document, choose <Restart File>. To cancel the queued printing altogether, choose <Stop Queue>.

Although it might take a while for the printer to get the message, Word responds as soon as you choose a command button. The <OK> and <Cancel> buttons simply close the File Print Queue dialog box; neither button has any effect on printing.

Printing a series of files

When you use the queued option, you can put more than one file in the printing queue. You don't have to wait for each document to be printed before you tell Word to print the next one. But you do have to wait for Word to create a printer file for each document before you tell it to print the next one. Again, you must have enough space on your document disk to hold extra copies of the files being printed. And you can continue to edit or create documents while Word is printing.

To print a series of documents, first follow the instructions in the previous section for printing while editing. Then follow these steps:

1. Move the cursor to the next document to be printed.

2. Choose and OK the File Print command.

3. Repeat steps 1 and 2 for each additional document that you want to print.

Each time you choose the File Print command, Word creates a temporary printer file. After Word prints a temporary printer file, that file is deleted, and Word begins printing the temporary printer file that was created next. Word starts each document on a new page.

As explained earlier, you can use the File Print Queue command to stop and restart queued printing. When you're printing a series of files, you can also use this command to find out what's going on. If Word is printing a file in the queue, the dialog box for the File Print Queue command tells you which file is being printed and how many files are in the queue. If no files are printing or in line to be printed, you see the message *Queue is empty*.

REPAGINATING WITHOUT PRINTING

Word usually decides where new pages in a document start as you type. But if you want to make changes to a document based on a previously printed copy, you can tell Word not to repaginate the document until it's printed again. To do this, choose the Utilities Customize command, and turn off the Background Pagination check box.

The advantage of postponing pagination until a document is printed is that the page numbers appearing on the screen match the page numbers in the last printed copy—no matter how many changes you've made to the document since you last printed it. The Edit Go To command can then easily find the page on the screen that corresponds to the printed page you have in hand.

If Background Pagination is turned off, you must wait until you print a document to see how many pages it contains and where new pages start. If you don't want to wait, use the Utilities Repaginate Now command or turn on Background Pagination. The document won't be printed, but the page breaks and the page numbers in the status bar will be updated as if the document were printed.

After you choose Utilities Repaginate Now, you see this dialog box:

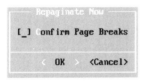

If the Confirm Page Breaks check box is turned off, Word paginates the document for you after you choose <OK>. Word inserts soft page breaks, each marked with a dotted line lighter than the line that marks a hard page break inserted manually with Ctrl-Enter or the Insert Break command. Soft page breaks can change if you revise a document; hard page breaks stay in place until you delete them.

Approving Page Breaks

If you turn on the Confirm Page Breaks check box and choose <OK>, Word stops to highlight the first character of each new page, and a message in the message bar asks you to confirm or move the page break. If the page break was inserted by Word, you see this message:

Press Enter to confirm page break or use direction keys to reposition it.

Press Enter to accept the page break, or press the Up direction key to move the page break up before you press Enter. If you move the page break, Word inserts a hard page break (a heavy dotted line) instead of a soft page break.

If Word finds a page break that you inserted, it highlights the break and gives you the opportunity to remove it:

Press Enter to confirm the page break or Del to remove it.

Press Enter to approve the break, or press the Del key to remove it. If you remove it, Word proposes a new break (if necessary) and asks you to approve it or move it up.

Although it's useful to be able to control where Word breaks pages, most documents don't require such close attention to every page break. Remember that you have other tools to prevent undesirable page breaks. You can insert manual page breaks wherever they're needed by pressing Ctrl-Enter or using the Insert Break command. The Format Paragraph command lets you specify that certain paragraphs not be broken (by turning on the Keep Paragraph Together check box) or that page breaks not occur between two paragraphs (by turning on the Keep Paragraph With Next check box). Preventing widows and orphans is another way to avoid awkward page breaks.

Controlling Widows and Orphans

As explained in Chapter 9, Word avoids creating widows and orphans by refusing to print single lines of paragraphs at either the top or the bottom of a page. But you might want to turn off this feature when you need to print the same number of lines on each page or when you're trying to print a document on as few pages as possible.

If you do not want Word to prevent widows and orphans, turn off the Widow/Orphan Control check box in the Utilities Customize dialog box. With this feature turned off, Word fills up the page, as defined by the margins, without regard for widows and orphans.

PREVIEWING BEFORE YOU PRINT

If your monitor can display graphics, you can get a preview of what your document will look like when it's printed. The File Print Preview command displays one or two pages at a time, scaled to fit your screen. You might not be able to read everything, but you can clearly see the layout of the document. Most notably, you can view the actual placement of headers and footers, footnotes, page numbers, line numbers, multiple columns, and graphics. Different fonts are scaled to represent their actual size.

After you choose the File Print Preview command, the display changes, and a new menu bar appears at the top of the screen. Commands on the View menu control the display. Choose the View 1-Page command to see one page, the View 2-Page command to see two pages, or the View Facing Pages command to see two pages that will face each other when the document is bound (for example, pages 2 and 3).

The only Edit command available is Edit Go To. This command lets you jump to specified page numbers, bookmarks, footnotes, and annotations, just as it does in the standard display. The status bar tells you what page you're looking at. You can scroll through the document with the PgUp and PgDn keys. Ctrl-Home and Ctrl-End take you quickly to the beginning or end of the document. With the mouse, you can use the vertical scroll bar.

From the File menu, you can choose the Print command to print the document, the Printer Setup command to change your printer setup, or the Exit Preview command to return to the regular editing display. You can also press the Esc key to exit the print preview display.

WHERE TO GO FROM HERE

The one printing command not discussed in this chapter is File Print Merge. To find out about this command as well as a host of other commands that represent Word's most advanced features, turn to Part III of this book.

Super Word

Chapter 13

Merge Printing

The File Print Merge command eliminates more repetitive, numbing work than any other word-processing command. Merge printing gives you a duplicating machine that can churn out countless copies of a document and alter each copy according to your instructions. Each copy can be tailored to suit its intended audience. As copies of a document are being printed, Word can methodically insert bits and pieces of text from another file, insert an entire document from another file, or prompt you to tell it what to insert.

This chapter discusses two applications of the File Print Merge command that can save you a lot of time without using a lot of disk space: mass mailings and chain printing.

MASS MAILINGS

To understand how mass mailings are generated, imagine what you would do if you were instructing an assistant to send the same letter to a number of people. If you wanted each person to receive an original, not a copy, you would hand your assistant two items: a draft of the basic letter that should go to everyone and a list of the names and addresses of the people to whom the letter should be sent.

On the basic letter, you might draw blank lines to indicate where the name and address go, and you might indicate what goes in each blank by labeling it, as blanks on a form are labeled. You would then tell your assistant to type a copy of the letter for each person on the list. When typing the letters, the assistant would refer to the mailing list and substitute information from the list for each labeled blank.

With Word, you can type the basic letter once, provide a mailing list, and then watch as Word prints a copy of the letter for each person on the list. Word plugs in names and addresses from the list as it prints the letters. The basic letter is called the *main document,* and the mailing list is called the *data document.* You must prepare both the main document and the data document in such a way that Word understands what you want to do.

Preparing the Main Document

The main document for a mass mailing is usually a letter, but it can be any kind of document that you want to mass-produce and yet personalize. You prepare the main document as you would any other document, with two exceptions: You use *field names* to represent the text that varies from one copy to another, and you include *instructions* that tell Word where to find the text to substitute for the field names.

Each field name or instruction that you type in the document must be enclosed in symbols called chevrons (« ») so that Word does not print the field name or instruction as part of the text. These special symbols do not appear on any of the key tops on your keyboard. To generate chevrons, you must press these keys:

Ctrl-[(left bracket)   to type «
Ctrl-] (right bracket)   to type »

The field names

The field names, like labeled blanks on a form, tell Word *what* information from the data document goes into the main document. The positions of the names tell Word *where* to put the information. You can use any name to identify a field (one item) of information. The name can contain as many as 64 characters and should clearly indicate what you're referring to. Include only letters and numbers, and use underscores instead of spaces. Begin each field name with a letter rather than a number or an underscore.

If your main document is a letter, it might start out looking like this on the screen:

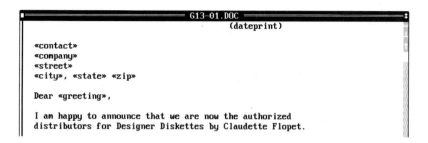

Notice that the glossary name *dateprint* is used in the sample letter. When you prepare documents that you plan to use for more than one mailing, you can use *dateprint* to instruct Word to insert the current date in printed copies of the letter. Wherever the current date should appear, type *dateprint* and press the F3 key. (See Chapter 8 for more information on *dateprint*.)

The DATA instruction

If you want Word to get names, addresses, or other variable information from a separately prepared list (the data document), you must use the DATA instruction to tell Word the filename and the location of the data document.

Type the DATA instruction at the very beginning of the main document. The instruction starts with the word DATA, followed by a space and the filename of the data document. Word needs to know the complete filename, including the extension if it is not .DOC. For example, if your data document is called CUSTOMER.LST, you would type

«DATA CUSTOMER.LST»

as the first line of your document. If the data document isn't in the default drive or directory, include the path to the file. For example, type

«DATA C:\SALES\CUSTOMER.LST»

to tell Word that the data document called CUSTOMER.LST is in the SALES directory in drive C.

Although you can type instructions and field names in either uppercase or lowercase letters, the sample documents here use uppercase letters for instructions and lowercase letters for field names.

PART III: SUPER WORD

Preparing the Data Document

A data document contains the information that replaces the field names in a main document. A data document resembles a table, with column headings and rows of information. Unlike entries in a table, however, the information in a data document is usually squeezed together to save space rather than aligned in neat columns. Here's a short data document that might be used with the sample letter from the previous section:

```
══════════════════════ G13-04.DOC ══════════════════════
company, contact, greeting, street, city, state, zip
PreFab Bridges Corp., George Girder, Mr. Girder, 1593
Suspension Rd., Birmingham, AL, 23098
Hedgerow Enterprises, Joseph Bush, Joe, 1302 Border Lane,
Evergreen Village, NH, 10386
Gemstone Jewellers, Ruby Rhinestone, Ruby, 433 Diamond
Blvd., Wichita, KS, 49708
```

In this data document, the first line, which is called the header record, is followed by three data records.

The header record

The first line of column headings in a data document is the *header record:*

```
══════════════════════ G13-05.DOC ══════════════════════
company, contact, greeting, street, city, state, zip
```

Notice that the field names in the header record match those in the sample letter. The field names tell you what's in the data document, and they must appear in the first line. As in the main document, each field name can contain as many as 64 characters.

To let Word know where one field name ends and the next one begins, you must separate the names with a single comma, semicolon, or tab character. (Don't use commas as separators if you're using them as decimal characters.) To end the header record, press the Enter key *once.* If you use commas or semicolons to separate field names, you can also put an optional space after each comma or semicolon to make the field names a little easier to read.

Using tabs instead of commas or semicolons lets you create a more readable data document. To align the columns of information, set tabs that allow for the longest entry in each column. Be careful not to insert more than one tab character between columns, or Word will misread your data document.

244

The data records

Each row of information under the header record is called a *data record*. Data records contain the pieces of information inserted in place of the field names in the main document. In a data document that stores a simple mailing list, a data record would include all the mailing information for one person or company, as in this example:

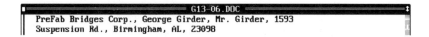

Each piece of information in a data record is called a *field entry*. The field entries in each data record must be in the same order as the corresponding field names in the header record. The number of field names in the header record must equal the number of field entries in each data record—that is, your information table must have as many columns as it has column headings. A data document can, however, contain more fields of information than are used by a main document.

Each field entry can be as long as you like, and each record can contain as many as 256 separate fields. Field entries, like field names, must be separated with a single comma, semicolon, or tab character; the separator should be the same as the one used in the header record. To let Word know where one record ends and the next one begins, end each record by pressing the Enter key *once*. If you press the Enter key *before* you get to the end of the data record, Word will look in the wrong places to find the information that corresponds to the field names. Pressing the Enter key more than once *after* a data record also confuses Word.

You can leave a field blank, but you must separate the blank field from the other fields with a comma, semicolon, or tab. For example, if the second record in the sample mailing list didn't have a street address, it would look like this:

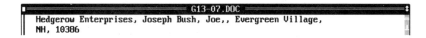

If a field entry already contains a comma, semicolon, or tab, you must enclose the entire entry in double quotes to signal Word that the character is not a field separator. If Gemstone Jewellers were located in Suite 303, its record would read as follows:

```
================================ G13-08.DOC ================================
  Gemstone Jewellers, Ruby Rhinestone, Ruby, "433 Diamond Blvd.,
  Suite 303", Wichita, KS, 49708
```

When a field entry itself contains double quotes, you must type each double quote twice and enclose the entire field entry in another set of double quotes. To include George Girder's nickname ''Chip'' (with quotes around it), for instance, enter this record:

```
================================ G13-09.DOC ================================
  PreFab Bridges Corp., George Girder, """Chip""", 1593
  Suspension Rd., Birmingham, AL, 23098
```

Saving the data document

Use the File Save command to name and save a data document. You might want to assign it a filename extension, such as .LST or .DAT, to indicate that it is a data document and not an ordinary document. Data documents created with Word can have the normal Word format. (Choose Word in the Format box of the File Save As dialog box.)

Preparing data documents with other programs

If you create a lot of data documents, you should consider purchasing a data-management program that makes entering, editing, and sorting data easier. Most mailing-list programs, filing programs, and database programs produce data files that Word can use: ASCII files with fields separated by commas, semicolons, or tab characters and each record terminated with a single carriage return (paragraph mark).

Data files created by other programs do not include header records. If you create a data document with another program, you need to create a separate file to store the header record. You must include the name of that file, along with the name of the data document, in the DATA instruction in the main document. Type the name of the header file first, and separate it from the name of the data document with a comma. For example, if your data document is called CLIENT.LST and your header file HCLIENT.LST, you would type this DATA instruction in the main document:

«DATA HCLIENT.LST,CLIENT.LST»

If you use a data-management program, you might need to experiment a little. The manual *Using Microsoft Word* offers some tips for using data documents that were not created with Word.

Merging the Main Document with the Data Document

After you prepare the main document and the data document, you're ready to merge them using the File Print Merge command. The two documents can be on separate disks, but both disks must be in the computer when you choose the File Print Merge command. Because the instructions in the main document tell Word what to do, start by opening the main document with the File Open command. Then choose the File Print Merge command to display the File Print Merge dialog box:

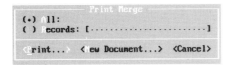

If you want to merge all records in the data document with the main document, turn on the All button. Word then prints a copy of the main document for each record in the data document.

If you want a copy of the main document for certain records only, type the numbers of those records in the Records box (*1* for the first record that appears in the data document, *2* for the second record, and so on). If you want to use a range of records, separate the beginning and ending numbers of the range with a hyphen. For example, type *10-20* to merge records 10 *through* 20 with the main document. List individual record numbers by separating them with commas. For example, type *10,20* to merge records 10 *and* 20 with the main document.

The command buttons at the bottom of the File Print Merge dialog box let you send the merged information directly to a printer or to a file. Choose the <Print> button to print the merged documents without viewing them on the screen. When you choose <Print>, Word displays the File Print dialog box. After you OK this dialog box, Word prints the first copy of the document, inserting the data from the first (or the first specified) record in the data document. It continues printing copies of the document until each data record specified in the File Print Merge dialog box has been used.

Neither the data document nor the main document is altered by the merge printing. The results of the merging appear only on the printed copies of the document. Figure 13-1 shows the results of merging the sample letter (the main document) and the data document shown earlier in the chapter.

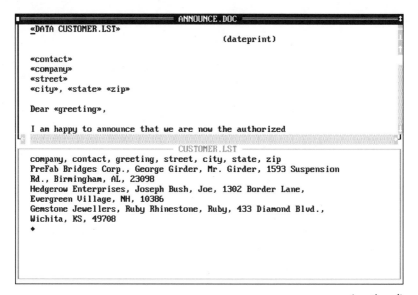

(continued)

Figure 13-1. *A main document, a data document, and the results of merge printing them.*

Figure 13-1. *continued*

```
                                      January 2, 1991

        George Girder
        PreFab Bridges Corp.
        1593 Suspension Rd.
        Birmingham, AL 23098

        Dear Mr. Girder,

        I am happy to announce that we are now the authorized
        distributors for Designer Diskettes by Claudette Flopet.
```

```
                                      January 2, 1991

        Joseph Bush
        Hedgerow Enterprises
        1302 Border Lane
        Evergreen Village, NH 10386

        Dear Joe,

        I am happy to announce that we are now the authorized
        distributors for Designer Diskettes by Claudette Flopet.
```

```
                                      January 2, 1991

        Ruby Rhinestone
        Gemstone Jewellers
        433 Diamond Blvd.
        Wichita, KS 49708

        Dear Ruby,

        I am happy to announce that we are now the authorized
        distributors for Designer Diskettes by Claudette Flopet.
```

If you want to check the merged output before printing it, choose the <New Document> button in the File Print Merge dialog box. This sends the merged documents to a file instead of directly to a printer. In the accompanying dialog box, you're asked to specify a filename:

Type a filename in the Document Name box and choose <OK>. If you type the name of an existing file, Word asks you to confirm that you want to overwrite the file. (Word will not overwrite an open file.) After Word prepares the new merged file, you can check, edit, format, and print it as you would any other file.

Using Other Print Merge Instructions

The DATA instruction tells Word to look in a data document for pieces of text that are missing from a form letter or other main document. Two other Print Merge instructions, ASK and SET, prompt you to provide the missing text when Word starts printing the document. All three of these instructions rely on field names embedded in the main document to tell Word what text is missing and where the replacement text should be inserted. A fourth instruction, INCLUDE, works independently of field names: It tells Word to insert an entire file into the main document.

The ASK instruction

The ASK instruction is useful when you don't want to create a data document or when your data document does not include all the information you want to put in the main document. When it encounters the ASK instruction, Word pauses before printing each copy of the document and prompts you to type in the replacement text for a particular field name.

An ASK instruction might look like this:

The instruction begins with the word ASK, followed by the field name of the information you need to supply, an equal sign, and then a question mark that tells Word to prompt you for that information. When it's ready to print the letter, Word prompts you with a message box identifying the field name:

```
Enter text for company

[.......................................................................]
 _

                                                    OK      <Cancel>
```

You can specify the exact wording of the prompt in the message box by typing it after the question mark in the ASK instruction. Writing screen prompts for yourself or for others can be fun. It's your chance to make the computer speak to you the way you'd like to be spoken to, and you can be as playful or as serious as you like.

One useful application of the ASK instruction is preparing customer response letters. You might, for example, want to send a timely response to individuals who request a catalog of your products. You could prepare these response letters each day, as the requests arrive, by setting up a standard response letter that's ready to print except for the name and address of the recipient. When Word prints the letter, it prompts you to supply the name and address as well as any other variable information you want to insert.

Instead of starting such a letter with a DATA instruction, you would begin with an ASK instruction for each field name in the letter, as shown in the following example:

```
============================ G13-15.DOC ============================
«ASK contact=?Type the name of the contact person.»
«ASK company=?Type the company name.»
«ASK street=?Type the street address.»
«ASK city=?Type the city.»
«ASK state=?Type the state.»
«ASK zip=?Type the zip code.»
«ASK greeting=?Type the name used in the salutation.»
                                        (dateprint)


«contact»
«company»
«street»
«city», «state»  «zip»

Dear «greeting»,

Thank you for your interest in our products. Enclosed, you will
find a catalog and price list describing our full line of
accessories designed to make your work more enjoyable.
```

Notice that the ASK instructions shown in this example include customized prompts. Before Word starts printing the first copy of the letter, it displays the prompt for the first ASK instruction:

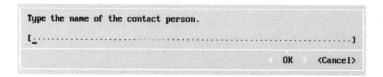

After you type the text (in this case, the name of the contact), choose <OK> (press Enter). Word displays the next prompt:

The prompts continue until Word has all the information it needs to print the first copy of the letter.

After the first copy is printed, Word starts again, displaying the same screen prompts for the next copy of the letter. Word continues to print letters and prompt you for information until you press the Esc key to cancel the merge printing.

Using the ASK instruction for a very large mailing is not practical. Someone has to stay by the computer to answer questions for each letter and then wait for the letter to print before answering the questions for the next letter. For large mailings, it's more efficient to prepare a data document.

The SET instruction

The SET instruction is similar to the ASK instruction in that both call for your input when it's time to print. When you use the SET instruction, however, Word prompts you to type replacement text for each field name only once. It then uses that text for all copies of the document.

The format for the SET instruction is the same as the format for the ASK instruction. A letter to sales representatives that includes a few SET instructions for entering information about a price change might look like this:

```
┌──────────────────────────── G13-18.DOC ────────────────────────────┐
│«DATA SALESREP.LST»                                                  ▲│
│«SET product=?Type the product name.»                               ▓│
│«SET newprice=?Type the new price.»                                 ▓│
│«SET effective=?Type the effective date for the new price.»         ▓│
│                                              (dateprint)            ▓│
│                                                                     ▓│
│«contact»                                                            ▓│
│«street»                                                             ▓│
│«city», «state»  «zip»                                               ▓│
│                                                                     ▓│
│Dear «greeting»,                                                     ▓│
│                                                                     ▓│
│Starting «effective», the new price for «product» will be           ▓│
│«newprice». Any orders for «product» prepared on or after           ▓│
│«effective» will be billed at the new rate. You should per-         ▓│
│sonally notify customers in your territory and urge them            ▓│
│to order before the price change.                                   ▓│
└─────────────────────────────────────────────────────────────────────┘
```

When you print the letter with the File Print Merge command, Word displays the prompts for each SET instruction, one at a time, and waits for you to respond to the first one before displaying the next one. After you supply the information, Word starts printing copies of the letter. The product name, new price, and effective date that you supply at printing time are inserted in each copy of the letter in place of the corresponding field names. All other field names in this sample letter are replaced by information from the data document named SALESREP.LST.

The INCLUDE instruction

The INCLUDE instruction lets you insert an entire file into your main document at printing time. This instruction is especially useful when you want to insert standardized paragraphs (boilerplate) that are used in a variety of documents. Storing these standardized paragraphs in separate files lets you create modules of text that you can plug into any document during printing.

To insert an entire file into your main document, type an INCLUDE instruction where the file should be inserted. The INCLUDE instruction contains the name of the file you want to insert. For example, to insert a file called PRICES.DOC, which stores a price list for your products, type

  «INCLUDE PRICES.DOC»

Include the filename extension if it is not .DOC. And if the file is not in the default drive or directory, include the path to the file.

Let's take a look at an INCLUDE instruction in the context of a letter. Suppose you want to include the current price list, which is stored in the file PRICES.DOC, in the following form letter:

```
═══════════════════════ G13-20.DOC ═══════════════════════
Thank you for your interest in Designer Diskettes by Claudette
Flopet. I'm sending you a few samples so you can see for yourself
that floppy diskettes don't have to be ugly. Try them out. In
addition to being works of art, they work! If that's not enough
to convince you that you should be using Designer Diskettes, take
a look at our prices:

«INCLUDE PRICES.DOC»
```

When you print the letter with the File Print Merge command, the price list is inserted. The letter (the main document) and the price list (the included document) can be on separate disks, but both disks must be in the computer when you choose the File Print Merge command.

To check the results of merging text with the INCLUDE instruction before printing, choose the <New Document> button in the File Print Merge dialog box to create a file copy that you can edit before printing.

Recall that glossaries also let you insert blocks of standardized text into documents. The File Print Merge command offers some advantages over glossaries, however. Using the INCLUDE instruction requires less disk space, and you can update the inserted text without changing every document that already includes it. In the preceding letter, for example, you can update the price list simply by editing the PRICES.DOC file. You don't need to change the letter or any other document that uses the INCLUDE instruction to insert the updated price list.

The Insert File command can also be used to insert all or part of one file into another. This command lets you link the files so that if the inserted file is changed, you can easily update the file that includes it. (For more information, see Chapter 27, "Spreadsheet or Document Linking," in the manual *Using Microsoft Word*.)

CHAIN PRINTING

Chain printing prints a series of separate documents as one long document. Pages and footnotes are renumbered to be continuous from the beginning to the end of the finished document.

To chain documents together for printing, you prepare a main document containing only INCLUDE instructions. You then use the File Print Merge command to print the main document. For example, to link the files named SECTION1.DOC, SECTION2.DOC, and SECTION3.DOC, you would prepare this main document:

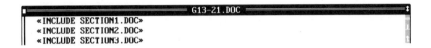

The chained documents are printed one after another, without page breaks between them. To start any of the documents on a new page, insert a new page mark (press Ctrl-Enter) before the INCLUDE instruction for that document.

THERE'S MORE

This chapter covers only the most basic merge printing operations. Word's other merge printing features include the use of conditional instructions, which let you insert text into a main document only if certain conditions are met. For example, you can tell Word to include a message in a letter only if the recipient lives in a particular state or orders a specified dollar amount of your product. The manual *Using Microsoft Word* contains information on using conditional instructions and other print merge features you might want to explore.

Chapter 14

Spelling, Hyphenation, and the Thesaurus

Despite some attempts to make the spelling of English words more phonetic and efficient, our language hasn't changed much. And adherence to traditional spelling and hyphenation rules, no matter how arbitrary, is still valued. Word can check your spelling, hyphenate words for you, and, with an electronic thesaurus, help you find words that precisely express what you want to say. But don't burn your bulky paper dictionary or thesaurus yet. Electronic spellers, hyphenators, and word finders are not perfect, although they can catch most of your typing and spelling errors, improve your writing, and save you a lot of time.

CHECKING SPELLING

With Word's Spell feature, you can proofread and correct spelling in your text without leaving the Word program. You have a good deal of control over how Spell works, and you can customize it to suit your needs.

Proofing Documents

When Spell examines a document or part of a document, it calls your attention to any words that aren't in its dictionaries. It also points out unusual capitalization (such as *dOg*), improper punctuation (such as *;cat*), and a common typing error: repeated words (such as *to to*).

Neither paper nor electronic dictionaries are all-inclusive, so you'll find that some of the words Spell doesn't recognize are correctly spelled. After Spell shows you a word it doesn't recognize, you can correct the word or leave it as it is. Whichever option you choose, you don't have to deal with the same word twice. If Spell encounters the word again during the same spell-checking session, it remembers how you treated the word the first time and corrects or ignores it accordingly.

To begin proofing a whole document or part of a document without leaving Word:

1. Open the document you want to proof.

2. If you want the *entire* document checked for spelling, move the cursor to the beginning of the document, or highlight the entire document. If you want only *part* of the document checked for spelling, move the cursor to the beginning of the part you want to check, or highlight the part you want to check.

3. Choose the Utilities Spelling command (Alt, U, S).

If you have a floppy-disk system, Word tells you to insert the Spell disk in place of the Word Program disk. After the Spell dictionaries are opened, Spell begins to check the spelling of each word in the document or in the highlighted part of the document. If you start Spell with the cursor located in the middle of a document, it checks spelling from the cursor's position to the end of the document. Then it gives you the opportunity to check the rest of the document, starting from the beginning.

If Spell doesn't find any errors, it reports *No incorrect words found* in the message bar. If it finds errors, it presents them one at a time in a dialog box, letting you choose whether to ignore or to correct each error. When Spell is finished, it reports in the message bar the number of words checked, corrected, and ignored.

Correcting errors

When Spell finds what seems to be an error, it highlights the word in the document, allowing you to see it in context. The Utilities Spelling dialog box explains the problem. For example, if Spell finds the word *bak* in your document, you see this dialog box:

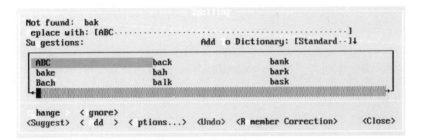

```
Not found: bak
  eplace with: [ABC................................]
Su gestions:                    Add  o Dictionary: [Standard··]↓

 ABC               back              bank
 bake              bah               bark
 Bach              balk              bask

  hange    < gnore>
<Suggest>  <  dd  >  < ptions...>  <Undo>  <R member Correction>    <Close>
```

The first line tells you that the word *bak* was not found in the dictionary. The Replace With box suggests a correction. Other possible corrections are listed in the Suggestions box. To choose a replacement from the Suggestions box, press Alt-G to go to the box, and use the direction keys to highlight the word you want. (With the mouse, point to your choice and click.) The word you choose appears in the Replace With box.

If the word you want is not listed, type it in the Replace With box. If you meant to type *beak* instead of *bak* in the preceding example, you would need to type in the correction because *beak* does not appear in the list of suggested spellings.

The next step is to carry out the change by choosing the <Change> or the <Remember Correction> command button. If you choose <Change> (press Enter), Spell remembers your correction and applies it during the remainder of the current spell-checking session. In our example, Spell replaces each occurrence of the word *bak* with *beak* or with the correction you chose the first time the word was brought to your attention. If you choose the <Remember Correction> button, Spell records the correction and applies it not only during the current session but also in all future spell-checking sessions.

Before finally carrying out the command, Spell checks any correction you type in the Replace With box. If the word is not found in the dictionary, you see this message:

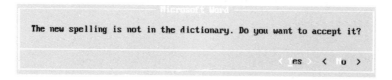

Choose <No> if you want to retype the correction or <Yes> to accept it as is.

Ignoring words

Occasionally, the Spell program finds and highlights a word that you know is correct. The word might not be in the dictionary Spell is using—it might be a person's name, an acronym, a technical term, or a possessive form. If you're certain that the word is spelled correctly, you can choose the <Ignore> command button to tell Word to pass over it. If Spell finds the word again in the same spell-checking session, it ignores the word without consulting you.

Adding words to a dictionary

Instead of ignoring words Spell doesn't recognize, you can add them to the standard dictionary by choosing the <Add> command button. Or you can easily create a special *user dictionary* to store words unique to your work or a *document dictionary* to store words unique to individual files. To create a user or document dictionary, choose User or Document from the drop-down list in the Add To Dictionary box before you choose <Add>.

User and document dictionaries supplement rather than replace the standard dictionary that comes with Word. Try to add only words that occur frequently—the more words in a dictionary and the more dictionaries you have, the longer it takes Spell to check a document. (Consult the *Using Microsoft Word* manual for more help with creating and altering dictionaries.)

Undoing changes

After you correct or ignore a word found by Spell, you can choose the <Undo> command button to go back to the word and undo the change you made, if any. Spell goes back to the previous word checked, restores it to its original form, and gives you another chance to change or ignore it.

To undo all changes made with the Utilities Spell command, use the Edit Undo command immediately after closing the Utilities Spelling dialog box.

Interrupting and quitting Spell

As you're running Spell, you might spot some text in the document that needs revising. Or you might encounter an error that Spell can't fix, such as an unwanted space in the middle of a word. For example, if you type *auto matically*, Spell would approve *auto* but would ask you to fix *matically*. To delete the unwanted space, you need to close the Utilities Spelling dialog box.

Word makes it easy to interrupt and restart Spell without losing your place or starting all over: Simply press the Esc key or choose the <Close> command button. Word returns to editing mode and moves the cursor to the last word checked in the document. Any changes already made by Spell are unaffected by the interruption. To restart Spell, choose the Utilities Spelling command again, and Spell continues checking the document from the cursor location.

Customizing the Spelling Checker

The <Options> button in the Utilities Spelling dialog box lets you customize the way Spell works. Choosing <Options> produces this dialog box:

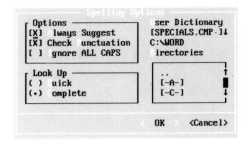

Spell normally looks for and lists alternative spellings when it finds a word it doesn't recognize. But if you find that you can correct most of your errors without the help of suggestion lists, you can save time by turning off the Always Suggest check box. Even with this check box turned off, you can see a list of suggestions when you need to: Just choose the <Suggest> command button in the Utilities Spelling dialog box.

When the Check Punctuation box is turned on, Spell looks for punctuation marks (. , ; : ! and ?) that are not followed by spaces and for symbols (such as @, #, %, &) and numbers embedded in words or immediately adjacent to words. Although Spell can't tell you whether you used the correct punctuation, it can help you find some common errors involving misplaced punctuation, symbols, and numbers. When the Check Punctuation box is turned off, Spell ignores punctuation marks, symbols, and numbers. It assumes that these characters, like spaces, simply separate words.

Some documents include many initials, acronyms, or program commands that appear in uppercase letters and that Spell won't recognize—for example, ASCII, COD, AWOL, or DIR. You can tell Spell to ignore these words from the start by turning on the Ignore ALL CAPS box. (Instead, however, you might want to add them to a dictionary.)

The Look Up box determines how many alternative words Spell searches for when it can't find a word in the dictionary. With Quick Look Up, the faster option, Spell assumes that the first two letters of the word are correct. With Complete Look Up, Spell assumes that every letter might be incorrect and therefore looks for many more possible alternatives.

The settings for all of these spell-checking options remain in effect from session to session until you change them.

HYPHENATING AUTOMATICALLY

If you want to avoid unsightly gaps of space in justified text or unpleasant raggedness in left-aligned or right-aligned text, you can let Word hyphenate words at the ends of lines. The Utilities Hyphenate command adds optional (nonrequired) hyphens whenever possible to even out the length of lines.

To hyphenate all or part of a document:

1. If you want to hyphenate the entire document, move the cursor to the beginning of the document, or highlight the entire document. If you want to hyphenate part of the document, move the cursor to the beginning of the part you want to hyphenate, or highlight that part.

2. Choose the Utilities Hyphenate command (Alt, U, H) to display the Utilities Hyphenate dialog box:

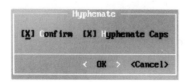

3. If you don't want to confirm the placement of each hyphen, turn off the Confirm check box. If you don't want to hyphenate words that begin with uppercase letters, turn off the Hyphenate Caps check box.

4. Choose <OK> (press Enter).

If you choose the Utilities Hyphenate command when the cursor is in the middle of a document, the text is hyphenated from that point until the end of the document. Word then gives you a chance to check the rest of the document, starting from the beginning. After optional hyphens are inserted, Word tells you how many words were hyphenated.

Word inserts hyphens where they will be needed in the printed copy. Unless the Show Line Breaks check box in the View Preferences dialog box is turned on, line breaks on the screen might not match the breaks in the printed copy, causing some hyphenated words to fall in the middle of lines on the screen. If an optional hyphen is not at the end of a line on the screen, you won't see it unless the Optional Hyphens check box or the Show All check box in the View Preferences dialog box is turned on.

Confirming Hyphenation

When the Confirm box of the Utilities Hyphenate command is turned on, Word stops to highlight each proposed hyphen and to display a dialog box so that you can approve the location before the hyphen is inserted. For example, if the word *optional* occurs at the end of a line, you might see this dialog box:

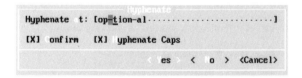

Choose <Yes> to confirm the position of the hyphen. Choose <No> only if you don't want to hyphenate the word at all. Choose <Cancel> to cancel the Utilities Hyphenate command.

To hyphenate the word but change the location of the hyphen, use the Up and Down direction keys to move the cursor to other recommended hyphen locations in the word, or use the Left and Right direction keys to reposition the hyphen elsewhere. When the cursor is at the place where you want to insert the hyphen, choose <Yes> to confirm the location.

Notice that the dialog box used to confirm hyphens includes both the Confirm and Hyphenate Caps check boxes, allowing you to turn them on or off at any time.

Stopping and Undoing Automatic Hyphenation

You can interrupt and cancel the Utilities Hyphenate command by choosing the <Cancel> button or pressing the Esc key. Any hyphens already inserted stay in place. To *remove* all optional hyphens inserted by the Utilities Hyphenate command, choose the Edit Undo command immediately after you interrupt the Utilities Hyphenate command or after you let it run its course.

To remove individual hyphens inserted by Word, delete them as you would delete any other text. Because optional hyphens must be visible before you can select and delete them, you must first choose the View Preferences command and turn on the Optional Hyphens check box to make them visible.

USING THE THESAURUS

To extend your vocabulary and sharpen your writing, you can look up words in a thesaurus to find synonyms or alternatives. To use Word's thesaurus, select the word you want to look up, and choose the Utilities Thesaurus command. Word displays the Utilities Thesaurus dialog box.

The dialog box contains a list of definitions for the word you selected and a list of synonyms for the first definition. For example, if you look up the word *spirit* in the thesaurus, you see a dialog box similar to the one shown in Figure 14-1.

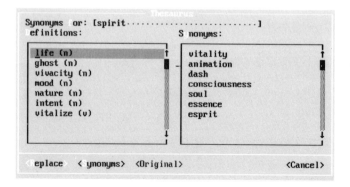

Figure 14-1. *A thesaurus dialog box.*

The words in the Definitions box are possible meanings for the word *spirit*. The words in the Synonyms box are synonyms for the highlighted definition, which is *life*. As you move the highlight in the Definitions box from one word to another, the list of synonyms changes to show synonyms for each definition as it is highlighted. For example, if you intended another meaning for *spirit*, such as *vivacity*, you could highlight *vivacity* to see a list of synonyms for that meaning, as shown in Figure 14-2.

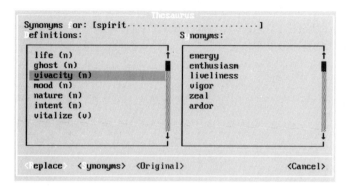

Figure 14-2. *Choosing another meaning for the word* spirit *and viewing synonyms for that meaning.*

You can choose a word from either the Definitions box or the Synonyms box to replace the word selected in the document. When you spot a good replacement word, highlight the replacement (in the Definitions box or the Synonyms box), and choose the <Replace> command button (press Enter).

Word closes the thesaurus window and substitutes the word you chose for the word selected in the document. If you want to close the thesaurus window without choosing a synonym, choose <Cancel> or press the Esc key.

Other Thesaurus Maneuvers

Sometimes the route to the best word is not so direct. You might need to scout around the thesaurus before you find a suitable word. You might, for example, look up synonyms for one of the words listed in the Synonyms box. To do this, highlight the synonym, and choose the <Synonyms> button. You can also choose <Synonyms> to see definitions and synonyms for a highlighted word in the Definitions box. With the mouse, double-click a synonym or definition to see definitions and synonyms for that word. You can choose a word from the new lists that appear to replace the word highlighted in the document, or you can go back to the original lists of definitions and synonyms by choosing the <Original> command button.

If, while the thesaurus window is open, you decide that you would like to see synonyms for another word, move the cursor to the Synonyms For box and type the word. Then choose the <Synonyms> button. In the Definitions box, choose the meaning you have in mind. Again, you can choose a word from either the Definitions box or the Synonyms box to replace the word highlighted in the document, or you can choose the <Original> button to go back to the original lists of definitions and synonyms.

Chapter 15

Finding and Managing Files

The File Management command on the File menu allows you to access a file by specifying its filename and location or by choosing it from a list, as you do with the File Open command. The main difference is that the File File Management command gives you more control over the list of files you see.

You can instruct Word to list files from more than one directory or to create a list of files that share common characteristics (independent of their location). For example, you can create a list of files written by the same author or prepared by the same operator. You can find files with common subject matter or files created on the same date or in a specific time frame.

After you find the files you want to work with, you can open, rename, copy, move, print, or delete them. You can view, update, and print their summary information sheets. The commands to copy, move, print, and delete files can be applied to batches of files as well as to a single file, which makes printing multiple files and organizing disks much easier.

FILLING OUT SUMMARY SHEETS

Word's ability to search for and identify files rests in part on the information you provide in summary sheets. When you first save a file, Word displays a dialog box titled Summary, shown on the following page.

```
┌──────────────────── Summary for PILLOWS.DOC ────────────────────┐
│                                                                  │
│  Title:     [_..............................................]    │
│  Author:    [................................................]    │
│  Operator:  [................................................]    │
│  Keywords:  [................................................]    │
│  Comments:  [................................................]    │
│                                                                  │
│  Version Number:  [...........]                                  │
│  Date Created:    [10/29/1990.]                                  │
│  Date Saved:      [10/29/1990.]                                  │
│                                                                  │
│                                      <  OK  >   <Cancel>         │
└──────────────────────────────────────────────────────────────────┘
```

The information you type in this dialog box is saved with the file as a summary sheet. You can view, revise, and print the summary sheet with the File Management command on the File menu. (You can also use the File Print command to print summary sheets, as explained in Chapter 12.)

Using the Search and Sort Boxes

Word can use information from the Author, Operator, Keywords, Date Created, and Date Saved boxes to find files. Information from the Author, Operator, Date Created, and Date Saved boxes helps to sort files.

The author is the person who wrote or created the document; the operator is the person who prepared or last saved the file. You can use as many as 40 characters in each box to specify an author or operator, and you can include more than one name in each box, separating them with spaces or commas.

Use the Keywords box to store words that identify the subject matter or purpose of the document. Although Word can search through the documents themselves to find those that include particular words or text, searching through summary sheets for keywords is much faster. Include keywords such as the main words in the title and important topic words from the text. Try to anticipate what topics and features in the document you might look for later, as you do when you set up subject files and cross-indexes for paper files. The Keywords box can contain 80 characters; separate multiple keywords with spaces or commas.

Word fills in the Date Created and the Date Saved (revision date) boxes for you. This lets you use these two dates to find and sort files whether you fill out the rest of the summary sheet or not. Word also includes the size of the file (in characters) with the summary sheet information after the file has been saved.

Using the Information-Only Boxes

The other three boxes in the Summary dialog box—Title, Version Number, and Comments—help you identify a file when you view its summary sheet. The information they contain is not used to sort or search for files.

The Title box, which can contain 40 characters, allows ample room to give the file a title that describes its contents more clearly than the eight-character DOS filename can. For example, a form letter used for reminding customers that their accounts are overdue might be identified with the title *Overdue Account Form Letter*.

The version number helps you distinguish between variations of the same basic document. You can assign a number or a word (or words) as long as 10 characters. For instance, if you have separate versions of the overdue account letter for accounts that are 30 days, 60 days, and 90 days past due, you can type *30 days*, *60 days*, or *90 days* in the Version Number box. You can also use the Comments box to explain what is unique about each version.

You have space for 220 characters in the Comments box. Use it to include any helpful information about a file, such as detailed summary information or reminders to yourself or others. You might, for example, include a reminder to use the document for a specific purpose or to edit the document further. Or you might keep notes on what has been done to the document so far: Has it been proofread for spelling? Has it been formatted? Who has reviewed it?

Figure 15-1 summarizes information about the Summary boxes.

Summary Box	Maximum Characters	Automatically Filled In	Search Key	Sort Key
Title	40	No	No	No
Author	40	No	Yes	Yes
Operator	40	No	Yes	Yes
Keywords	80	No	Yes	No
Comments	220	No	No	No
Version Number	10	No	No	No
Date Created	8	Yes	Yes	Yes
Date Saved	8	Yes	Yes	Yes
Size		Yes	No	Yes

Figure 15-1. *The Summary boxes.*

Choosing Not to Fill Out Summary Sheets

Filling out summary sheets is optional. When the Summary dialog box appears, you can either choose <OK> (press Enter) or choose <Cancel> (press Esc) to skip it. Or, by choosing the Utilities Customize command and turning off the Prompt for Summary Info check box, you can tell Word not to request summary information for new files. You also have the option of filling in some boxes but not others in the summary. If you change your mind, you can add information to a summary sheet or revise information later using the File File Management command. (See the section "Updating Summary Sheets" later in this chapter.)

Remember that you can still search for files based on the creation date, the revision date, or the text, even if you don't fill out summary sheets. Because Word fills in the Date Created and the Date Saved boxes, you can search for files that were created or revised in a specific period of time. Because the text contained in files is independent of summary sheets, you can also search for files that share common text, although this procedure is slower than searching for keywords from the summary sheet.

THE FILE MANAGEMENT DIALOG BOX

After you choose the File Management command from the File menu, Word displays a dialog box similar to the one shown here:

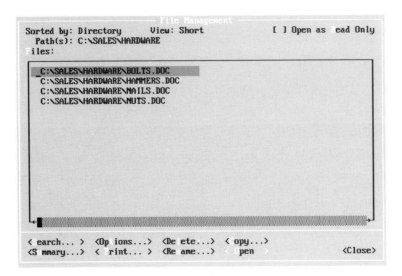

The first two lines of the dialog box describe the list of files shown in the Files box: how the files are sorted; how much information you see about each file (View); and the location, or path, of the files. The first line also includes an Open as Read Only check box, which is useful when you open a file that you don't want to change.

Initially, the files listed in the Files box are sorted by the directory in which they reside and are the .DOC files found in the default path. Short View is specified, which means that you see only the filenames for each file.

The File Management dialog box contains nine command buttons:

- <Search> lets you find files and determines which documents are listed in the Files box. After you tell Word what to search for, the Files box lists only those files that match your search criteria. You can then use the other command buttons to open, rename, delete, copy, or print the listed files or to revise the summary information for those files.

- <Summary> lets you revise the summary information for a file.

- <Options> determines how much information about each file is shown in the Files box and how files are sorted within the list.

- <Print> allows you to print one or more files or their summary sheets or both.

- <Delete> erases one or more files.

- <Rename> lets you change the name or location of a file.

- <Copy> copies one or more files to a different drive or directory.

- <Open> lets you load a file and leave the dialog box.

- <Close> closes the dialog box.

SEARCHING FOR DOCUMENTS

With the <Search> command button, you can tell Word to find a file or a group of files and list them in the Files box. After you choose the <Search> button, the Search dialog box appears, as illustrated on the next page.

```
┌──────────────────────── Search ────────────────────────┐
│ Search  aths: [C:\SALES\HARDWARE_·····················]  │
│                                     C:\SALES\HARDWARE    │
│  uthor:   [······································]        │
│  perator: [······································]  irectories: │
│  eywords: [······································]        │
│  ext:     [······································]  ┌──────────┐ │
│ Date  aved:   [·····················]              │ ..    ↑│ │
│ Date  reated: [·····················]              │[-A-]  ▓│ │
│                                                    │[-C-]  ▓│ │
│ [ ]  atch Case   [ ] Selected  iles Only           │[-D-]  ↓│ │
│                                                    └──────────┘ │
│                                        <  OK  >   <Cancel>  │
└─────────────────────────────────────────────────────────┘
```

Specifying Search Paths

The Search Paths box in the Search dialog box tells Word where to look for files and, optionally, which filenames to include. If you don't specify a path, Word looks in the default path shown under the Search Paths box. You can specify more than one path, separating the pathnames with commas and optional spaces. For example, typing

c:\sales\hardware, c:\sales\software

tells Word to look in the Hardware and Software subdirectories of the Sales directory in drive C.

Instead of typing a directory name, you can easily choose a directory from the Directories box to add to the Search Paths box. Highlight the directory you want to add, and type a comma; the directory appears in the Search Paths box. You can add a series of directories to the Search Paths box using this method.

If you don't specify any filenames, Word looks for all .DOC files in the specified or default path. When you specify files, you can include the wildcards ? and * in the filenames. Use the question mark to stand for a single unspecified character and the asterisk to stand for any number of unspecified characters. For example, to search for all documents with the filename extension .RPT in the Hardware and Software subdirectories, type

c:\sales\hardware*.rpt, c:\sales\software*.rpt

You can also specify individual filenames in the Search Paths box. Type the filenames and their paths (if the files are not in the default path) in the Search Paths box. Separate multiple filenames with commas, adding spaces after the commas if you choose.

You can use as many as 128 characters to specify filenames and paths in the Search Paths box. Only the files described in this box will be listed in the Files box of the File Management dialog box after you OK the search.

Word remembers the paths you specify in the Search Paths box until you change them. If you set a new default path for storing and saving files with the <Options> button of the File Save or the File Open command, the paths specified in the Search Paths box do not change.

Specifying Other Search Criteria

The other options in the Search dialog box help to narrow down the list of files found by the Search Paths box. You can tell Word to include only those files that have specific authors, operators, keywords, text, revision dates, or creation dates. When you fill in the Author, Operator, Keywords, Date Saved, or Date Created box, Word looks for files in the specified paths that have matching information in their summary sheets. When you type text in the Text box, Word looks for files that have matching text in the file itself. The Match Case check box is related only to the Text box: Turn it on if you want to search for text that matches the letter case of the specified text (the *search string*), or turn it off to ignore letter case.

When you search for authors, operators, keywords, or document text, Word finds your search string whether or not it is embedded in other text. For example, if you specify *opera* in the Text box as a search criterion, Word finds all documents that contain the words *operator, cooperate,* and *operation,* as well as files that include the word *opera.* You do not have a Whole Word option, as you do when you search for text with the Edit Search command.

One way to avoid finding embedded words is to make use of the Keywords box. If *opera* has been entered as a keyword in the summary sheets for documents related to opera, you can search for *opera* as a keyword rather than as document text. Doing this reduces the chances of finding documents you don't want. Matching letter case can also help: When you are searching for an acronym such as *RAM* as document text, you can turn on the Match Case check box to avoid finding *ram, tram, frame, bramble,* and so on.

Another way to avoid finding embedded words is to specify what you *don't* want to find. Word uses the tilde symbol (~) to represent NOT. For example, if you're searching for documents authored by someone named Hart, you could type

Hart~Hartford~Hartley

in the Author box to find *Hart* but not *Hartford* or *Hartley*.

You can use 80 characters to specify authors, operators, keywords, or document text and 25 characters to specify the creation or revision date.

Specifying multiple search entries

You can search for more than one author, operator, keyword, piece of document text, creation date, or revision date. Multiple entries in any Search box must be separated with a comma, which means OR, or an ampersand (&), which means AND. (A space can also be used to represent AND.) For example, if you want to find documents authored by either Carlo *or* Larry, type

Carlo, Larry

in the Author box. But if you want to find documents coauthored by Carlo *and* Larry, type

Carlo & Larry

in the Author box.

You can use parentheses to clarify expressions. For example, type

(Pete & David),(Carlo & Larry)

if you want to find documents coauthored by Pete and David or coauthored by Carlo and Larry.

Sometimes it's easier to specify what you don't want to find than to specify what you do want to find. For example, suppose you have access to the work of five authors (Carlo, Larry, Pete, David, and Clyde) and you want to locate files created by the first four. You can use a tilde in the Author box to specify the one you don't want rather than specifying the four you do want by typing

~Clyde

The AND symbol (ampersand or space), the OR symbol (comma), and the NOT symbol (tilde) are called *logical operators*. They can be used in all Search boxes except the Search Paths box. You can also use the wildcards ∗ and ? in all Search boxes except the date boxes.

Searching for a range of dates

You can specify an open-ended range of dates rather than single dates by using the greater than (>) and less than (<) symbols. These symbols can be included only in the Date Created and Date Saved boxes. When used with dates, the > symbol means *after* and the < symbol means *before*. For example, to find files created after December 31, 1989, type

>*12-31-89*

in the Date Created box. To find files created before January 1, 1990, type

<*1-1-90*

in the Date Created box.

You can search for a closed range of dates by combining an ampersand (for AND) with the > and < symbols. For example, to find documents revised in 1990, type

>*12-31-89 & <1-1-91*

which means after 12-31-89 and before 1-1-91.

You can exclude a range of dates from a search by combining a comma (for OR) with the > and < symbols. For example, to exclude documents revised during the last six months of 1989, type

<*7-1-89, >12-31-89*

which means before 7-1-89 or after 12-31-89.

You cannot combine a tilde (for NOT) with the > or < symbol.

Searching for special symbols

If you want to search for text that includes any of the logical-operator symbols, enclose the text in double quotes to signal Word that the symbol is not being used as an operator. For example, to search for references to *Bluff & Blunder, Inc.*, in documents, type

"Bluff & Blunder, Inc."

in the Text box. If you omit the quotes, Word looks for documents that contain either *Bluff* and *Blunder* or *Inc.* Remember that spaces are symbols for the logical operator AND. If you want to search for a phrase containing one or more spaces, enclose the phrase in quotes. For example, to search for documents containing the name *John Gregory*, type

"*John Gregory*"

in the Text box. Otherwise, Word searches for documents with the name *John* and the name *Gregory* in them. A document with the names *John Jones* and *Gregory Smith* would satisfy the search criteria.

Because quotation marks also have a special meaning to Word, you must *double* them when you want to include quotation marks in a search string. For example, searching for

""*pursuit of happiness*""

finds

"*pursuit of happiness*"

To include either of the symbols used for wildcards (? or *) as part of a search string, precede the symbol with a caret (^).

Putting It All Together

Use the <Search> command button to determine which files are listed in the Files box of the File Management dialog box. After you choose the <Search> button, specify your search criteria in the Search dialog box. Figure 15-2 summarizes key facts about filling out the Search dialog box.

Search Box	Maximum Length	Use Logical Operators & , ~	Use > <	Use Wildcards
Search Paths	128	Comma only	No	In filename only
Author	80	Yes	No	Yes
Operator	80	Yes	No	Yes
Keywords	80	Yes	No	Yes
Text	80	Yes	No	Yes
Date Saved	25	Yes	Yes	No
Date Created	25	Yes	Yes	No

Figure 15-2. *The Search boxes.*

You can enter search criteria in more than one Search box to pinpoint the files you want to see. For example, if you want to examine all documents prepared in 1990 that are related to a customer named Huntington Industries, your responses in the Search dialog box might look like this:

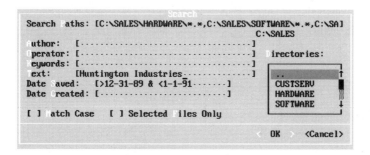

Notice that although you don't need to know the filenames, you do need to specify which directories Word should search. The wildcard expression *.* is used in the paths to include all filenames and filename extensions.

After your search is defined, choose <OK> (press Enter). Word responds by displaying—in the Files box of the File Management dialog box—the list of files that meet your search criteria. The files can be from any of the directories in the search path.

You can further refine the list by using the <Search> command button again. For example, if you want to find documents pertaining only to complaints, you could add the word *complain* in the Text box of the Search dialog box to find documents in the search path containing the words *complain, complaint, complained,* and other derivatives:

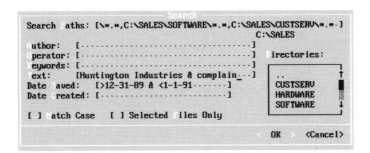

ADJUSTING THE DISPLAY OF LISTED FILES

With the <Options> command button in the File Management dialog box, you can adjust the display to see more information about the files listed in the

Files box or to change the order in which the filenames appear. After you choose the <Options> button, you see the Options dialog box:

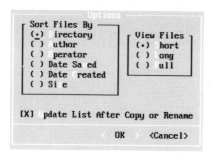

The Sort Files By box determines the order in which the files appear. The View Files box controls how much information about each file is displayed. With the proposed responses, Short View and Directory Sort, Word shows the path and filename of each file, with the directories listed alphabetically and the files listed alphabetically within each directory, as shown in Figure 15-3. The files list in Figure 15-3 results from looking for the chapters in this book that contain the document text *search*.

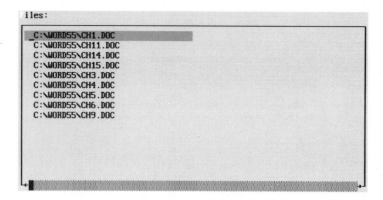

Figure 15-3. *A short view sorted by directory.*

A short view lists the files in a two-column format that allows 33 characters for each file. If the path and filename are too long to fit, Word shortens them by replacing characters in the middle with an ellipsis (...).

If you choose Long View, you see the path and filename of each file as well as the sort criterion and the file title from the summary sheet. For example, if you choose Long View and sort the files by the date saved, the display in the Files Box resembles that shown in Figure 15-4.

```
iles:                          Date Saved     Title
┌─────────────────────────────────────────────────────────────────┐
│ C:\WORD55\CH1.DOC             09/17/1990  Getting Acquainted      │↑
│ C:\WORD55\CH5.DOC             09/24/1990  Selecting Text and Using│■
│ C:\WORD55\CH6.DOC             09/24/1990  Searching and Replacing │
│ C:\WORD55\CH3.DOC             09/24/1990  Revising a Document     │
│ C:\WORD55\CH9.DOC             10/11/1990  Formatting              │
│ C:\WORD55\CH4.DOC             10/20/1990  Saving, Retrieving, and │
│ C:\WORD55\CH11.DOC            10/22/1990  Filing                  │
│ C:\WORD55\CH14.DOC            10/28/1990  Spelling, Hyphenation, a│
│ C:\WORD55\CH15.DOC            10/28/1990  Finding and Managing Fil│
│                                                                   │
│                                                                   │↓
└─────────────────────────────────────────────────────────────────┘
```

Figure 15-4. *A long view sorted by date saved.*

If the files are sorted by directory, a long view displays the author's name in the second column because the name of the directory is already shown in the first column.

When you choose Full View, you can see the entire summary sheet for the highlighted file in the Files Box, as shown in Figure 15-5. With the direction keys, move the highlight to any file in the list to see its summary sheet. With the mouse, just point and click. If necessary, you can use the scroll keys, PgUp and PgDn, or the scroll bar to see more of the list.

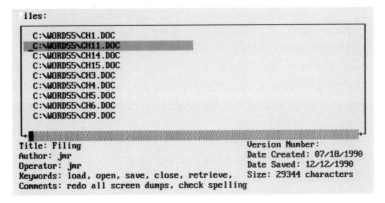

Figure 15-5. *A full view sorted by date saved.*

UPDATING SUMMARY SHEETS

To update a summary sheet for a file listed in the Files box, highlight the filename and choose the <Summary> command button. Word opens a Summary dialog box that includes any summary information you previously provided, as shown in this example:

```
                              Summary
  File Name: CH15.DOC          Size: 28403 characters
  Directory: C:\WORD55

   itle:    [Finding and Managing Files.............]
   uthor:   [jr...................................]
   perator: [...................................]
   eywords: [files, search, summary, batch.........]
   omments: [Insert dialog boxes for new version......]

   ersion Number: [...........]
  Date C eated:   [06/30/1990.]
  Date  aved:    [10/28/1990.]

                          <   OK   >   <Cancel>
```

To edit an existing entry, position the cursor where you want to insert or delete text. Press the Del key to delete characters highlighted by the cursor, and press the Backspace key to delete the character to the left of the cursor. When you finish revising the information, choose <OK> (press Enter).

If you want to update a summary sheet for a file not currently listed in the Files box, you must first use the <Search> button to find and list the file.

OPENING FILES

To open a file listed in the Files box, highlight the filename and choose the <Open> command button. With the mouse, double-click a filename to open the file. If you want to protect a file from accidental changes while you view it, turn on the Open as Read Only check box before you choose the <Open> button. After you choose the <Open> button or double-click the filename, Word closes the File Management dialog box and opens the file.

If you want to open a file that isn't listed in the Files box, first use the <Search> button to find and list the file.

MARKING FILES

You can copy, move, delete, or print more than one file at a time by marking each file in the Files box before choosing the appropriate command button. After you mark a file, an asterisk appears to the left of its filename.

To mark or unmark a file with the keyboard, highlight the filename and press the Spacebar. With a two-button mouse, mark or unmark a file by pointing to the filename and clicking the right mouse button. You can mark or unmark all listed files by pressing Ctrl-Spacebar. By turning on the Selected Files Only check box in the Search dialog box, you can tell Word to display only the marked files.

COPYING, MOVING, RENAMING, AND DELETING FILES

The <Copy> command button lets you copy or move files to another drive or directory, the <Rename> button lets you change the name of a file, and the <Delete> button lets you delete files.

To copy or move a file listed in the Files box, highlight the filename and choose the <Copy> command button. To copy or move more than one file to the same location, mark the files to be copied or moved before you choose the <Copy> button. When you see the Copy dialog box, type the new location for the files in the Path Name box or choose a location from the Directories box.

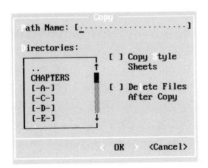

Turn on the Delete Files After Copy check box if you want each marked file moved instead of copied. Turn on the Copy Style Sheets check box if you want to copy or move any attached style sheets along with the files. Choose <OK> (press Enter) to carry out the command.

To rename a file listed in the Files box, highlight the filename and choose the <Rename> command button. When you see the Rename dialog box, type the new filename in the Rename To box and choose <OK> (press Enter):

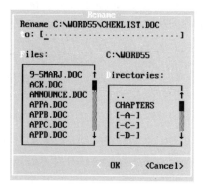

To delete a file listed in the Files box, highlight the filename and choose the <Delete> command button. To delete several files, mark them before you choose <Delete>. Word asks for confirmation that you want to delete the highlighted or marked files before it deletes them. Be sure to check which files are highlighted or marked before you choose <OK>. You can choose <Cancel> (press Esc) in the message box to cancel the command if necessary.

PRINTING FILES

To print a file listed in the Files box, highlight the filename and choose the <Print> command button. To print a batch of files, mark each file you want to print before you choose <Print>. Word then displays the File Print dialog box with the same options you see when you choose the File Print command:

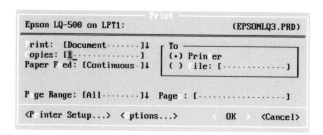

To print only documents or only summary sheets, choose Document or Summary Info from the drop-down list in the Print box. To print both documents and summary sheets, first choose Document in the Print box. Then choose the <Options> button to display the Print Options dialog box, and turn on the Summary Info check box. After you OK the File Print dialog box, Word starts printing the specified documents.

Chapter 16

Macros: Custom-Made Commands

Macros are custom-made commands that speed up word processing and make it easier. The building blocks for macros are all the keys on the keyboard, the commands you find on menus and on keys, and a group of special instructions. After a sequence of commands and keystrokes is recorded in a macro, you can play back the macro by using the macro name, by choosing the Macro Run command, or by pressing a key code of one to three keys. You store macros in glossaries, along with glossary entries that consist of text only. Any key on your keyboard can be recorded in a macro.

With macros, you can reduce complicated tasks to a few keystrokes, combine several steps into one, remind yourself of what needs to be done, assign new tasks to function keys, customize the way Word works, or make Word imitate a word processor that you're more familiar with.

In this chapter, you learn how to run the ready-made macros Word provides, how to edit macros, and how to create macros from scratch by recording them. You'll find that creating macros can save you time and that it does not require special knowledge or skills.

USING READY-MADE MACROS

Word supplies some ready-made macros that are waiting for you to try. To use the supplied macros, you need access to MACRO.GLY, the glossary file in which they are stored. You can open MACRO.GLY, or you can merge it with the currently open glossary.

Opening MACRO.GLY

If you have a floppy-disk system, you can find MACRO.GLY on the Sample Documents disk created by the Setup program. If you have a hard-disk system, the Setup program copied MACRO.GLY to the same directory as the Word program.

To close the currently open glossary and open MACRO.GLY:

1. If you have a floppy-disk system, insert the Sample Documents disk in drive B.

2. Choose the Macro Edit command (Alt, M, E).

3. Choose the <Open Glossary> command button from the Edit Macro dialog box:

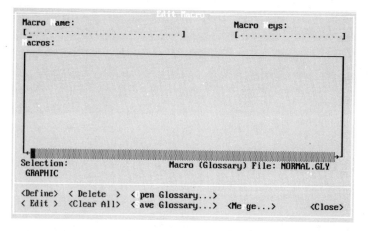

4. When the Open Glossary dialog box appears, type *macro.gly* in the File Name box. Include the path if MACRO.GLY is not in the path shown under the File Name box. Instead of typing the names, you can choose the path from the Directories box and MACRO.GLY from the Files box.

5. Choose <OK> (press Enter).

Word gives you the opportunity to save the currently open glossary before closing it if you have not saved all your changes. The Edit Macro dialog box stays open so that you can view the list of macros and create (define), edit, or delete macros. For now, choose <Close> to return to the window.

Merging MACRO.GLY

Because the glossary file NORMAL.GLY is opened whenever you start Word, merging MACRO.GLY with NORMAL.GLY and saving the resulting glossary as NORMAL.GLY makes the supplied macros available for use each time you start Word.

To merge the supplied macros with the glossary currently in memory:

1. If you have a floppy-disk system, insert the Sample Documents disk in drive B.

2. Choose the Macro Edit command (Alt, M, E).

3. Choose the <Merge> command button.

4. When the Merge Glossary dialog box appears, type *macro.gly* in the File Name box. Include the path if MACRO.GLY is not in the path shown under the File Name box. Instead of typing the names, you can choose the path from the Directories box and MACRO.GLY from the Files box.

5. Choose <OK> (press Enter).

6. Choose <Close> to close the Edit Macro dialog box and return to a window.

If you have not saved all your changes, Word gives you a chance to save the currently open glossary before merging it with MACRO.GLY.

If you want to make the supplied macros a permanent part of the glossary in memory, use the Macro Edit command. Choose the <Save Glossary> command button, and then choose <OK> (press Enter). The Save Glossary dialog box proposes the current glossary name as the filename for the merged glossary. Whether you save them or not, the supplied macros are now in glossary memory and ready for you to use.

Experimenting with Macros

The quickest way to find out what macros can do is to try the ready-made macros. Open any long document, and begin experimenting with the macros described in the next sections. When you finish experimenting, use the File Close command without saving the document so that the document is not permanently altered.

To copy or move text

Let's start with a macro that copies text. Named *text_copy*, it has been assigned the key code Ctrl-V6. Although this macro doesn't really save keystrokes, it leads you through the steps of copying text without your having to remember the sequence of selecting text, choosing the Edit Copy command, selecting a location, and choosing the Edit Paste command.

Your cursor can be anywhere in the window when you start this macro. Simply press Ctrl-V, 6. (Hold down the Ctrl key while you press and release V; it doesn't matter whether Ctrl is held down when you press 6.) The message bar prompts you to highlight the text you want to copy:

> Select text to be copied. Press enter when done.

For trial purposes, highlight any text and press the Enter key. Now the macro prompts you to move the cursor to the place where you want to insert the copy of the text:

> Select the destination point. Press enter when done.

When you press the Enter key, a copy of the selected text is inserted to the left of the cursor.

A similar macro, *move_text*, works in the same way to move text. Press Ctrl-V, T to see how it works. (Take care not to hold the V key down too long, or Word will assume you want to run the macro that has the key code Ctrl-VV. If this happens, press the Esc key twice to cancel the macro.) Look for prompts in the message bar. Highlight any piece of text when you are prompted, and follow the instructions in the message bar to move the text to a new location.

To move the cursor a page at a time

If you have a document longer than one page, you can try out the macros *next_page* and *prev_page*. As their names suggest, these macros allow you to jump to the beginning of the next or the previous page. Their key codes are Ctrl-VN and Ctrl-VP. The macros choose the Edit Go To command for you and determine the page number that will take you to the next or the previous page. You can press Ctrl-V, N or Ctrl-V, P to move through documents one full page at a time.

To save part of a document in a new file

To see the timesaving power of macros, try the macro called *save_selection*. Assigned the key code Ctrl-VS, this macro opens a new window, copies highlighted text to the new window, saves the text in the new window as a new file, prompts you to name the file, and then closes the new window. All you need to do is highlight the text you want to copy and save in a new file and then give the new file a name when prompted.

Try it: Press Ctrl-V, S. The message bar prompts you to select the text you want to copy and to press the Enter key. Then Word asks you to give the excerpt a filename. Type a name like *erase-me* to remind yourself to delete this test file later, and then press the Enter key. Before you know it, the process is complete, and the screen that was visible when you started the macro is restored.

Viewing a List of Macros

Now that you've tried using some macros, take a look at the complete list of supplied macros. After you open MACRO.GLY or merge it with the glossary in memory, you can see the names of all supplied macros by choosing the Macro Run command. Word displays a dialog box that lists the macro names:

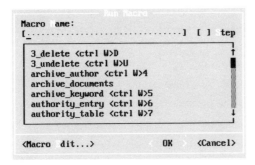

You can scroll to see more of the list. (With the keyboard, press the Down direction key to move to the list box.) Notice that each macro is followed by the key code used to run the macro. Angle brackets (< >) around two keys indicate that those two keys must be held down together.

You can run a macro after choosing the Macro Run command by typing the macro name (*save_selection*, for example) in the Macro Name box or by highlighting the macro name in the list box and choosing <OK> (pressing Enter). With the mouse, double-click your choice in the list of macros to choose it and to OK the command.

Choose the <Cancel> command button now to close the dialog box so that you can examine the contents of a macro in the next section.

Examining a Macro

You can insert a macro in a document (without running the macro) to examine the macro's contents:

1. Move the cursor to the place where you want to insert the macro text. You can use the File New command to have the macro inserted in a separate file.

2. Choose the Macro Edit command.

3. Type the macro name in the Macro Name box, or choose it from the list in the Macros box.

4. Choose the <Edit> command button.

Word closes the dialog box and inserts the macro text at the cursor position. When it is inserted in a document, the macro called *save_selection* looks like this:

```
═══════════════════ Document2 ═══════════════════
*  «SET echo="off"»
*  «PAUSE If the text to be saved has not been selected, do so now.
   Press Enter.»<ctrl ins>
*  <enter>store<f3><backspace>
*  <ctrl esc>fn<enter><ins>
*  «ASK fileName=? Enter the name of this new file where the
   selection will be saved.»<ctrl esc>fcy«fileName»<enter><enter>
*  <enter>restore<f3><backspace>•
```

The individual steps of this macro are listed and explained in Figure 16-1. Notice that special keys are represented by words or abbreviations enclosed in angle brackets. The Insert key, for example, is represented by <*ins*>, and the Enter key appears as <*enter*>.

This macro contains some special instructions, which are enclosed in chevrons (« »). The PAUSE instruction tells Word to display a message telling you what to do. The message in this PAUSE instruction tells you to select the text you want to save and to press the Enter key. (When given a PAUSE instruction, Word waits until you press the Enter key before it proceeds with the next step.)

Macro Step	Purpose
«SET echo="off"»	Turns off the screen updates while the macro chooses menus and commands and fills in dialog boxes unseen.
«PAUSE If the text...»	Pauses, displays a message in the message bar, and waits for the user to select the text to be copied and to press Enter.
<ctrl ins>	Copies the selected text to the scrap.
<enter>store<f3>	Runs a macro called store, which chooses the Utilities Customize command and then turns on the Use Word 5.0 Function Keys check box and turns off the Use INS for Overtype Key check box.
<backspace>	Deletes the paragraph mark inserted in the document by the previous step.
<ctrl esc>	Activates the menu bar. (The Control-Escape key combination is used instead of the Alternate key in case the menu is already activated.)
fn	Chooses the File New command.
<enter>	OKs the File New dialog box.
<ins>	Inserts text from the scrap in the new file.
«ASK fileName=? Enter...»	Displays a message box asking the user to type the filename and press the Enter key. Waits until the user presses the Enter key.
<ctrl esc>fc	Chooses the File Close command.
y	Chooses Yes when prompted to save the file to be closed.
«fileName»	Inserts the filename the user typed (when prompted by the ASK instruction) into the File Save As dialog box.
<enter>	OKs the File Save As dialog box.
<enter>	Closes the Summary dialog box.
<enter>restore<f3>	Runs the macro called restore, which restores the previous settings for the Use Word 5.0 Function Keys and the Use INS for Overtype Key check boxes.
<backspace>	Deletes the paragraph mark inserted by the previous step.

Figure 16-1. *Examining the steps in a macro.*

Editing Macros

Once you have a macro in view in a window, you can edit it with the tools you use to edit any other text. Word has a number of specific rules about writing and editing macros. Every character in a macro is significant. Minor changes can easily be made; here you learn how to create new macros by making minor changes to existing macros.

Suppose you want to change *save_selection* so that it deletes selected text and saves it in a new file—thus moving the text instead of copying it. You can add a comment at the beginning of the macro that explains what it does, and you can change the macro's name and key code when you save it.

Comments explain the purpose of a macro or specific steps in a macro. Because Word ignores comments when it executes a macro, you can include in a comment any text that helps you remember what the macro does.

To alter *save_selection:*

1. With the macro visible in a window, move the cursor to the first character of the macro. Insert a comment at the beginning of the macro by typing

    «*COMMENT Prompts you to select text, which it then deletes and saves in a new file.*»

    and pressing Enter. (To type chevrons, press Ctrl-[and Ctrl-].)

2. Change the wording of the prompt in the PAUSE instruction so that the user knows exactly what to do. For example, revise the first sentence of the PAUSE instruction as follows:

    Select the text to be deleted and saved in a new file.

3. In the first group of keystrokes after the PAUSE instruction, change *<ctrl ins>* to *<shift del>* to have the macro delete the selected text instead of copying it. The macro now looks like this:

```
════════════════════════ CH16.DOC ════════════════════════
*   «COMMENT Prompts you to select text, which it then deletes and
    saves in a new file.»
*   «SET echo="off"»
*   «PAUSE Select the text to be deleted and saved in a new file.
    Press Enter.»<shift del>
*   <enter>store<f3><backspace>
*   <ctrl esc>fn<enter><ins>
*   «ASK fileName=? Enter the name of this new file where the
    selection will be saved.»<ctrl esc>fcy«fileName»<enter><enter>
*   <enter>restore<f3><backspace>♦
```

4. Highlight the entire macro, and choose the Macro Edit command to save the new macro.

5. Type a new name in the Macro Name box. For example, type

   save_deletion

   to clarify the purpose of the new macro (and also to preserve the original macro).

6. To assign a new key code, move the cursor to the Macro Keys box. To type the key code Ctrl-SD, press Ctrl-S and then press D. The key code appears in the Macro Keys box as follows:

```
Macro eys:
[<ctrl S>d ...........]
```

7. Choose the <Define> command button to record the new macro.

Now press Ctrl-S, D to see if the new macro works. Because you saved the edited macro under a new name, the original macro, *save_selection*, remains in the glossary unchanged. This new macro provides a fast way to break a long file into two separate files. It prompts you to highlight the text you want to move to a new file, deletes the text from the existing file, and saves it in the new file.

CREATING MACROS FROM SCRATCH

The easiest way to create macros from scratch is to type the actual commands and keystrokes that you want to include in the macro while Word records them. (Mouse actions cannot be recorded.) When you finish recording the macro, you give it a name and store it in a glossary.

Naming Macros

Naming a macro is similar to naming a glossary entry. Choose a name that indicates what the macro does. The name can contain as many as 30 characters, including the key code. It can include any letters or numbers but no spaces and only a few symbols. You can use an underscore, a hyphen, or a period where you would normally use a space. For example, a macro that prints and saves a file might be called *print_save*.

Assigning Key Codes

When naming a macro, you can assign a key code to reduce the number of keys you must press to use the macro. For example, when you want to use the *print_save* macro, it is more convenient to press Ctrl-P, S than to type the macro name and press the F3 key or to choose the Macro Run command and choose the name from the list in the dialog box.

As with glossary entries, key codes for macros can be a combination of the Control key plus one or, preferably, two characters (such as Ctrl-SL); a function key (such as F4); or a function-key combination (such as Shift-F4 or Ctrl-F4). Remember that Word has already assigned tasks to many Control-key combinations, all function keys, and most function-key combinations. When you use Control-key combinations as key codes, it's best to use two-character key codes whose first character is a letter or number not used for speed formatting.

If you assign a speed formatting key, a function key, or a function-key combination to a macro, you must press Ctrl-A before you press the function key or speed formatting key to use it for its original purpose.

Key codes are assigned by pressing the keys to be included in the code when the cursor is in the Macro Keys box (found in the dialog box of the Macro Edit or the Macro Record command). For example, to assign the key code Ctrl-PS, hold down Ctrl while you press P, and then either hold down or release Ctrl while you press S. (To allow more space for long macro names, *release* the Ctrl key before you press the second letter. This results in an abbreviated key code such as *<ctrl P>s* rather than *<ctrl P><ctrl S>*, which uses 7 more of the possible 30 characters for the macro name.)

Recording Macros

Recording keystrokes is the easiest way to create macros. To record a macro:

1. Choose the Macro Record command (Alt, M, C).

2. Type a macro name in the Macro Name box.

3. To assign a key code, move the cursor to the Macro Keys box, and press the keys you want to use for the key code.

4. Choose <OK> to turn on the macro recorder. When it is on, MR (for Macro Record) appears in the status bar.

5. Type the keystrokes and commands you want to record.

6. Choose the Macro Stop Recorder command (Alt, M, C), which now appears on the Macro menu.

After you stop recording, Word inserts the new macro into the current glossary.

Suppose that you want to hyphenate your entire document from any point within it. A macro that moves the cursor to the beginning of the document and starts the hyphenation process without hesitating at menus saves time and keystrokes. To create this macro:

1. Choose the Macro Record command.

2. Type a macro name in the Macro Name box. For example, type

   hyphenate_all

3. If you want to assign a key code to the macro, press Alt-K to move to the Macro Keys box, and then press the keys you want to use for the code. For example, press Ctrl-G and then press H to assign the key code Ctrl-GH.

4. Choose <OK> (press Enter).

5. Press the keys that move the cursor to the top of the document, and then press the keys that choose and carry out the Utilities Hyphenate command: Ctrl-Home, Alt, U, H, Enter.

6. Choose the Macro Stop Recorder command to turn off the macro recorder.

If you make a mistake while recording

If you press the wrong keys while recording a macro, choose the Macro Stop Recorder command to stop recording. Then start all over by choosing the Macro Record command to begin recording again. Type in the same name and key code for the macro to replace the macro recorded in error. If you type the name of an existing macro, Word asks you to confirm that you want to replace it with the new recording.

You can also delete macros recorded in error by choosing the Macro Edit command, highlighting the macro you want to delete in the Macros box, and choosing the <Delete> command button.

Creating Macros to Imitate Other Word Processors

Old habits are hard to break. If you've been working with another word processor, your hands might reflexively choose the more familiar commands and keys before you can think of the new ones that Word uses. If you or your hands are reluctant to learn new commands and key assignments, you can make Word imitate the word processor you know. You won't get a complete match, but you can simulate the most frequently used commands.

For example, if you're accustomed to reaching for the F10 key to save files, record

Alt, F, S

as a macro and assign the F10 key as the key code.

If you want the new key assignments activated each time you start Word, save the macros that change key assignments in NORMAL.GLY. If, instead, you want to choose when to activate them, save the macros in a separate glossary named, for example, KEY-MAP.GLY. Then, when you want to activate the new key assignments, open or merge KEY-MAP.GLY. Either way, you can change your mind about key assignments by deleting these macros. Deleting macros and opening, merging, and saving glossaries are done with the Macro Edit command.

In some cases, familiarity with another word processor is more a matter of being accustomed to different features. For example, a common typing error is switching the order of two letters. If you notice the error as you type it, you might want to correct it immediately. Correcting this kind of error is not difficult with Word, but if you've been using another word processor, you might be accustomed to having a special command to transpose characters. To make a macro that transposes two characters that were typed in the wrong order, record this sequence of keystrokes:

Shift-Del, Left direction key, Shift-Ins

You can name the macro *switch_char* and assign Ctrl-SC as the key code. Then, when you want to correct two transposed letters, move the cursor to the second letter and press Ctrl-S, C. Try using the macro now: Type the word *form,* move the cursor to *r,* and press Ctrl-S, C. The word *form* becomes *from.*

Similarly, you can make a macro that transposes two words by recording these keystrokes:

Alt-F6, Shift-Del, Ctrl-Left direction key, Shift-Ins

You can even make a macro that transposes two complete sentences with these keystrokes:

Alt-F8, Shift-Del, Left direction key, Left direction key, Alt-F8, Shift-Ins

Before you run either of these macros, you must move the cursor to any character in the second word or sentence.

WORKING WITH MACROS

Whether you use macros that you create or macros that Word supplies, the techniques for working with them are the same. The following sections summarize information about running macros and deleting macros. In addition, you learn how to repeat, cancel, and print macros.

Running Macros

When you're using a macro for the first time, it's wise to protect your work by saving all changes before you run the macro. The Edit Undo command can undo the last command or action taken by the macro—but it cannot undo the entire macro. If the macro does something dreadful, you can use the File Close command to clear the document without saving the damage, and you can then reload the previously saved copy of the document.

You have three ways to run a macro that's in glossary memory. To begin, first move the cursor to where you want to start running the macro, unless you're sure the macro does that for you. Then use one of these three methods:

- If the macro has been assigned a key code, such as Ctrl-SC, simply type the key code. The commands and keystrokes contained in the macro are carried out, starting at the cursor position.

- If you know the name of the macro, type the name and press the F3 key. The macro name disappears, and the macro starts running from the cursor's location.

- Choose the Macro Run command. Choose a macro from the list by highlighting the macro name, and press the Enter key to run the macro. If you're using a mouse, double-click your choice.

After you initiate a macro, the words Running Macro are displayed in the status bar until the macro completes its task.

Repeating and Canceling Macros

You can repeat macros the same way you repeat single commands: by pressing the F4 key. To interrupt a macro, press the Esc key. Word stops and displays this message box:

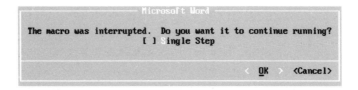

At this point, you can either cancel the macro or restart it to continue from where it left off. If you want to stop the macro altogether, choose <Cancel> (press Esc). Only the commands and keystrokes that have not yet been carried out are canceled; those already carried out are unchanged. If you want to restart the macro instead of canceling it, choose <OK> (press Enter). If you turn on the Single Step check box before restarting the macro, Word pauses after each step so that you can check the effect it has on the document. Press any letter key to proceed to the next step. After you turn on the Single Step check box, all macros are run in this step mode unless you turn off the check box in the Run Macro dialog box or in the message box displayed after you interrupt a macro.

Some of Word's supplied macros include an instruction to turn off the Use INS for Overtype Key check box on the Utilities Customize command and a later instruction to turn the check box back on. If you interrupt such a macro after it has turned off the check box and before the check box is turned back on, you might be puzzled by the new behavior of the Insert and Delete keys. To restore them to their usual functions, choose the Utilities Customize command, and turn on the Use INS for Overtype Key check box yourself.

Printing Macros

Macros are printed the same way other glossary entries are printed. Choose the File Print command, and choose Glossary in the Print box. After you OK the command, Word prints the entire contents of the glossary currently in memory, including macros as well as other entries.

THERE'S MORE

In this chapter, you became acquainted with macros, started using them, learned how to run the macros Word supplies, and created a macro by recording keystrokes.

Word offers another way to create macros: writing them. When you write macros, you can include special instructions (such as the PAUSE instruction) that can't be recorded in macros. These special instructions let you program macros to calculate, to repeat themselves conditionally, to ask you for information, and to perform tasks only if specified conditions are met or perform alternative tasks if the conditions are not met. When you're comfortable with the notion of macros and with the techniques for recording and running them, explore the more advanced macro options described in the manual *Using Microsoft Word*.

Chapter 17

Style Sheets

In the book-publishing field, book designers draw up ''spec sheets'' to record the formatting specifications for published works. Typesetters, proofreaders, editors, and artists use these spec sheets to guide them as they transform an author's raw text and sketches into an attractive and marketable book. Adherence to the spec sheet ensures consistency from one page to the next. In the business world, companies often have style manuals to guide employees as they prepare memos, letters, and reports.

By adding built-in *style sheets* to Word, Microsoft took a giant step toward accommodating the need for formatting standards. Word lets you create style sheets that map out the format of documents. Instead of looking up the format specifications on a spec sheet or in a style manual, you tell Word to look them up for you. Instead of having you issue all the commands necessary to produce that format, Word issues them for you.

Equally important, style sheets can save you time—whether you're trying to conform to specific formatting guidelines or not. Like a macro, each style can replace several formatting commands with a single command. Unlike a macro, a style becomes linked to the text after you apply it to that text. If you change the formatting instructions of the style, any text linked to it is also changed. A macro that is changed has no effect on text to which it was previously applied.

Creating and using styles for frequently repeated formatting instructions and for seldom-used but complex formats can save you much time and effort.

USING A STYLE SHEET

Even without knowing much about the content or makeup of style sheets, you can begin using them to format documents. Word provides a few ready-made style sheets that you can try. Before you can use a style sheet to format a document, however, you must first attach it to the document.

Attaching a Style Sheet

Let's create a letter and format it as we type it, using the style sheet called SEMI.STY that Word provides. SEMI.STY is designed to format letters in a standard semiblock style. If you have a floppy-disk system, you can find SEMI.STY and a style sheet called FULL.STY (for full-block letters) on the Sample Documents disk created by the Setup program. Use the DOS command COPY to copy SEMI.STY and FULL.STY from the Sample Documents disk to your default document disk or directory if these style sheets are not already there. Start Word or use the File New command to produce a blank window in which you can start typing a new document.

You can attach a style sheet to a document before you begin typing the document or after you type it. To attach a style sheet to a document:

1. Choose the Format Attach Style Sheet command (Alt, T, A).

2. The Format Attach Style Sheet dialog box appears:

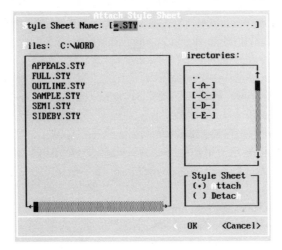

Type the name and, if necessary, the path of the style sheet in the Style Sheet Name box. In this case, type *semi*. As usual, you can use the Directories and Files boxes to choose the style sheet.

3. Choose <OK> (press Enter).

SEMI.STY is now available for use and will be available each time you open the document. The next step is to find out what's in the style sheet.

Looking at Available Styles

A style sheet can contain three kinds of styles: character styles, paragraph styles, and section styles. *Character styles* specify character formats only, such as font, font size, boldface, italics, underlining, and all the options available through the Format Character command. *Paragraph styles* control the formatting options available through the Format Paragraph, Format Tabs, Format Borders, and Format Position commands. As a bonus, paragraph styles can also include character formats, allowing you, for example, to center a heading and make it boldface with one command. *Section styles* determine the general layout: the margins, page size, page numbering, and all the other options of the Format Section, Format Margins, and Format Header/Footer commands.

An individual style usually governs the formatting of a distinct part of a document. For example, one style might control the placement and format of the date in a letter, another style might control the format of the complimentary closing, and another might determine the treatment of a numbered list within the document.

When you're not familiar with the styles in a style sheet, you can use the Format Apply Style command simply to see what styles are available. You must specify whether you want to see character, paragraph, or section styles. Let's first take a look at the character styles in SEMI.STY. If you haven't already done so, open a new file and attach SEMI.STY as instructed earlier. To see a list of available character styles, choose the Format Apply Style command, and choose Character in the Style Type box. For SEMI.STY, you see the dialog box that appears on the following page.

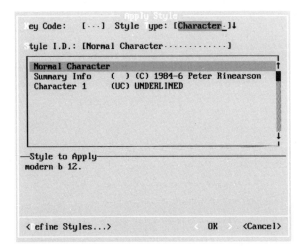

All the character styles found in SEMI.STY are listed in the Style I.D. list box. Normal Character is Word's default character style. Word adds this style to all style sheets (although you don't see it in the style sheets themselves unless you redefine it). Applying this character style is the equivalent of pressing Ctrl-Spacebar to restore characters to normal format. The second listing, Summary Info, is not really a style; rather, it's a copyright message embedded in the style sheet. The third listing, Character 1, is more typical:

Three pieces of information are given about each style in the list: the style I.D., the key code, and a remark. The *style I.D.* is a name for the style. A set of special style I.D.s (such as Normal Character, Page Number, and Footnote Ref) is used for styles that Word initially defines and applies automatically. These automatic styles control the default formatting for various parts of a document. You can redefine the defaults by changing the automatic styles. Generic names with numbers (such as Character 1, Paragraph 1, and Section 1) represent styles that you define and apply yourself.

The *key code* tells you what keys to press in combination with the Control and Shift keys to apply the style to selected text. Much like the key codes used to play back macros or like the speed formatting keys, key codes provide a shortcut for applying styles. Key codes consist of one or, preferably, two keys. In this example, UC is the key code for the style that underlines characters. Pressing Ctrl-Shift-U, C applies that character style. (It's not necessary to hold down Ctrl-Shift while you press the second letter of the key code.)

The *remark* tells you the purpose of the style. In this case, the remark explains that this style underlines selected characters. In a well-written style sheet, the remarks and the key codes provide good clues to what a style does and what it's used for.

When you highlight a style in the Style I.D. list box, the formatting instructions for the style are displayed in the Style to Apply box. Press Alt-S to move to the Style I.D. list box, and press the Down direction key to highlight Character 1. With the mouse, point to Character 1 and click. The formatting instructions that appear in the Style to Apply box tell you the font, the font size, and the special attribute applied to characters when the Character 1 style is chosen:

```
─Style to Apply──────────────────────────────
 modern b 12 Underlined.
```

Now let's look at the paragraph styles available with SEMI.STY. Choose Paragraph in the Style Type box. You see this list of paragraph styles in the Style I.D. list box:

```
 tyle I.D.: [Normal····················]

 Normal        (SP) NORMAL PARAGRAPH               ↑
 Paragraph 7   (DA) DATE
 Paragraph 8   (NA) AUTHOR'S NAME (BELOW SIGNTR)
 Paragraph 9   (TI) AUTHOR'S TITLE (AFTER NAME)
 Paragraph 10  (LH) ADJUSTABLE LETTERHEAD SPACE
 Paragraph 11  (IA) INSIDE ADDRESS/Mr. Jim Smith
 Paragraph 13  (SA) SALUTATION / Dear...
 Paragraph 14  (RA) shift-←┘ RETURN NAME, ADDR    ↓
```

Move the cursor to the box, and scroll to see more of the list. A paragraph style is available for each distinct part of a letter (shown in Figure 17-1 on the next page).

As you can see, remarks are a vital part of a style sheet. The remark for the return address style, for example, reminds you to press Shift-Enter at the end of each line of the address rather than the Enter key alone. (The formatting of the return address in this style sheet requires that the entire address be treated as one paragraph.) Remarks can include as many as 28 characters.

Part of Letter	Corresponding Style	
	Key Code	Remark
Return address	(RA)	Shift-⏎ RETURN NAME, ADDR
Date	(DA)	DATE
Recipient's address	(IA)	INSIDE ADDRESS/ Mr. Jim Smith
Salutation	(SA)	SALUTATION/Dear…
Body of letter	(SP)	NORMAL PARAGRAPH
Complimentary closing	(CL)	COMPLMNTRY CLOSING/Sincerely
Author's name	(NA)	AUTHOR'S NAME (BELOW SIGNTR)
Author's title	(TI)	AUTHOR'S TITLE (AFTER NAME)
Reference information: Initials (author/ preparer), enclosures, CC (copies to)	(RI)	REF INITIALS, ENCLOSURES, CC

Figure 17-1. *Parts of a letter and their corresponding styles in the SEMI.STY style sheet.*

You will see one additional style, with the key code LH and the remark ADJUSTABLE LETTERHEAD SPACE. This style was added to accommodate letterhead stationery. When you prepare a letter to be printed on letterhead stationery, you don't need to type a return address. Instead, you must allow extra space for the letterhead, which the LH style does for you.

Most formatting in a letter is done with paragraph formats. But margins and page size are determined by section formats. Choose Section in the Style Type box to see the list of section styles:

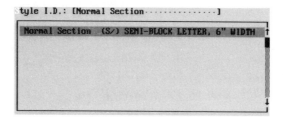

Because most letters, as well as other kinds of documents, have only one section, this style sheet contains only one section style, Normal Section. This automatic style defines the default section format.

Now that you've examined the SEMI.STY style sheet, press the Esc key to close the Format Apply Style dialog box.

Applying Styles from a Style Sheet

Style sheet formatting works like direct formatting with the Format commands: You can format text as you type by applying styles before you type the text, or you can return to previously typed text and apply styles. If you format as you type, the style you choose affects everything you type until you choose another style or change the format with various formatting commands. If you apply a style to previously typed text, the style you choose affects selected text only.

After you've attached a style sheet, you can apply styles to a document in three ways: with the key codes, with the formatting ribbon, or with the Format Apply Style command. If you don't have a mouse, pressing a key code is the fastest method. If you don't know the key codes, you can use the formatting ribbon or the Format Apply Style command to view a list of character, paragraph, or section styles and to choose a style from the list.

Using the ribbon to apply styles

When it is turned on, the formatting ribbon appears below the menu bar at the top of the screen. If you're using the ribbon with the keyboard, press Ctrl-S to turn on the ribbon and to move the cursor to the Style box on the ribbon. The Style box displays paragraph styles only. It initially displays the style I.D. and the key code assigned to the selected paragraph. You can press the Up and Down direction keys to travel through the list of available paragraph styles, or you can press Alt-Down direction key to make the list drop down and then use the direction keys to highlight your choice. In either case, press Enter when the style you want to apply is highlighted. If you drop down the list, you can see the style I.D., the key code, and the first 10 characters of the remark for each style, as shown on the next page.

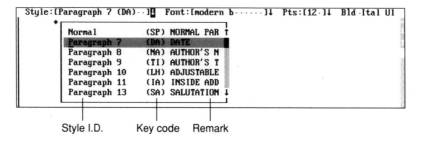

Style I.D.   Key code   Remark

With a mouse, the formatting ribbon offers the quickest way to apply paragraph styles. To turn on the ribbon using the mouse, choose the View Ribbon command, or point to the ruler icon (⌐) in the upper right corner and click the right mouse button. When the ribbon is visible, click the arrow next to the Style box to make the list drop down, and click a style to apply it to text. Use the scroll bar if necessary to see more of the list. To apply a character or section style with the mouse, you need to use the Format Apply Style command. A quick way to choose this command is to double-click the word Style on the ribbon.

Applying styles to a sample letter

Let's type a letter and format it with the style sheet SEMI.STY. If you format as you type, you can see the letter take shape as you work. The style sheet inserts all the extra tabs and the necessary line spacing; you don't need to press the Tab key or the Enter key to add the indents and the blank lines you normally want in a letter. The instructions that follow call for using the key codes to format the letter, but feel free to choose styles from the formatting ribbon instead.

When using a style sheet, turn on the *style bar* so that the key codes for the styles will appear next to the left window border as you apply them. To turn on the style bar, choose the View Preferences command, turn on the Style Bar check box, and choose <OK>.

Let's suppose you'll be printing on letterhead stationery and thus need extra space at the top for the preprinted name, logo, address, and so on. Press Ctrl-Shift-L, H. LH appears in the style bar to the left of the cursor to indicate that the first paragraph has the letterhead format. This first paragraph won't contain any text—it's only a space maker that adds two blank lines. Combined with the top margin, it allows 2 inches at the top of the page for the letterhead.

Now press the Enter key to move to the next paragraph. LH appears next to the second paragraph. All paragraphs will have the letterhead format until you choose a new format.

Usually, the first item you type in a letter is the date. When you press Ctrl-Shift-D, A, the style code for the second paragraph changes to DA, and the cursor jumps to the middle of the screen, where the date appears in a semiblock-style letter. Now type the date. For example, type

January 2, 1991

and press Enter.

To type the inside (recipient's) address, press Ctrl-Shift-I, A. The cursor jumps back to the left margin to position the address. Type the name and address of the person receiving the letter, pressing the Enter key at the end of each line. In this case, type

Johnny Appleseed
25 Apple Blossom Road
Springfield, IL 60432

Press Ctrl-Shift-S, A to prepare for the salutation. The cursor skips down a line to leave a blank space between the address and the salutation. Type

Dear Johnny,

and press Enter.

Now you're ready to type the body of the letter. Press Ctrl-Shift-S, P to indicate that you want to switch to standard (or normal) paragraph formatting. For semiblock style, standard formatting indents the first line of each paragraph. After you apply the standard paragraph format, the cursor moves five spaces to the right for the first-line indent. Type the body of the letter, pressing the Enter key once at the end of each paragraph:

I am pleased to offer you a position with our firm as Horticultural Consultant
for the Midwest region. What impressed us most about your background are
the volunteer activities you have engaged in throughout the prairie states.

As you know, PlantRight is sprouting several new branches and can offer an
industrious young twig like yourself ample growth opportunity. Please call
me at your earliest convenience so that we can discuss salary, benefits, and
starting date.

Notice that the standard paragraph style not only indents each paragraph but also adds a blank line between paragraphs.

To close the letter, press Ctrl-Shift-C, L, type the closing

Sincerely,

and press Enter. Now press Ctrl-Shift-N, A to position the author's name under the closing, type the name

Pete Moss

and press Enter. The style adds enough space for a signature above the name.

Press Ctrl-Shift-T, I to type the author's title under the name. You might want to break long titles by pressing Shift-Enter when you want to start a new line. Shift-Enter starts a new line without starting a new paragraph, and the title style indents the second line three spaces. Type

Vice President,

and press Shift-Enter. Then type

Trees and Shrubs

and press Enter.

It's customary to put both the author's and the typist's initials at the end of a letter. Notes about enclosures and who receives copies are also appended. Suppose you forget the key code for formatting this reference information. In that case, choose the Format Apply Style command. Press Alt-S to move to the list, and use the direction keys to move the highlight to the style labeled with the remark REF INITIALS, ENCLOSURES, CC. Press Enter to OK the command. The command then applies the highlighted style to the currently selected paragraph. Now type the initials

PM:vn

and you're done. Figure 17-2 shows you what the letter formatted with the semiblock style sheet looks like when it's printed.

After formatting a document with one style sheet, you can easily reformat the document by attaching a new style sheet if the new style sheet contains the same key codes and corresponding (though different) style definitions. (Default styles, such as Normal Paragraph, are applied automatically and do not require the same key codes.) For example, Word provides another style sheet, called FULL.STY, for letters. It includes the formatting instructions

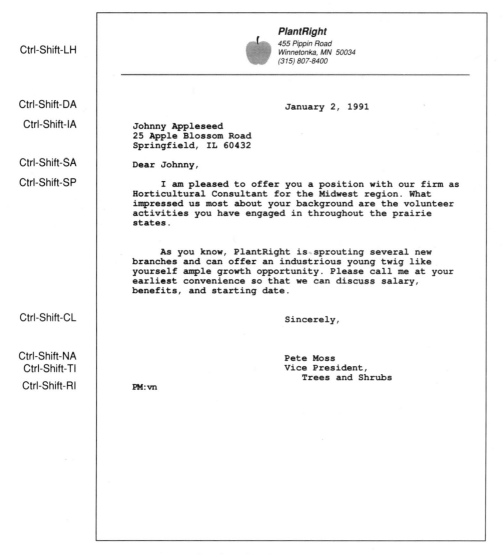

Ctrl-Shift-LH

Ctrl-Shift-DA

Ctrl-Shift-IA

Ctrl-Shift-SA

Ctrl-Shift-SP

Ctrl-Shift-CL

Ctrl-Shift-NA
Ctrl-Shift-TI
Ctrl-Shift-RI

PlantRight
455 Pippin Road
Winnetonka, MN 50034
(315) 807-8400

January 2, 1991

Johnny Appleseed
25 Apple Blossom Road
Springfield, IL 60432

Dear Johnny,

I am pleased to offer you a position with our firm as Horticultural Consultant for the Midwest region. What impressed us most about your background are the volunteer activities you have engaged in throughout the prairie states.

As you know, PlantRight is sprouting several new branches and can offer an industrious young twig like yourself ample growth opportunity. Please call me at your earliest convenience so that we can discuss salary, benefits, and starting date.

Sincerely,

Pete Moss
Vice President,
    Trees and Shrubs

PM:vn

Figure 17-2. *Letter formatted by SEMI.STY.*

needed to produce a letter in full-block style, in which none of the main parts of the letter are indented. If you attach FULL.STY to the letter you just prepared, you'll see an immediate transformation. Choose the Format Attach Style Sheet command, and type *full* in the Style Sheet Name box, or use the Directories and Files boxes to choose the FULL.STY style sheet. Then

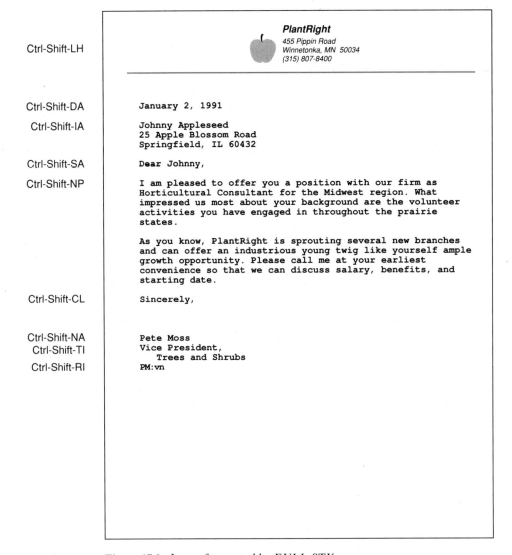

Ctrl-Shift-LH

Ctrl-Shift-DA

Ctrl-Shift-IA

Ctrl-Shift-SA

Ctrl-Shift-NP

Ctrl-Shift-CL

Ctrl-Shift-NA
Ctrl-Shift-TI

Ctrl-Shift-RI

PlantRight
455 Pippin Road
Winnetonka, MN 50034
(315) 807-8400

January 2, 1991

Johnny Appleseed
25 Apple Blossom Road
Springfield, IL 60432

Dear Johnny,

I am pleased to offer you a position with our firm as
Horticultural Consultant for the Midwest region. What
impressed us most about your background are the volunteer
activities you have engaged in throughout the prairie
states.

As you know, PlantRight is sprouting several new branches
and can offer an industrious young twig like yourself ample
growth opportunity. Please call me at your earliest
convenience so that we can discuss salary, benefits, and
starting date.

Sincerely,

Pete Moss
Vice President,
    Trees and Shrubs
PM:vn

Figure 17-3. *Letter formatted by FULL.STY.*

choose <OK> (press Enter) to carry out the command. The results of attaching FULL.STY to your letter are shown in Figure 17-3.

Now use the Format Attach Style Sheet command to switch back to SEMI.STY. We'll revise SEMI.STY by recording a style and adding it to the style sheet.

Recording Styles

The easiest way to alter existing styles or to add new styles to a style sheet is to type and format text in a document and then record the format in the style sheet. If you record the format under an unassigned name, you create a new style. If you record it under a name already assigned to a style, you change that style.

Frequently, letters and other documents include numbered or unnumbered lists. You can create a style for formatting both kinds of lists. Hanging indents, in which item numbers or markers (sometimes called bullets) stick out from the rest of the text, are an attractive list format. Each item in the list is treated as a separate paragraph, and the first line of each paragraph is "outdented" (given a negative left indent).

Let's add a section that includes a list to the Johnny Appleseed letter. Move the cursor to the end of the first paragraph and press Enter. Start typing the new section:

Your duties will include:

Press the Enter key again before beginning the list. The list will be indented from the rest of the letter, and each item in the list will be marked by a hyphen. You'll type the first item in the list and format it with the Format Paragraph command. Type the following, pressing the Tab key before and after you type the hyphen:

- Preparation of budgets, forecasts, and quarterly reports for submission to the Head Office.

To create the hanging indent:

1. With the cursor still in the first item of the list, press Alt, T, P to choose the Format Paragraph command.

2. Press Alt-F to move to the From Left box, and type *1*.

3. Press Alt-N to move to the First Line box, and type *-.5*.

4. Press Alt-B to move to the Spacing Before box, and type *.5* to allow one-half line of extra space between items in the list.

5. Press the Enter key to choose <OK>.

6. Press Alt, T, T to choose the Format Tabs command.

7. Type *.8* in the Tab Position box. Press Alt-R to turn on the Right Alignment button, and press Alt-S to choose the <Set> button.

8. Type *1* in the Tab Position box. Press Alt-L to turn on the Left Alignment button, and press Alt-S to choose <Set>.

9. Press the Enter key to OK the Format Tabs command.

The right-aligned tab positions the markers or numbers for the entries in a list. Right alignment ensures that numbers line up like this:

    8.
    9.
  10.
  11.

and not like this:

    8.
    9.
  10.
  11.

The left-aligned tab ensures that the first character following a number or marker is aligned with the rest of the paragraph. After formatting, the first item in the list should look like this:

```
┌─────────────────────── FIG17-3.DOC ───────────────────────┐
│     ‐   Preparation of budgets, forecasts, and quarterly   │
│         reports for submission to the Head Office._         │
└────────────────────────────────────────────────────────────┘
```

Now let's record this format in the style sheet that is already attached to the letter. To record a new style or to record a new format for an existing style, you can use either the Format Record Style command or the Styles box on the formatting ribbon:

1. Move the cursor to the text that has the format you want to record. In this case, move the cursor to the list item you just formatted.

2. Choose the Format Record Style command (Alt, T, R). Or, to activate the formatting ribbon, press Ctrl-S or click the arrow next to the Style box.

3. If you're using the ribbon, choose the next unassigned style I.D. from the Style list by highlighting it and pressing Enter or by click-ing the unassigned, generic style I.D. (An unassigned style I.D. has no accompanying key code or remark.) In this case, choose Para-graph 1.

4. The Format Record Style dialog box appears:

```
Record Style
 ey Code:    [...]  Style  ype: [Paragraph·]↓
 emark:         [............................]
 tyle I.D.: [Paragraph 1.................]↓

─Style to Record──────────────────────────
modern b 12. Flush left, Left indent 1" (first line
indent -0.5"), space before 0.5 li. Tabs at: 0.8"
(right flush), 1" (left flush).


< efine Styles...>              <  OK  >  <Cancel>
```

Type an easy-to-remember two-letter code for the style in the Key Code box. For example, type *IL* in the Key Code box for the in-dented list format you're recording now.

5. In the Style Type box, choose the kind of style you're recording: Character, Paragraph, or Section. In this case, choose Paragraph.

6. Type a note in the Remark box telling you what the style does or what kind of text it is used for. For example, type *INDENTED LIST* to identify the format you're recording now. Use uppercase letters to make the remark easy to spot in a style sheet.

7. The Style I.D. box proposes the next unassigned style I.D. (or the one you chose from the Styles box on the ribbon). In this example, it proposes Paragraph 1.

8. Choose <OK> (press Enter) to carry out the command.

If you choose not to use the proposed style I.D., type another I.D. in the Style I.D. box or drop down the Style I.D. list and choose one from the list. If a style I.D. is already assigned to a style, the key code for the style is shown next to the style I.D. in the list.

You can usually accept the proposed style I.D. But if you're recording a format to change an existing style, you must choose the style I.D. for that style. Word replaces its format with the newly recorded format after asking for confirmation. If you want to record an automatic style that will determine the default formatting of parts of a document and that will be automatically applied by Word, you need to use one of the special automatic style I.D.s. Automatic style I.D.s appear at the beginning of the style I.D. drop-down list (and are listed in Figure 17-4).

Character	*Paragraph*	*Section*
Normal	Normal	Normal
Annotation Ref	Annotation	
Footnote Ref	Footnote	
Line Draw	Header/Footer	
Line Number	Heading 1–7*	
Page Number	Index 1–4*	
Summary Info	Table 1–4*	

*Numbers refer to levels of headings, index entries, or entries in a table of contents.

Figure 17-4. *Automatic style I.D.s for character, paragraph, and section styles.*

If you've been following the instructions, you've just added a new style (for indented lists) to the style sheet (SEMI.STY) attached to the current document (the Johnny Appleseed letter). In addition to creating a new style, you assigned the style to the first item in the list. You should see the key code IL to the left of that paragraph.

Continue typing the rest of the list, and watch the newly recorded style do the formatting for you. Remember to press the Tab key before and after each hyphen marking an entry in the list and to press the Enter key after each entry. Type the following entries:

 - *Hiring and firing.*
 - *Start-up of local nurseries and seed beds.*
 - *Field management of planting crews.*

So far, you've learned to attach and use a style sheet and to alter it by recording a new style. You can easily perform these tasks without learning the details of how style sheets are composed. When you're ready to examine style sheets more closely, move on to the next sections.

WORKING IN A STYLE SHEET WINDOW

You can view an entire style sheet in a style sheet window by opening it with the File Open command or the Format Define Styles command. The File Open command can open any style sheet. The Format Define Styles command opens the style sheet that is attached to the document the cursor is in when you choose the command. After you open a style sheet, you can directly edit individual styles or create new styles from scratch.

A style sheet window looks like any other window. When a style sheet window is active, the menu bar looks the same, but some of the commands listed on the menus are different.

Filing Style Sheets and Managing Windows

When a style sheet window is active, the commands on the File and Window menus are almost identical to those you see when a document is in a window. You can open style sheets with the File Open command, save them with the File Save commands, clear them from memory with the File Close or the Window Close command, and set a default directory for finding and saving style sheets with the <Options> command button of the File Open or File Save command. You can size, move, split, arrange, maximize, and close style sheet windows with the Window commands.

The File Open command does not attach a style sheet to a document. That can be done only with the Format Attach Style Sheet command when a document is in the window. The File Close and Window Close commands do not detach style sheets from documents. To detach a style sheet from a document, activate the document, choose the Format Attach Style Sheet command, and turn on the Detach button in the Style Sheet box before you OK the command.

Opening, Viewing, and Printing Style Sheets

To see the style sheet attached to a document, choose the Format Define Styles command when the cursor is in that document. To see any style sheet, choose the File Open command and specify the location, filename, and filename extension (.STY) of the style sheet. Instead of typing the path and the filename in the File Open dialog box, you can turn on the Style Sheet button in the Show Files box and use the Directories and Files boxes to choose a style sheet.

317

After you use the File Open command or the Format Define Styles command, the style sheet appears in a window with the name of the style sheet in the title bar. Choose the Format Define Styles command now to display SEMI.STY. Figure 17-5 shows what you see after you open SEMI.STY.

```
═══════════════════════ SEMI.STY ═══════════════════════
(S) S/ Normal Section                    SEMI-BLOCK LETTER, 6" WIDTH
         Page break. Page length 11"; width 8.5". Page # format Arabic. Top
         margin 1.67"; bottom 1"; left 1.25"; right 1.25". Header at 1"
         from top. Footer at 0.83" from bottom. Footnotes on same page.
(P) LH Paragraph 10                       ADJUSTABLE LETTERHEAD SPACE
         modern b 12. Flush left, space after 2 li.
(P) RA Paragraph 14                    shift-⏎ RETURN NAME, ADDR
         modern b 12. Flush left, Left indent 3.2", space before 1 li (keep
         in one column, keep with following paragraph).
(P) DA Paragraph 7                        DATE
         modern b 12. Flush left, Left indent 3.2", space after 1 li (keep
         in one column, keep with following paragraph).
(P) IA Paragraph 11                       INSIDE ADDRESS/Mr. Jim Smith
         modern b 12. Flush left, Left indent 0.5" (first line indent -
         0.5"), right indent 2.8" (keep in one column, keep with following
         paragraph).
(P) SA Paragraph 13                       SALUTATION / Dear...
         modern b 12. Flush left, space before 1 li (keep in one column,
         keep with following paragraph).
(P) SP Normal                             NORMAL PARAGRAPH
         modern b 12. Flush left (first line indent 0.5"), space before 1
         li.
(P) CL Paragraph 21                       COMPLMNTRY CLOSING/Sincerely
         modern b 12. Flush left, Left indent 3.2", space before 1 li (keep
```

Figure 17-5. *Display of the style sheet SEMI.STY.*

Each paragraph in the style sheet represents one style, or set of formatting instructions. For example, the style that formats normal sections (the default section style) looks like this:

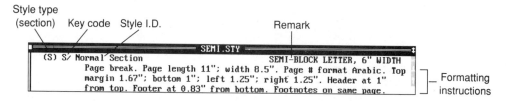

The first line of the style shows you the style type, the key code, the style I.D., and the remark. The remaining lines detail the formatting instructions for the style.

You can scroll up and down to see more of the style sheet, as you do with a document. Press Ctrl-End now (and the Up direction key, if necessary) to see the end of the style sheet, where the style that you recorded for indenting lists is stored:

```
================================ SEM1.STY ==================================
(P) IL Paragraph 1                              INDENTED LIST
         modern b 12. Flush left, Left indent 1" (first line indent -0.5"),
         space before 0.5 li. Tabs at: 0.8" (right flush), 1" (left flush).
```

When you are in a style sheet window, you can print a copy of the displayed style sheet by choosing the File Print command. (With a document in the window, you can print the style sheet attached to the document by using the File Print command and choosing Style Sheet in the Print box of the File Print dialog box.)

Editing Style Sheets

While in the style sheet window, you can revise a style sheet with the commands on the Edit, Insert, and Format menus and with the Insert and Delete keys. You cannot type directly in the style sheet window.

Use the direction keys to move the highlight in the window up and down from one style to another. The highlight always selects at least one entire style at a time. It is used to mark the style you want to edit or the place where you want to insert a new style. You can extend the highlight to select more than one style at a time—for example, when you want to delete two or more adjacent styles.

In addition to the Format commands, the following commands can be used to revise style sheets:

Edit Copy	Edit Rename Style	Insert New Style
Edit Cut	Edit Repeat	Insert Style Sheet
Edit Paste	Edit Undo	

The Edit Copy command (or Ctrl-Ins) copies the highlighted style to the scrap, and the Edit Cut command (or Shift-Del) deletes the highlighted style to the scrap. From the scrap you can, if desired, reinsert the style with the Edit Paste command (or Shift-Ins). You can insert the style back into the same style sheet or into another style sheet. You would, for example, reinsert a style into the same style sheet when you create a new style by copying an existing one and making minor changes to it. You can move a style from one location to another in a style sheet by first deleting the style and then inserting it. You might want to move styles around within a style sheet to group related styles together.

You can change a style's key code, style I.D., or remark with the Edit Rename Style command, and you can change the style's formatting instructions with the Format commands. The Edit Repeat command lets you repeat the last editing or formatting change made, and the Edit Undo command reverses the last change.

Use the Insert New Style command to create new styles from scratch. It lets you assign the new style a key code, style type, style I.D., and remark. Then use the Format commands to define the format for the style. The Insert Style Sheet command allows you to combine two or more style sheets by inserting one into the other.

After making changes to a style sheet file, you must save the file to preserve the changes. As it does for document files, Word checks for unsaved changes to a style sheet file before it allows you to exit the Word program or clear memory with the File Close or the File Close All command.

In the next sections, we'll use the Edit Copy and Edit Paste commands to copy styles from one style sheet to another, the Insert New Style and Format commands to create a new style, and the Format commands to change an existing style.

Copying styles from one style sheet to another

Some standard elements of a document rarely vary from one document to another. Although you might want different style sheets for different kinds of documents, you'll probably find some styles, such as the style for formatting lists, suitable for more than one style sheet. Rather than creating those styles in each style sheet, you can copy them from one style sheet to another.

Let's copy the indented list style you created earlier from the style sheet named SEMI.STY to the one named FULL.STY. To copy a style from one style sheet to another:

1. If it is not already open, open the style sheet you want to copy *from*. You can use the Format Define Styles command to open a style sheet attached to the active document, or you can use the File Open command. In this example, open the SEMI.STY style sheet.

2. Highlight the style you want to copy. In this case, highlight the style labeled with the remark INDENTED LIST.

3. Choose the Edit Copy command, or press Ctrl-Ins. The style appears in the scrap without being removed from the style sheet.

4. Use the File Open command to open the style sheet in which you want to insert the copy. In this example, open FULL.STY. Word opens another style sheet window to display FULL.STY.

5. Move the highlight to the place where you want to insert the copied style.

6. Choose the Edit Paste command, or press Shift-Ins.

Now that you have FULL.STY in view, try adding another style to it. This time, you'll create the style from scratch instead of creating it by recording a format as you did before.

Creating styles from scratch

The Insert New Style command and the Format commands come into play when you create a style from scratch. First you use the Insert New Style command to name the style; then you use the Format commands to specify the format for the style.

Let's create a style that formats characters in boldface italics. Move the highlight to where you want to insert the style. Because you're creating a character style, it's best to move the highlight to the other character style in the style sheet, which has the key code UC and the remark UNDERLINED. You can insert styles anywhere, but grouping similar styles together makes it easier to read style sheets and find styles. After the highlight is in position:

1. Choose the Insert New Style command (Alt, I, N). You see the Insert New Style dialog box (which is shown on the next page).

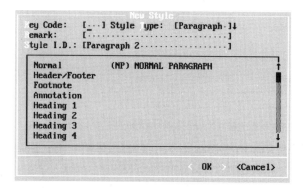

2. Type *BI* in the Key Code box, and choose Character in the Style Type box.

3. Move to the Remark box, and type

   BOLDFACE-ITALICS

4. Choose <OK> (press Enter).

You can usually accept the proposed style I.D. But if you're creating a style that you want Word to apply automatically, choose one of the automatic style I.D.s from the list box before you OK the command.

The boldface-italics style is now inserted in the style sheet and highlighted, but it does not yet include the formatting instructions that make characters bold and italic.

To define the format for the new style:

1. Choose the Format Character command while the new style is highlighted.

2. Turn on the Bold check box and the Italics check box.

3. Choose <OK> (press Enter).

The style now includes instructions to format characters in both boldface and italics:

You can create paragraph and section styles in the same way you create character styles. First use the Insert New Style command to identify the style, and then use the Format commands to specify the formatting instructions. The formatting commands available for a style depend on the style type. Commands that are not available are dimmed on the Format menu. You can use the Format Paragraph, Format Character, Format Tabs, Format Borders, and Format Position commands to assign formats to a paragraph style. If you're formatting a section style, you can use the Format Section, Format Margins, and Format Header/Footer commands.

Changing a style

You can use the Format commands while in a style sheet window to check and change the format of an existing style. With the style sheet in view, simply highlight the style you want to change and choose the appropriate Format command. To see how it's done, let's change the margins in the section style of FULL.STY:

1. If you haven't already done so, use the File Open command to open FULL.STY.

2. Highlight the style that has the key code S/ and the style I.D. Normal Section.

3. Choose the Format Margins command. In the Margins box, type *1* in both the Left and Right boxes to reduce the margins from 1.25 inches to 1 inch.

4. Choose <OK> (press Enter).

The instructions in the style are immediately changed. If you open a document to which FULL.STY is attached, you see that the document has changed to fit the new margins.

USING THE DEFAULT STYLE SHEET: NORMAL.STY

When you create a new document, Word looks for and attaches a style sheet called NORMAL.STY. Because NORMAL.STY does not contain style definitions until you insert them, it does not have any initial effect on the documents you create.

You can change the default formats that Word usually applies to documents by adding normal character, paragraph, and section styles to the style sheet NORMAL.STY. You might, for example, want page numbers printed for most documents and the first lines of paragraphs indented. You can add a section style to NORMAL.STY that includes instructions to print page numbers and a paragraph style that indents the first lines of paragraphs. By assigning either of these styles the style I.D. Normal, you ensure that Word will automatically apply the formatting instructions in that style to your text. They become the new default formats. You can override these formatting instructions by attaching a different style sheet to the document, by applying different styles to the text, or by formatting the document directly with the Format commands.

In addition to using NORMAL.STY to change default formats for most (or standard) text, use it to store your most commonly used formats for special text such as lists, titles, headings, and tables. What you put in NORMAL.STY depends on the kind of documents you most often prepare. For example, if you usually prepare letters, you might store formats for the various parts of a letter in NORMAL.STY. You are not confined to using the formats you define in NORMAL.STY. When styles are assigned a style I.D. that is not automatic, they are not applied to text unless you apply them with the key code, the Format Apply Style command, or the formatting ribbon. By putting commonly used formats in NORMAL.STY, you simply make them readily available. You can have more than one style sheet called NORMAL.STY, but they must be on separate disks or in separate directories.

Part IV

Appendixes

Appendix A

Getting Acquainted with DOS

Before you can start Word, you must first start DOS, the disk operating system. By familiarizing yourself with the most useful DOS commands, you'll feel comfortable working in the DOS environment and be ready to use some very handy tools that DOS provides.

STARTING THE DISK OPERATING SYSTEM

When you start your computer, it looks for DOS on the floppy disk in drive A and loads it into memory. If no disk is in drive A, the computer checks to see if DOS is on a hard disk in the C drive. This book assumes that DOS is already installed on your hard disk.

After DOS is loaded into memory, it normally asks you to enter the date and the time or (if you have a built-in, battery-operated calendar/clock) to confirm the current date and time. DOS uses this information to record the date and time that each file is created or changed.

When you answer questions or give commands to DOS, always complete your answer or command by pressing the Enter key. If you make a mistake while typing, you can back up and erase it with the Backspace key. When you type numbers on a computer keyboard, be sure to use the number keys and not, for example, the letter *l* (for one) or the letter *O* (for zero).

To start DOS:

1. If you have a floppy-disk system, put your DOS disk in drive A. Drive A is the left-hand or top drive in a two-drive system. If you have a hard disk (drive C), DOS should be on it, so leave drive A empty with the door open.

2. If your computer is off, turn it on. If the components of your system must be turned on individually, turn on your printer, your monitor, your disk drive(s), and then your computer. If your computer is already on, restart it by holding down the Ctrl and the Alt keys as you press the Del key (press Ctrl-Alt-Del).

3. If the current date displayed by DOS is correct, press the Enter key to confirm it. If it needs to be changed, type the correct date and then press the Enter key. Use hyphens or slashes to separate parts of the date. For example, type

    1/2/91

    if today's date is January 2, 1991.

4. If the current time displayed is correct, press the Enter key to confirm it. If it needs to be changed, type the correct time and then press the Enter key. Use colons to separate units of time. For example, type

    8:00

    if the correct time is 8 o'clock in the morning. DOS uses a 24-hour clock, so add 12 hours to afternoon or evening times. For example, type *14:00* for 2 o'clock in the afternoon. (Although it's rarely necessary to be so precise, seconds and hundredths of seconds can be appended to the time, using colons to separate units of time.)

When you see the *A>* prompt (on a floppy-disk system) or the *C>* prompt (on a hard-disk system), you know that DOS is running and ready for you to give the command to start Word.

UNDERSTANDING DOS FILENAMES

Programs and documents are stored on a disk as *files,* each with a unique name. When you create a new document, you give it a *filename*. A filename can be one to eight characters long and can include letters, numbers, and many of the symbols found on your keyboard, but no spaces. These symbols are acceptable:

! @ # $ % & ( ) - _ { } ' ^

The following symbols cannot be used as part of a filename:

* ? . , ; : [ ] + = \ ¦ / < >

A filename can be followed by an *extension,* which can be as many as three characters long. You can use any of the characters allowed in a filename. A period separates the filename from the extension. (Often, programs reserve certain extensions for their own use.)

Here are a few sample document filenames with extensions:

CHAPTER1.DOC	README.DOC
PICKLES.DOC	RESUME.DOC
8-15MEMO.DOC	JAN_SALE.RPT

Notice how symbols are used instead of spaces to separate words or numbers. Filename extensions usually indicate, in a general way, what is in a file. For example, the extension .DOC tells you (and Word) that the file is a document.

THE DOS PROMPT AND THE CURRENT DRIVE

The *DOS prompt A>* (or *C>* for a hard disk) tells you that DOS is started and is waiting for you to tell it what to do next by typing a *command.* The DOS prompt also tells you which drive is the *current drive.* That's where DOS looks for any files that it needs to carry out your commands.

Initially, the current drive is the drive where DOS resides. You can change the current drive so that DOS automatically looks in another drive for files. To make another drive the current drive, type the letter of the drive followed by a colon at the DOS prompt. For example, at the *A>* prompt, type

b:

and press the Enter key to change the current drive from A to B.

In most cases, instead of *changing* the current drive, you can simply tell DOS where to look for individual files that aren't located in the current drive. You do this by including the name of the disk drive with the filename. For example, typing

b:chapter1.doc

tells DOS that it can find the file CHAPTER1.DOC on the floppy disk in drive B. When specifying a file, always put a colon after the drive name, and don't put any spaces between the drive name and the filename or between the filename and the extension.

NOTE: When you give commands and information to DOS, you can type either uppercase or lowercase letters. It's usually easier to type lowercase letters.

LOOKING AT A DISK'S DIRECTORY

A *directory* is a list of files grouped together on a disk. The DOS directory command DIR displays the name of each file in the directory, the date and time each file was created or last changed, the size of each file (measured in bytes), the total number of files, and the amount of free space (in bytes) remaining on the disk. Recall that a byte is the amount of space needed to store one character. It takes about 3000 bytes (3 KB) to store one single-spaced document page.

When checking a directory to see if you have room for more documents, allow twice the space you think you'll need for additional documents. Word always keeps the previous copy of a revised document (and assigns the previous copy the same filename as the new document, with the extension .BAK, which stands for backup). In addition, Word needs some disk space to jot down notes to itself in temporary files. So allow some extra space (from 20 to 40 KB) for Word. Don't be too concerned with exact amounts of disk space: Word lets you know when you're running out. If you don't have enough room left on a disk to store a file, Word lets you put it on another disk.

To view the directory of a disk in the current drive, type

dir

at the DOS prompt (*A>* or *C>*) and press the Enter key. To view the directory of a disk that is not in the current drive, type the drive name and a colon after the DIR command. Let's try it now. Insert one of the Word disks in drive B. (If you have a hard disk and one floppy-disk drive, the floppy-disk drive is referred to as both A and B.) Now type

dir b:

and press the Enter key.

You should see a list of files similar to the one shown in Figure A-1. For now, don't try to figure out what's inside each file. Simply try to get a general idea of the kind of information you see in a directory. (The dollar sign, $, in a filename extension indicates that the file is compressed to save space. You must run Word's Setup program before you can use the compressed files on the Word disks.) Figure A-2 focuses on a single entry from the directory and identifies each column of information.

```
Volume in drive A is UTIL2_55
Directory of  A:\

MERGEPRD EX$    78605  10-04-90   1:59p
MW       HLP   270360  10-04-90   1:59p
        2 File(s)     12288 bytes free
```

Figure A-1. *The directory display of a Word disk (a single-level directory).*

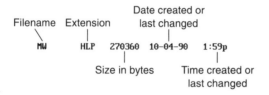

Figure A-2. *A directory entry.*

To view a long directory, type

dir/p

to make the computer pause after showing the first screenful of filenames. Then press any key to see the next screenful or the rest of the directory.

HIGHER-CAPACITY FLOPPY-DISK AND HARD-DISK DIRECTORIES

Higher-capacity floppy disks and hard disks can contain hundreds of files. Because it would be very time-consuming if you had to view all of them in the same directory or if DOS had to search through hundreds of files to find the one you want, DOS provides a way to organize files into subdirectories.

Setting up subdirectories is similar to setting up a filing system for paper files. If you had a filing cabinet full of folders, you'd want to avoid searching through the entire cabinet to find one file. You might assign a different category of files to each drawer. Then, within each drawer, you might further subdivide your files by grouping related files together and inserting labeled partitions that identify the subdivisions. To find a particular file, you would first go to the right drawer and then find the right subdivision in that drawer. If the organization is logical, the labels on the drawer and on the subdivisions guide you to the file you want.

Making a Subdirectory

To create a subdirectory, use the MD (Make Directory) command. You create and name the subdirectory at the same time. For example, type

> *md \sales*

at the DOS prompt and then press the Enter key to create a subdirectory called Sales. The rules for naming subdirectories are the same as the rules for naming files, except that subdirectory names do not have extensions. Each subdirectory must have a unique name. If you try to create a subdirectory with a name that is already in use, DOS tells you it is unable to create the directory.

The Root Directory and the Current Directory

Like the current drive, the *current directory* is the place where DOS expects to find any programs or files that you refer to in DOS commands. When you start DOS, the current directory is the *root directory* and is represented by a single backslash (\).

The root directory is created by DOS when you format a disk. If no subdirectories exist, the root directory is the only directory. If you create subdirectories, the root directory is the top-level directory and usually contains only a few DOS files that must be in the root directory, such as the files AUTOEXEC.BAT and CONFIG.SYS (discussed later in this appendix).

You can change the current directory before giving a command, or you can include a subdirectory's name in a command so that DOS can find what it needs to carry out the command.

To change the current directory, use the CD (Change Directory) command. For example, if you want to change the current directory to the Sales subdirectory, type

> *cd \sales*

at the DOS prompt and press the Enter key.

Now that the Sales directory is the current directory, you can subdivide it by creating new subdirectories with the MD (Make Directory) command. For example, type

md software

and press the Enter key. Then type

md hardware

and press the Enter key again. Because these commands are given while Sales is the current directory, they create two subdirectories—Hardware and Software—that are on a level below the Sales directory:

A directory on any level can be designated the current directory; in the preceding example, you could change the current directory to Hardware.

Paths and Pathnames

A *path,* or *pathname,* spells out the route that DOS must travel to get to a file. DOS first wants to see the drive, then the root directory, the subdirectory, the sub-subdirectory, and finally the filename, with parts of the path separated by backslashes. For example, the complete path to a file called HAMMER.RPT in the Hardware subdirectory would look like this:

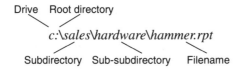

If C is the current drive and the Sales directory is the current directory, you can drop *c:\sales* from the path because DOS assumes that's where you want to start looking. The path now looks like this:

hardware\hammer.rpt

A subdirectory is actually a special kind of file. When you refer to it, DOS expects you to give its address or path. For example, if you wanted to see a list of all files in the Hardware subdirectory, you would type

dir c:\sales\hardware

and press the Enter key. Or, if you wanted to make Hardware the current directory, you would type

cd c:\sales\hardware

As usual, if C is the current drive, you don't need to include *c:* in the path.

Subdirectories, like other kinds of files, are listed in the directory where they reside. For example, if you asked to see the Sales directory, you might see a directory listing similar to the one shown in Figure A-3.

```
Volume in drive C is CCCC
Directory of   C:\SALES

.              <DIR>      10-28-90  11:32p
..             <DIR>      10-28-90  11:32p
HARDWARE       <DIR>      10-28-90  11:32p
SOFTWARE       <DIR>      10-28-90  11:33p
CUSTSERV       <DIR>      10-28-90  11:34p
ANNUAL   RPT   47616       1-29-91  10:57a
HOTLIST  DOC    2048       1-29-91  10:59a
EMPLOYEE DOC    6144      11-26-90   9:09a
        8 File(s)  13264896 bytes free
```

Figure A-3. *The directory display of the Sales subdirectory (a multilevel directory).*

Notice that in Figure A-3 both the names of files and the names of subdirectories (labeled <DIR>) are in the directory for Sales. (The first two subdirectories displayed are special names DOS gives the *current directory* [.] and the *parent directory* [..] immediately above it.) Just as you might store miscellaneous or broad category files at the beginning of a file drawer labeled Sales, you can put files in the directory called Sales rather than in the Hardware or Software subdirectory.

Changing the DOS Prompt

When you have multiple directories, it's easy to lose track of which directory you're in. With the PROMPT command, you can change the DOS prompt so that it displays the current directory along with the current drive. (You can also customize the prompt to have DOS greet you with any message you like.)

You might want to create a prompt that tells you the current drive and the current directory with a minimum number of characters, such as the following:

c:\sales\hardware>

This prompt tells you that C is the current drive and that the current directory is Hardware, which is a subdirectory of Sales. To create this kind of prompt, type

prompt pg

at the *A>* or *C>* prompt, and press the Enter key. The *$p* tells DOS to display the current drive and directory. The *$g* tells DOS to append an angle bracket (>) to the end of the prompt. Once you give this PROMPT command, DOS displays the customized prompt throughout your work session. Each time you start DOS, you must give the PROMPT command again—unless you put it in an AUTOEXEC.BAT file so that the command is automatically executed each time you start DOS. (See the end of this appendix for more information about AUTOEXEC.BAT files.)

To restore your prompt to a simple current drive indicator such as *A>* or *C>*, type

prompt

and press the Enter key.

Removing a Subdirectory

If you decide that you don't need a subdirectory, you can remove it with the RD (Remove Directory) command, which erases empty directories. For example, to remove the subdirectory called Software, you would type

rd c:\sales\software

To remove the current directory, you must first change to a different directory (with the CD command) because DOS won't remove the current directory. DOS also won't remove a directory that contains files or other subdirectories: You must first copy the files you want to save to another directory and then delete all files and remove any subdirectories.

The PATH Command

Application programs such as Word are started by typing a command. DOS finds the instructions for carrying out the command in a file with a .COM or .EXE filename extension. When you type the command *word* to start the Word program, DOS looks for the executable file WORD.EXE.

If you use multiple directories, you must type the full path to the WORD.EXE file if it is not in the current directory. To enable you to start Word from any directory without specifying the path, you can give a PATH command to DOS that tells it where to search for the WORD.EXE file.

For example, if you have stored the Word program in a directory called WORDIR in the C drive, the following PATH command tells DOS where to look for WORD.EXE:

path c:\wordir

When you give the command to start Word, DOS looks for WORD.EXE in WORDIR if it can't find it in the current directory. You can list more than one path in a PATH command by separating the paths with semicolons. If, for example, you have a program that starts with the command DRAW, and the DRAW.EXE file resides in a directory called Artwork, you might type your PATH command like this:

path c:\wordir;c:\artwork

This PATH command would enable you to simply type *word* or *draw* to start the Word or Draw program, regardless of which directory is currently active.

DOS remembers a PATH command throughout a work session. Each time you start DOS, you must give the PATH command again unless you put it in an AUTOEXEC.BAT file. The Setup program described in Appendix B can create or alter an AUTOEXEC.BAT file to include a PATH command that tells DOS where to find Word.

FORMATTING A DISK

Before you can store files on a document disk, you must format the disk. *Formatting a disk* is similar to drawing lines on the unlined pages of a notebook and numbering the pages before you start writing. You need to format a disk only once—the first time you use it.

Hard disks are usually formatted when they are installed. The intricacies of formatting a hard disk are beyond the scope of this book. If your hard disk has never been formatted, see your DOS manual or, better yet, get expert help. If you have a hard disk, you still need to know how to format floppy disks because you use them to make backup copies of files on your hard disk. Should the hard disk ever fail or become damaged, all is not lost if you have backup copies on floppy disks.

Formatting a floppy disk erases everything on the disk. Although you don't have to format a used disk that you want to recycle, formatting is a fast way to erase everything, freeing all the storage space for new files. Always check a disk's directory before formatting it to be sure you don't want to keep any of the files on it.

The program you use to format floppy disks is part of DOS, but it's in a separate file, called FORMAT.COM, on the DOS disk. FORMAT.COM is usually stored in the DOS directory of a hard disk. (As explained in Appendix B, you can also format floppy disks with Word's Setup program if you set up Word on a floppy-disk system. This is a roundabout method that requires more disk handling, however.)

 CAUTION: Use extreme care to avoid formatting a hard disk by mistake. Always include the floppy-disk drive name (A: or B:) when you type the FORMAT command.

Let's format a floppy disk now so that it'll be ready to use. To start, insert the disk you want to format in drive B and close the drive door. (If you have a hard disk and only one floppy-disk drive, the floppy-disk drive is referred to as both A and B.) If you have a dual-drive floppy-disk system, insert your DOS disk in drive A. When you see the *A>* or *C>* prompt, type

dir b:

If the disk in drive B contains files, replace it with another disk unless you're sure you want to erase the files. If the disk has never been formatted, DOS displays this message to tell you it can't use the disk yet:

```
General Failure error reading drive B
Abort, Retry, Fail?
```

Press A (for Abort) to cancel the DIR command and to return to the *A>* or the *C>* prompt.

When you're sure you want to format the disk in drive B, type

format b:

and press the Enter key. This message appears:

```
Insert new diskette for drive B:
and strike ENTER when ready
```

The term *new diskette* refers to the floppy disk you want to format. If you're not sure you put the correct disk in drive B, now is your last chance to check. If you are sure, press the Enter key. (Some versions of DOS prompt you to give the disk a volume name, which identifies the disk's contents and which can be as long as 11 characters.)

When DOS finishes formatting the floppy disk, you see the following message:

```
Format complete

    1213952 bytes total disk space
    1213952 bytes available on disk

Format another (Y/N)?
```

This time, press N for No, followed by the Enter key, to leave the FORMAT program. Notice that DOS tells you how much storage space is available on your blank disk. (The example above shows available storage space on a high-density 5¼-inch disk.) When DOS displays the system prompt, remove the formatted disk from drive B and label it to indicate that it is formatted and ready to use.

DELETING AND RENAMING FILES

Although Word provides commands for deleting files and changing file-names, it's often more convenient to delete or rename files with the DOS commands DEL (Delete file) and REN (Rename file).

To delete a file called OUTADATE.DOC, type

del outadate.doc

and press the Enter key. As with all DOS commands, you must tell DOS the complete path to the file you want to delete, unless the file is in the current drive and current directory. For example, if the current drive is A and you want to delete OUTADATE.DOC from the disk in drive B, you would type

del b:outadate.doc

If the same file is in a subdirectory called Sales, you would type

del b:\sales\outadate.doc

To change the name of a file called OLDNAME.DOC to NEWNAME.DOC, you would type

ren oldname.doc newname.doc

and press the Enter key. You must specify the drive and directory where OLDNAME.DOC can be found if it is not in the current drive and directory.

MAKING BACKUP COPIES

To protect your work, develop the habit of making backup copies of any word-processing work at least once a day. When you receive new software packages, such as Word, it's wise to make a backup copy of each disk in the package before you do anything else with it.

If you have two floppy-disk drives, you can easily copy files from one floppy disk to another. Many computer systems have a hard disk and only one floppy-disk drive. With one floppy-disk drive, you copy an entire floppy disk or single files from one floppy disk to another by exchanging disks during the copying process. DOS calls the disk you copy *from* the *source disk* and the disk you copy *to* the *target disk*. The commands DISKCOPY and COPY are handy tools for copying entire floppy disks or individual files.

The DISKCOPY Command

The DISKCOPY command makes an exact duplicate of an entire disk. Unlike the COPY command, DISKCOPY works only with floppy disks (not with hard disks), and it formats the target disk before it begins copying if the disk is not formatted. If the floppy disk you're copying is a DOS disk, DISKCOPY copies the entire disk, including any parts of the operating system that are stored in hidden files.

If you have no backup copies of your Word disks, make them now with the DISKCOPY command. DISKCOPY resides in a file called DISKCOPY.COM on the DOS disk or in the DOS directory or the root directory of a hard disk.

You should first write-protect your original Word disks by placing a write-protect tab over the notch on the side of each 5¼-inch disk or by opening the write-protect window of each 3½-inch disk (as shown in Figure 1-2 in Chapter 1). This prevents you from accidentally altering or erasing your original disks.

Now check to see that the *A>* or *C>* prompt is on the screen. If you have two floppy-disk drives, put the DOS disk in drive A. Then type

diskcopy a: b:

and press the Enter key. When DOS prompts you to insert the source disk in drive A, put one of your Word disks in drive A and press any key to confirm that the disk is in place and the drive door is closed. When DOS prompts you to insert the target disk in drive B, put a blank disk (or one that does not contain any files you want to keep) in drive B and press any key.

If you have only one floppy-disk drive, type

diskcopy

and press the Enter key. DOS prompts you to insert the source disk (in this case, the Word disk you want to copy) and exchange it with the target disk (the blank disk you are copying to) when necessary. Depending on the amount of memory in your computer, you might be prompted to switch disks repeatedly.

You know that the copy is complete when DOS asks you whether you want another copy. You can remove both disks, label the copy, and store the original in a safe place. Use the copy when you set up and work with Word.

Now press Y for Yes to copy another Word disk. As it did before, Word prompts you to insert the source and target disks. You can repeat this process until all your original Word disks have been copied. After all disks are copied, press N for No when asked if you want to make another copy.

Using the COPY Command

You can back up individual files or an entire directory with the COPY command that comes with (and is an intrinsic part of) DOS. When you use the COPY command, the target disk must be a previously formatted disk. If the target disk already contains files, the newly copied files are added without affecting the existing files unless you try to add a file with the same name as an existing file. In that case, the newly copied file replaces the existing file.

To see how to copy a single file, let's copy the README.DOC file from Word's Setup disk to another formatted disk. README.DOC includes last-minute information on the Word program that isn't in the user manuals. (When you run the Setup program, take a look at this file to see if it has any information that is useful to you, but don't worry if you don't understand everything in the file the first time you read it.)

First look for the *A>* or *C>* prompt. If you have two floppy-disk drives, insert the Setup disk in drive A and a formatted disk in drive B. Then type

    copy a:readme.doc b:

and press the Enter key.

If you have only one floppy-disk drive, insert the source disk (in this case, the Setup disk) in the drive. Type

    copy a:readme.doc b:

and press the Enter key.

When DOS prompts you to insert the disk for drive B, remove the Setup disk and put in a formatted disk. When you're ready to proceed, press any key. DOS continues to ask you to exchange disks until it finishes copying.

When the copy operation is complete, a message tells you that one file was copied. The copy of the file also has the name README.DOC.

Wildcards

When specifying files to be copied with the COPY command or deleted with the DEL command, you can use what DOS calls *wildcards*. An asterisk (∗) stands for any number of unspecified characters. A question mark (?) stands for a single unspecified character. For example, you can type

    ∗.doc

to represent all document files (all filenames with the extension .DOC). If you want to copy all files in a directory, you can use ∗.∗ to represent all filenames and filename extensions.

If only one directory—the root directory—is on a disk, ∗.∗ represents all files on the disk. For example, if you do not have multiple directories, the command

    copy a:∗.∗ b:

tells DOS to copy all the files on the disk in drive A to the disk in drive B.

(When no directory is specified, DOS assumes you mean the current directory.) The copied files are given the same names as the original files, and DOS displays the name of each file on the screen as it's being copied. After all the files are copied, a message tells you how many files were copied.

Copying to and from a Hard Disk

Files on a hard disk should be copied onto floppy disks in case the hard disk becomes damaged. You can use the COPY command to copy files to and from the hard disk. Follow the instructions that were given in the preceding section, substituting *c:* for *a:* or *b:* when appropriate. Because your hard disk probably has multiple directories, be sure to specify the directory path for a file being copied to or from the hard disk whenever the file's directory is not the current directory. COPY can also be used to copy files from one directory to another on the same disk.

The COPY command is easy to use and will serve your initial backup needs. When you're willing to invest more time in learning what DOS has to offer, investigate a pair of commands called BACKUP and RESTORE. These are powerful tools that can save time and floppy-disk space when you are backing up a hard disk. With BACKUP, you can choose individual files or groups of files based on their filenames, the directory where they reside, the date they were last changed, and whether or not they were changed since they were last backed up. Files copied with BACKUP can be used only after they have been recopied to a hard disk with the RESTORE command. For more information on BACKUP and RESTORE, see your DOS manual or *Running MS-DOS*, by Van Wolverton (Microsoft Press).

CONFIG.SYS AND AUTOEXEC.BAT FILES

Each time you start the operating system, DOS looks for two special files named CONFIG.SYS and AUTOEXEC.BAT. Both files can contain lists of special setup commands that you want DOS to execute automatically.

You can create and edit these files as you would text files, but they are saved without Word's usual formatting. (They must be saved with a *Text Only* format.) Each line of text in a CONFIG.SYS or AUTOEXEC.BAT file is a separate DOS command. DOS looks for CONFIG.SYS and AUTOEXEC.BAT files on the DOS disk or in the root directory of the disk used to start DOS. The Setup program (described in Appendix B) helps you create or alter CONFIG.SYS and AUTOEXEC.BAT files.

A CONFIG.SYS file contains commands that can't be given simply by typing them at the keyboard like other DOS commands. These commands tell DOS the special configuration requirements for your particular hardware and software system. For example, if you use a mouse with your system, the command DEVICE=MOUSE.SYS tells DOS to look for and read a file called MOUSE.SYS, which tells DOS how to use the mouse.

An AUTOEXEC.BAT file contains commands that can be typed at the keyboard but are put in an AUTOEXEC.BAT file so that you don't have to type them each time you start DOS. The PROMPT and PATH commands, for example, are found in an AUTOEXEC.BAT file.

Appendix B

Setting Up and Starting Word

The Setup program that comes with Word leads you through the steps of copying the Word program and accessory files that you will need or find helpful when using Word. In most cases, you'll use the Setup program only once—before you use Word for the first time.

WHAT'S ON THE DISKS YOU RECEIVE?

The following table lists the disks contained in your Word 5.5 package.

5¼-inch Disks (360 KB)	*3½-inch Disks (720 KB)*
Setup	Setup
Program (3 disks)	Program 1
Thesaurus/Sample Files	Program 2/Thesaurus
Utilities (2 disks)	Utilities
Printers (2 disks)	Printers
Optional (2 disks)	Optional
Learning Microsoft Word (2 disks)	Learning Microsoft Word

The Setup disk contains the program that sets up Word on your system. Most of the files on the Word disks are compressed to save space. You cannot use them until the Setup program decompresses and copies them to other disks. The Setup disk also contains a file called README.DOC. This file contains corrections to the Word manuals and notes about changes made to Word after the manuals were printed. The Setup program offers you the opportunity to look at the README.DOC file.

The other disks contain various parts of the Word program and accessories. For instance, if you are using 5¼-inch disks:

- Program disks 1 and 2 both contain the Microsoft Word word-processing program files. Program disk 3 contains sample macros, files for using the mouse, the Spell file, and other files for setting up Word.

- The Thesaurus/Sample Files disk puts an electronic thesaurus at your fingertips and includes some sample style sheets.

- The Utilities disks store useful tools such as programs to convert Word files to other formats, the Help files, and a program to create custom-made printer support files.

- Printers disks 1 and 2 store files that contain information Word needs to work with specific printers. Most of these files, when decompressed, have the filename extension .PRD, which stands for printer description or printer driver.

- Optional disks 1 and 2 contain files that are needed to support your equipment or options you might choose during setup.

- The Learning Microsoft Word disks contain tutorials that help you get a hands-on feel for how Word works. You can use the Learn program by itself, or you can access lessons while you're working with the Word program.

WHAT DOES THE SETUP PROGRAM DO?

For both hard-disk and floppy-disk systems, the Setup program

- Creates *working copies* of the Word program and accessories on other floppy disks or in the directory you specify on a hard disk. Setup modifies Word to suit the components of your system.

- Displays the file called README.DOC. Choose this option to see if the file contains any material relevant to your specific system or application.

- Installs printer drivers that enable Word to use your printer(s). The Install Printer Drivers option requires you to choose one or more printers from the list that Setup presents. If you will be using more than one printer, you'll want Setup to install a printer driver for each printer. If you can't find your printer on the list displayed by Setup, see "Additional Setup Tasks" later in this appendix.

- Updates the mouse driver. If you have a mouse, choose this option when Setup presents it, in order to have Setup copy the mouse information file to your DOS disk or into the Word program directory of a hard disk.

- Updates system files. Choose this option when Setup offers it so that Setup will create or alter the AUTOEXEC.BAT file to help Word run more effectively. If you have a mouse, Setup creates or alters the CONFIG.SYS file to include a DEVICE command that tells DOS where to find the mouse information file.

- Customizes Word settings to change how the display looks or how the keyboard works or to change the default paper size. If you have a color monitor, choose this option so that you can specify the color capabilities of your monitor. When you are asked to describe the colors you see, choose the appropriate response.

It's easiest to accept (by pressing the Enter key) Setup's default responses to most of the customizing options. The default responses are to run Word in text mode, to use Word 5.5 function keys, to use Insert as the overtype key, and to specify an 8½-by-11-inch paper size. You can change these options after you set up and run Word: Use the View Preferences command to change the display mode (text or graphics), the Utilities Customize command to change the keyboard assignments, or the Format Margins command to change the paper size for individual documents. For more information on these options, see the *Getting Started* booklet included in your Word package.

Setup Tasks for Floppy Disks

If you are setting up a floppy-disk system, the Setup program offers to

- Format blank floppy disks for storing documents
- Copy Help and Hyphenation files to a document disk if they won't fit on your copy of the Word Program (Startup Word) disk

Because the Help and Hyphenation files won't fit on a 360-KB Word Program disk, the Setup program offers to copy them onto document disks, which are blank, unformatted disks that you provide and that you will use to store documents. The Help and Hyphenation files take up about 295 KB of space on each disk, but having these files on your document disks might be more convenient than switching to other disks each time you ask for help or automatic hyphenation.

Setup Tasks for Hard Disks

If you're setting up a hard-disk system, the Setup program can

- Copy the Learning Microsoft Word program and the Help and Hyphenation files to the hard disk

- Copy the Spell program to the hard disk

- Copy the Thesaurus program to the hard disk

Because of the greater storage capacity of hard disks, the Setup program offers you the option of copying the major accessory programs to the Word program directory of your hard disk. Copy as many of the accessories as you have room for, because they will be faster to access and easier to use if they are on the hard disk. To include everything on your disk, Word requires about 3 MB of disk space.

HOW TO USE THE SETUP PROGRAM

How you use the Setup program depends on whether you are setting up a floppy-disk system or a hard-disk system. (If you are running Setup on a network, see the *Getting Started* booklet for setup procedures.)

Setting Up a Floppy-Disk System

To set up Word on a floppy-disk system, you need

- The Word disks.

- A DOS disk (version 2.11 or later). The DOS disk should be a copy, not the original, and it should contain the FORMAT.COM file. Check the disk directory, using the DIR/P command, to see if FORMAT.COM is there.

- Blank, unformatted floppy disks for creating working copies of Word and Word utilities. If you're setting up on 720-KB disks, you need 7 blank disks. If you're setting up on 360-KB disks, you need 12 blank disks. If you're setting up on 1.2-MB or 1.44-MB disks, you need 5 blank disks.

■ At least one additional unformatted disk for storing documents. If you have a system with 360-KB floppy disks, Setup puts the printer description file and the Help and Hyphenation files on this document disk.

In addition, you need to know

■ The type of computer you have

■ The type of display unit and adapter card you have

■ The brand name and model of your printer(s)

To run the Setup program, you must first start DOS (as explained in Appendix A). When you see the *A>* prompt, replace the DOS disk in drive A with the Setup disk. Then type *setup* and press the Enter key to start the Setup program.

The Setup program leads you through the setup procedure by telling you what to do next, asking you questions, giving you lists of options to choose from, and telling you when to remove or insert disks. Be sure to label each disk as instructed by the Setup program when it prompts you to insert a new disk. Setup creates from 5 to 12 disks, depending on the storage capacity of your disks. The following table lists the disks created by the Setup program.

360-KB Disks *(5¹/₄-inch)*	*720-KB Disks* *(3¹/₂-inch)*	*1.2-MB or 1.44-MB Disks* *(5¹/₄-inch or 3¹/₂-inch)*
Program (Startup Word)	Program (Startup Word)	Program (Startup Word)
Document	Thesaurus/Help	Thesaurus/Help
Program 2	Help	Utilities
Spell/Hyphenation	Utilities	Learning Word
Thesaurus	Printer Driver Utilities	Sample Documents
Help	Learning Word	
Utilities 1	Sample Documents	
Utilities 2		
Printer Driver Utilities		
Learning Word 1		
Learning Word 2		
Sample Documents		

If you have a mouse, Setup alters your *working copy* of the DOS disk. You must use this altered DOS disk to start the operating system when you want to use the mouse with Word.

If you have a system with 360-KB floppy disks, Setup copies the printer information and, optionally, the Help and Hyphenation files onto a document disk because there isn't room to store them with the Word program. To use your printer most effectively, you must copy the .PRD file(s) from a document disk that Word creates during setup to each document disk you use to store documents. This can be done with the DOS command COPY.

Setting Up a Hard-Disk System

To set up Word on a hard-disk system, you need to know

- The name of the directory you want to copy the Word program to. If the directory doesn't exist yet, Setup creates it and assigns the name you want. Whatever name you choose, this directory is referred to as the *Word program directory*.

- The type of computer you have.

- The type of display unit and adapter card you have.

- The brand name and model of your printer(s).

To run the Setup program, you must first start DOS (as explained in Appendix A). When you see the *C>* prompt, insert the Setup disk in drive A. Then type

   a:

and press the Enter key. Then type

   setup

and press the Enter key to start the Setup program.

The Setup program tells you what to do next, asks you questions, gives you lists of possible answers to choose from, and tells you when to remove or insert disks.

ADDITIONAL SETUP TASKS

In some situations, you'll need to or choose to perform additional setup tasks. Most of these situations depend on what kind of equipment you have. Glance through the sections that follow to see if any of them apply to you. Consult the *Getting Started* booklet to find out how to use Word on a network, with expanded memory, with a RAMDrive, with more than one display adapter, or with a variety of operating environments (such as Microsoft Windows) and other programs (such as Presentation Manager).

If You Can't Find Your Printer on the List

If you can't find your printer on the list the Setup program displays, you can choose one of Word's generic printers. These are listed at the end of the printer list. Choose *Standard printer* for dot-matrix printers that don't have backspace capability and *Standard printer with support for backspace* for dot-matrix printers with backspace capability. Choose *Standard printer with support for formfeeds* for dot-matrix printers that recognize a formfeed character at the end of a page. And choose *Standard daisywheel printer* if you have a daisy-wheel or thimble printer. The generic printer description files enable almost any printer to work, but they do not support advanced features such as proportional spacing, italics, boldface, or other special printing effects.

In addition to providing ready-made files that let you use the most common printers, Word provides programs (in files called MAKEPRD.EXE and MERGEPRD.EXE) that allow you to tailor-make printer description files for less widely used printers or printer-font combinations. See the manual *Printer Information for Microsoft Word* for instructions on using these programs.

If You Have a Serial Printer

If you have a serial printer, you must regulate how the computer sends characters to the printer. You do this through the MODE command that comes with DOS. If, after consulting your DOS manual and printer manual, you're not sure how to use the MODE command or what parameters to include in it, ask your dealer for help. After you learn how to use MODE, it's a good idea to put the MODE command into an AUTOEXEC.BAT file so that the computer is prepared to work with your printer each time you start DOS.

If You Have Higher-Capacity Disks

If you don't have a hard disk but do have 5¼-inch or 3½-inch disks that hold 720 KB or more, you can take advantage of their greater storage capacity by combining Word and part of DOS on one disk. This way, you will need only one disk to start both DOS and Word.

To combine Word and DOS on one disk:

1. Format a blank disk as a *system start* disk. To do this, insert your DOS disk in drive A. Then type

   format b:/s

   at the *A>* prompt and press the Enter key.

2. When the FORMAT program asks for a new disk, insert a blank, unformatted disk in drive B. (If you have only one floppy-disk drive, remove your DOS disk from drive A and insert the blank, unformatted disk. DOS will treat the drive as both drive A and drive B.)

3. Press the Enter key to format the disk and copy DOS to it.

4. When the FORMAT program is finished, it asks whether you want to format another disk. Press N for No, and then press Enter.

5. Insert in drive A the copy of the Word Program (Startup Word) disk created by Setup. (Do not use the original Word Program disk 1 shipped with Word.) At the *A>* prompt, type

   *copy *.* b:*

   and press Enter to copy all the files from the Word Program (Startup Word) disk created by Setup to the new system start disk.

You can now use the disk to start DOS and then, without changing disks, to start Word.

If You Add Equipment Later

You might purchase a mouse or a printer after you've set up your working copy of Word. In that case, run the Setup program again. Choose the Modify Existing Version option when it appears, and choose only those options that apply to the new equipment. If you have a floppy-disk system, insert your *working copy* of the Word Program disk when the Setup program asks you to insert the Word Program disk.

Appendix C

Summary of Commands

STARTING AND STOPPING WORD

Starting Word

	Type:
Start Word without loading a document	word
Start Word and load specified document	word *filename*
Start Word and load document last worked with	word/l

Stopping Word

	Keys/Command
Stop the Word program and return to DOS	Alt-F4 or File Exit Word

ENTERING TEXT

	Keys/Command
Start new paragraph	Enter
Start new line (within same paragraph)	Shift-Enter
Start new section	Insert Break
Start new column	Ctrl-Shift-Enter
Start new page	Ctrl-Enter
Enter nonrequired hyphen	Ctrl-hyphen key
Enter nonbreaking hyphen	Ctrl-Shift-hyphen key
Enter long hyphen (em dash)	Alt-Ctrl-hyphen key
Enter nonbreaking space	Ctrl-Shift-Spacebar
Enter character not found on key top	Num Lock ON, Alt-*ASCII code for character* (use numeric keypad to type code)

USING COMMANDS WITH THE KEYBOARD

	Keys/Command
Move to and from menu	Alt or F10
Choose menu or command	Bold letter
Cancel menu, command, or dialog box	Esc
Get help with specific command	F1
Repeat last command or macro	F4 or Edit Repeat
Repeat last search command	Shift-F4
Reverse last edit or format change	Alt-Backspace or Edit Undo
Inside Dialog Boxes	
Move to option in dialog box	Alt-bold letter
Move to next option	Tab
Move to previous option	Shift-Tab
Turn check box on/off	Spacebar or Alt-bold letter
Turn option button on	Spacebar or Alt-bold letter
Choose command button	Alt-bold letter
View drop-down list	F4 or Alt-Down direction key

(continued)

Using Commands with the Keyboard, *continued*

	Keys/Command
Choose item in list	Direction keys
Carry out command	Enter
Cancel command	Esc
Get help	F1
Macro Commands	
Record macro or end recording	Ctrl-F3 or Macro Record
Run macro	Ctrl-*key code* or Macro Run
Interrupt or cancel macro	Esc

SCROLLING

	Keys
Up	
Up one line	Scroll Lock ON, Up direction key
Up one windowful	PgUp
Up to beginning of document	Ctrl-Home
Down	
Down one line	Scroll Lock ON, Down direction key
Down one windowful	PgDn
Down to end of document	Ctrl-End
Left	
Left one-third windowful (if document is wider than window)	Scroll Lock ON, Left direction key
Left to beginning of line	Home
Right	
Right one-third windowful (if document is wider than window)	Scroll Lock ON, Right direction key
Right to end of line	End

MOVING THE CURSOR

	Keys/Command
Up	
Up one line	Up direction key
Up to beginning of paragraph or to previous paragraph	Ctrl-Up direction key
Up to top of window	Ctrl-PgUp
Up to beginning of document	Ctrl-Home
Down	
Down one line	Down direction key
Down to next paragraph	Ctrl-Down direction key
Down to bottom of window	Ctrl-PgDn
Down to end of document	Ctrl-End
Left	
Left one character	Left direction key
Left to previous word	Ctrl-Left direction key
Left to beginning of line	Home
Right	
Right one character	Right direction key
Right to next word	Ctrl-Right direction key
Right to end of line	End
To a Specific Place	
To next window pane	F6
To previous window pane	Shift-F6
To next window	Ctrl-F6
To previous window	Ctrl-Shift-F6
To specified page number	F5 or Edit Go To
To next footnote/annotation or from reference mark to related footnote/annotation text and back	F5 or Edit Go To
To specified bookmark	F5 or Edit Go To
To specified text	Edit Search
To specified format	Edit Search, <Search for Formatting Only>

SELECTING TEXT

	Keys
Previous word	Alt-F6, Ctrl-Left direction key, Alt-F6
Current or next word	Alt-F6
Current line	Home, Shift-End
Previous sentence	Alt-F8, Ctrl-Left direction key, Alt-F8
Current or next sentence	Alt-F8
Previous paragraph	Alt-F10, Ctrl-Left direction key, Alt-F10
Current or next paragraph	Alt-F10
Entire document	Ctrl-5 (numeric keypad) or Shift-F10
Turn on extend mode	F8
Extend selection to next word, sentence, paragraph, document	Repeat F8 until selected
Shrink selection	Shift-F8
Turn off extend mode	Esc
Turn column selection on/off	Ctrl-Shift-F8
Select column when column selection is turned on	Direction keys

EDITING TEXT

	Shortcut Keys	Command	Command Button
Deleting			
Delete character left of cursor	Backspace		
Delete selected text to scrap	Shift-Del	Edit Cut	
Delete selected text (no scrap)	Del		

(continued)

Editing Text, *continued*

	Shortcut Keys	*Command*	*Command Button*
Inserting			
Insert contents of scrap	Shift-Ins	Edit Paste	
Insert glossary entry; choose glossary name from list		Edit Glossary	\<Insert\>
Replace glossary name in document with glossary entry	F3		
Copying			
Copy highlighted text to new location:			
1. Copy to scrap	Ctrl-Ins or Alt-F3	Edit Copy	
2. Move cursor to new location	Direction keys		
3. Insert from scrap	Shift-Ins	Edit Paste	
Copy highlighted text to glossary		Edit Glossary	\<Define\>
Moving			
Move highlighted text to new location:			
1. Delete to scrap	Shift-Del	Edit Cut	
2. Move cursor to new location	Direction keys		
3. Insert from scrap	Shift-Ins	Edit Paste	
Searching and Replacing			
Find text		Edit Search	
Find and replace text		Edit Replace	
Find format		Edit Search	\<Search for Formatting Only\>
Replace format		Edit Replace	\<Replace Formatting Only\>
Find page, bookmark, footnote, or annotation	F5	Edit Go To	

(continued)

Editing Text, *continued*

	Shortcut Keys	Command	Command Button
Miscellaneous			
Turn overtype on/off	Ins or Alt-F5		
Insert/remove bookmark	Ctrl-Shift-F5	Insert Bookmark	
Calculate	F2	Utilities Calculate	
Help:			
General		Help Index	
Tutorial		Help Learning Word	
With Help		Help Using Help	
Help specific to highlighted command	F1		
Run other programs		File DOS Commands	

WORKING WITH WINDOWS

	Shortcut Keys	Command
Window Panes		
Split window into panes		Window Split (use direction keys to move split line, and then press Enter)
Open or close footnote/annotation pane		View Footnotes/ Annotations
Move to next pane	F6	
Move to previous pane	Shift-F6	
Close pane		Window Split (use direction keys to move split line to top, and then press Enter)

(continued)

Working with Windows, *continued*

	Shortcut Keys	*Command*
Multiple Windows		
Open window		File Open or File New
Open new window on same document		Window New Window
Close window	Ctrl-F4	Window Close or File Close
Move to next window	Ctrl-F6	Window *window number*
Move to previous window	Ctrl-Shift-F6	Window *window number*
Arrange windows		Window Arrange All
Size window	Ctrl-F8	Window Size (use direction keys to move right or bottom window border, and then press Enter)
Move window	Ctrl-F7	Window Move (use direction keys to move, and then press Enter)
Maximize window	Ctrl-F10	Window Maximize
Restore window	Ctrl-F5	Window Restore

FORMATTING CHARACTERS

You can assign character formats by using speed formatting keys, the Format Character command, or the formatting ribbon. Speed formatting keys for character formats toggle between turning a format on and turning it off. You can use the Format Character command to view character formats that have already been assigned. If you use macros or glossary entries whose key codes begin with the same letters as speed formatting keys, you must first press Ctrl-A to use the speed formatting keys—for example, press Ctrl-A, B for Ctrl-B.

Formatting Characters, *continued*

	Speed Formatting Keys and Shortcut Keys	*Command*	*Dialog Box Option*
Change font	Ctrl-F2 or Ctrl-F (ribbon)	Format Character	Font
Change font size	Ctrl-F2 or Ctrl-P (ribbon)	Format Character	Point Size
Change font color	Ctrl-F2	Format Character	Color
Change case	Shift-F3 (repeat until desired case)		
Bold	Ctrl-B	Format Character	Bold ON
Italic	Ctrl-I	Format Character	Italic ON
Underline	Ctrl-U	Format Character	Underline ON
Double underline	Ctrl-D	Format Character	Double Underline ON
Small capitals	Ctrl-K	Format Character	Small Kaps ON
Uppercase		Format Character	All Caps ON
Strikethrough		Format Character	Strikethru ON
Hidden text	Ctrl-H	Format Character	Hidden ON
Superscript	Ctrl-plus sign key	Format Character	Superscript ON
Subscript	Ctrl-equal sign key	Format Character	Subscript ON
Remove all character formats or styles (normal character)	Ctrl-Spacebar	Format Character	
Remove all character formats or styles except font and font size	Ctrl-Z	Format Character	

FORMATTING PARAGRAPHS

You can assign paragraph formats by using speed formatting keys, the Format Paragraph command, or the ruler. When a paragraph format requires a measurement, speed formatting keys assign a fixed measurement (shown below in parentheses with the keys). You can use the Format Paragraph command to view paragraph formats that have already been assigned. If you use macros or glossary entries whose key codes begin with the same letters as speed formatting keys, you must first press Ctrl-A to use the speed formatting keys.

Formatting Paragraphs, *continued*

	Speed Formatting Keys	*Command*	*Dialog Box Option*
Paragraph Alignment			
Align paragraph flush left	Ctrl-L	Format Paragraph	Left Alignment ON
Align paragraph flush right	Ctrl-R	Format Paragraph	Right Alignment ON
Center paragraph	Ctrl-C	Format Paragraph	Center Alignment ON
Justify paragraph	Ctrl-J	Format Paragraph	Justified Alignment ON
Paragraph Indents			
Indent first line		Format Paragraph	First Line: *positive measure greater than left indent*
"Outdent" first line (create hanging indent)	Ctrl-T (0.5 inches)	Format Paragraph	First Line: *negative measure equal to or smaller than left indent*
Indent left side	Ctrl-N (to next tab)	Format Paragraph	From Left
Indent right side		Format Paragraph	From Right
Increase left indent (nest)	Ctrl-N (to next tab)		
Decrease left indent	Ctrl-M (to previous tab)		
Increase left and right indents	Ctrl-Q		
Line Spacing			
Set spacing between lines in paragraph	Ctrl-1 (single) Ctrl-2 (double)	Format Paragraph	Spacing Line
Add extra space before paragraph	Ctrl-O [letter *O*] (1 line)	Format Paragraph	Spacing Before
Add extra space after paragraph		Format Paragraph	Spacing After

(continued)

Formatting Paragraphs, *continued*

	Speed Formatting Keys	Command	Dialog Box Option
Miscellaneous			
Remove paragraph formatting or style (apply normal paragraph formatting)	Ctrl-X	Format Paragraph	
Prevent page break in paragraph		Format Paragraph	Keep Paragraph Together ON
Prevent page break between paragraphs		Format Paragraph	Keep Paragraph With Next ON
Avoid widows and orphans when printing		Utilities Customize	Widow/Orphan Control ON
Tabs			
Set or move tabs		Format Tabs	<Set>
Clear tabs		Format Tabs	<Clear>
Clear all tabs and reset tabs at ½-inch intervals		Format Tabs	<Clear All>
Change preset intervals for tabs		Utilities Customize	Default Tab

FORMATTING SECTIONS

	Shortcut Keys	Command	Dialog Box Option
Section Boundaries			
Start section on same page and column		Format Section or Insert Break	Section Start: Continuous Section ON Continuous ON
Start section in new column		Format Section	Section Start: Column

(continued)

Formatting Sections, *continued*

	Shortcut Keys	*Command*	*Dialog Box Option*
Start section on new page		Format Section	Section Start: New Page
		or Insert Break	Section ON Next Page ON
Start section on next odd-numbered page		Format Section	Section Start: Odd Page
		or Insert Break	Section ON Odd Page ON
Start section on next even-numbered page		Format Section	Section Start: Even Page
		or Insert Break	Section ON Even Page ON

Page Numbers

Print page numbers and specify their vertical position		Insert Page Numbers or Format Section	From Top or From Bottom; <Page Numbers>
Specify horizontal position of page numbers		Insert Page Numbers	Align Page Number At
Specify starting number		Insert Page Numbers	Start At
Specify format of page numbers		Insert Page Numbers	Format

Margins and Page Size

Set page size		Format Margins	Width, Height
Set top and bottom margins		Format Margins	Top, Bottom
Set left and right margins		Format Margins	Left, Right
Set gutter margins		Format Margins	Gutter
Mirror margins		Format Margins	Mirror Margins ON

Multiple Columns

Format into multiple columns		Format Section	Columns Number

(continued)

Formatting Sections, *continued*

	Shortcut Keys	*Command*	*Dialog Box Option*
Assign space between multiple columns		Format Section	Columns Spacing
View columns		View Layout or File Print Preview	
Start new column	Ctrl-Shift-Enter		
Select column	Ctrl-Shift-F8		
Move to next column (while in View Layout)	Alt-5, Right direction key		
Move to previous column (while in View Layout)	Alt-5, Left direction key		

Footnotes and Annotations

Create footnote		Insert Footnote	
Specify footnote reference mark		Insert Footnote	Footnote Reference Mark
Create annotation		Insert Annotation	
Specify annotation reference mark		Insert Annotation	Annotation Mark
Position footnotes/ annotations on same page as reference marks		Format Section	Place Footnotes Same Page ON
Position footnotes/ annotations at end of section		Format Section	Place Footnotes End of Section ON
Move between footnote/annotation text and reference mark	F5	Edit Go To	
Open or close footnote/annotation window		View Footnotes/ Annotations	

(continued)

Formatting Sections, *continued*

	Shortcut Keys	*Command*	*Dialog Box Option*
Headers and Footers			
Create headers or footers and assign general position		Format Header/ Footer	
Assign exact position for headers or footers		Format Header/ Footer	<Options>
Format text of header or footer		Format Paragraph	
Insert page number in header or footer	Type *page* in header or footer and press F3		

STYLE SHEETS

	Shortcut Keys	*Command*	*Dialog Box Option*
Attach style sheet		Format Attach Style Sheet	
Display style key codes in style bar		View Preferences	Style Bar ON
Apply style		Format Apply Style	
Record style		Format Record Style	
Print style sheet		File Print	Print: Style Sheet
Open style sheet window and view style sheet		Format Define Styles or File Open	Show Files: Style Sheets
Open style sheet window and create new style sheet		File New	Style Sheet ON

(continued)

Style Sheets, *continued*

	Shortcut Keys	*Command*	*Dialog Box Option*
Working in a Style Sheet Window *(created with Format Define Styles command)*			
Create new style		Insert New Style	
Format new style or change format of selected style		various Format commands	
Change name of highlighted style		Edit Rename Style	
Copy style	Ctrl-Ins, Shift-Ins	Edit Copy, Edit Paste	
Delete style	Del	Edit Cut	
Move style	Shift-Del, Shift-Ins	Edit Cut, Edit Paste	
Undo last change to style sheet	Alt-Backspace	Edit Undo	
Repeat last change to style sheet	F4	Edit Repeat	
Merge style sheets		Insert Style Sheet	
Save style sheet	Alt-F2 or Alt-Shift-F2	File Save As or File Save	
Print style sheet	Shift-F9	File Print	
Close style sheet window		File Close or Window Close	

FILING

	Shortcut Keys	*Command*	*Dialog Box Option*
Document and Style Sheet Files			
Open file	Ctrl-F1 or Alt-Ctrl-F2 or Ctrl-F12	File Open	
Open new file		File New	
Merge files		Insert File	

(continued)

Filing, *continued*

	Shortcut Keys	*Command*	*Dialog Box Option*
Save file	Alt-Shift-F2 or Shift-F12	File Save	
Save file under new name or in new location	Alt-F2 or F12	File Save As	
Save all open document, style sheet, and glossary files		File Save All	
Autosave document, style sheet, and glossary files		Utilities Customize	Autosave Frequency
Turn summary sheet prompt on/off		Utilities Customize	Prompt for Summary Info ON/OFF
Change default path for files		File Open or File Save	<Options>
Close file	Ctrl-F4	File Close	
Close all document, style sheet, and glossary files		File Close All	

Glossary Files

	Shortcut Keys	*Command*	*Dialog Box Option*
Open glossary file		Edit Glossary	<Open Glossary>
Merge glossary files		Edit Glossary	<Merge>
Save glossary file		Edit Glossary	<Save Glossary>
Clear glossary memory		Edit Glossary	<Clear All>
Print glossary	F5	File Print	Print: Glossary

FINDING AND MANAGING FILES

	Command	Dialog Box Option
Search for files	File File Management	<Search>
Sort files	File File Management	<Options>, Sort Files By
Load file	File File Management	<Open>
Rename file	File File Management	<Rename>
Make changes to summary sheet	File File Management	<Summary>
Mark files for copying, moving, deleting, or printing	File File Management	Files (use direction keys to highlight and then press Spacebar, or point and click right mouse button)
Copy marked files	File File Management	<Copy>, Delete Files After Copy OFF
Move marked files	File File Management	<Copy>, Delete Files After Copy ON
Delete marked files	File File Management	<Delete>
Print marked files	File File Management	<Print>
Print summary sheets for marked files	File File Management	<Print>, Print: Summary Info
Print summary sheets with marked files	File File Management	<Print>, <Options>, Include Summary Info ON

PRINTING

	Shortcut Keys	Command	Dialog Box Option
Print document	Shift-F9 or Ctrl-Shift-F12	File Print	Print: Document
Print glossary	Shift-F9 or Ctrl-Shift-F12	File Print	Print: Glossary

(continued)

Printing, *continued*

	Shortcut Keys	*Command*	*Dialog Box Option*
Print style sheet	Shift-F9 or Ctrl-Shift-F12	File Print	Print: Style Sheet
Print summary sheet	Shift-F9 or Ctrl-Shift-F12	File Print	Print: Summary Info
Print summary sheet with document	Shift-F9 or Ctrl-Shift-F12	File Print	<Options>, Include Summary Info ON
Use computer as typewriter	Shift-F9 or Ctrl-Shift-F12	File Print	Print: Direct Text
Send printer output to file instead of to printer	Shift-F9 or Ctrl-Shift-F12	File Print	To File ON
Merge documents while printing		File Print Merge	
Stop printing	Esc		
Preview printing	Ctrl-F9	File Print Preview	
Exit print preview mode	Esc	File Exit Preview	
Change printers		File Printer Setup	
Repaginate without printing		Utilities Repaginate Now	
Printing Options			
Change paper feed		File Printer Setup	Paper Feed
Print more than one copy	Shift-F9 or Ctrl-Shift-F12	File Print	Copies
Print highlighted section of document	Shift-F9 or Ctrl-Shift-F12	File Print	Page Range: Selection
Print specified pages	Shift-F9 or Ctrl-Shift-F12	File Print	Pages
Print on both sides of paper		File Print	<Options>, Duplex ON
Print draft	Shift-F9 or Ctrl-Shift-F12	File Print	<Options>, Draft ON

(continued)

Printing, *continued*

	Shortcut Keys	*Command*	*Dialog Box Option*
Print hidden text	Shift-F9 or Ctrl-Shift-F12	File Print	<Options>, Hidden Text ON
Print summary sheet with document	Shift-F9 or Ctrl-Shift-F12	File Print	<Options>, Summary Info ON
Avoid widows and orphans		Utilities Customize	Widow/Orphan Control ON
Queued Printing			
Print while editing (queued printing)		File Printer Setup	Use Print Queue ON
Temporarily stop queued printing		File Print Queue	<Pause>
Restart queued printing, continuing from where you left off		File Print Queue	<Continue>
Restart queued printing from beginning of file		File Print Queue	<Restart File>
Cancel queued printing		File Print Queue	<Stop Queue>

HYPHENATION, THESAURUS, AND SPELLING

	Shortcut Keys	*Command*	*Dialog Box Option*
Check document for spelling errors	F7	Utilities Spelling	
Find synonyms for highlighted word	Shift-F7	Utilities Thesaurus	
Automatically hyphenate words		Utilities Hyphenate	

(continued)

Hyphenation, Thesaurus, and Spelling, *continued*

	Shortcut Keys	*Command*	*Dialog Box Option*
Spelling Options			
See suggested corrections without requesting them		Utilities Spelling	\<Options\>, Always Suggest ON
Check for punctuation errors		Utilities Spelling	\<Options\>, Check Punctuation ON
Ignore words in all caps		Utilities Spelling	\<Options\>, Ignore ALL CAPS ON
Assume first two letters of words are correct		Utilities Spelling	\<Options\>, Quick Look Up ON
Check all letters in words		Utilities Spelling	\<Options\>, Complete Look Up ON

CUSTOMIZING WORD

Viewing Options

	Shortcut Keys	*Command*	*Dialog Box Option*
Turn display of all nonprinting characters on/off		View Preferences	Show All
Turn display of some nonprinting characters on/off: tabs, optional hyphens, paragraph marks, spaces, and hidden text		View Preferences	Check boxes for characters you want displayed or hidden

(continued)

Viewing Options, *continued*

	Shortcut Keys	*Command*	*Dialog Box Option*
Turn display of actual line breaks on/off	Alt-F7	View Preferences	Line Breaks
Turn menu on/off		View Preferences	Menu
Turn style bar on/off		View Preferences	Style Bar
Turn window borders on/off		View Preferences	Window Borders
Turn message bar on/off		View Preferences	Message Bar
Turn scroll bars on/off		View Preferences	Horizontal or Vertical
Turn line-number display in status bar on/off		View Preferences	Show Line Numbers
Turn ruler on/off		View Ruler	
Turn ribbon on/off		View Ribbon	
Turn status bar on/off		View Status Bar	
Turn layout view on/off		View Layout	
Turn print preview on	Ctrl-F9	File Print Preview	
Turn print preview off	Esc	File Exit Preview	
Turn outline view on/off	Shift-F2	View Outline	
Change cursor speed		View Preferences	Cursor Control Speed
Change display mode	Alt-F9	View Preferences	Display Mode
Change colors		View Preferences	<Colors>

Operating Options

	Command	Dialog Box Option
Turn on autosave and set frequency	Utilities Customize	Autosave Frequency
Turn off autosave	Utilities Customize	Autosave Frequency: 0
Turn background pagination on/off	Utilities Customize	Background Pagination
Turn summary sheet prompt on/off	Utilities Customize	Prompt for Summary Info
Turn widow/orphan control on/off	Utilities Customize	Widow/Orphan Control
Turn Word 5.0 function key assignments on/off	Utilities Customize	Use Word 5.0 Function Keys
Turn Insert key as overtype key on/off	Utilities Customize	Use INS for Overtype Key
Display shortcut keys on menus	Utilities Customize	Show Keys on Menus
Turn audible alarm on/off	Utilities Customize	Mute (ON turns alarm off, OFF turns alarm on)
Change decimal character	Utilities Customize	Decimal
Change automatic date or time formats	Utilities Customize	Date or Time
Change default unit of measure	Utilities Customize	Measure
Change line draw character	Utilities Customize	Line Draw Character
Change default tab width	Utilities Customize	Default Tab
Change dictionary for Spell program	Utilities Customize	Speller Name

Appendix D

Toggle Keys and Commands

Toggle keys and commands alternate between turning a feature on and turning it off. For most toggle keys and commands, Word displays a two-letter code in the status bar to let you know when the feature is turned on. A few of the features listed here are not strictly toggles; they are turned on by one key or command and turned off by another. (Some keys and commands listed here are not covered in this book. They are included so that you will know which keys to press to turn them off if you accidentally turn them on.)

Feature	Toggle Keys or Command	Code Displayed When On
Type uppercase letters	Caps Lock	CL
Select column	Ctrl-Shift-F8	CS
Extend selection	F8 (on), Esc (off)	EX
Use direction keys to draw lines	Utilities Line Draw (on), Esc (off)	LD
Show layout	View Layout	LY
Mark revisions	Utilities Revision Marks (turn Mark Revisions check box on/off)	RM

(continued)

Toggle Keys and Commands, *continued*

Feature	Toggle Keys or Command	Code Displayed When On
Use direction keys to type numbers	Num Lock	NL
Overtype	Ins or Alt-F5	OT
Record macro	Ctrl-F3 or Macro Record	MR
Use direction keys to scroll	Scroll Lock	SL*
Run macros step by step	Esc (to interrupt macro), Macro Run, Alt-S to turn step mode on/off	ST
Maximize window	Ctrl-F10 or Window Maximize (on), Ctrl-F5 or Window Restore (off)	MX
Choose text/graphics display mode	Alt-F9	Display changes, no code
View print preview	Ctrl-F9 (on/off) or Esc (off)	Display changes, no code
View outline	Shift-F2 or View Outline	The word Text appears at left end of status bar
Organize outline	Shift-F5 (in outline view)	ORGANIZE appears at left end of status bar
Display ribbon	View Ribbon	Ribbon appears
Display ruler	View Ruler	Ruler appears
Turn ruler mode on/off	Ctrl-Shift-F10 (on), Esc (off)	Cursor moves to ruler
Display status bar	View Status Bar	Status bar appears

* If a window is maximized, the code MX appears in the status bar, and the code SL is not visible even if Scroll Lock is turned on.

Appendix E

Summary of Mouse Activities

CHOOSING COMMANDS AND USING DIALOG BOXES

	Location of Pointer	Point to	Mouse Action
Browse through menus	Menu bar	Menu names	Drag pointer across menu names
Choose menu	Menu bar	Menu name	Click
Choose command	Menu	Command name	Click
Choose dialog box option, list item, or command button	Dialog box	Option, list item, or command button	Click
Turn check box or option button on/off	Dialog box	Check box or option button	Click
View drop-down list	Dialog box	Drop-down arrow	Click
Choose list item and carry out command	List box	Item in list	Double-click
Carry out command	Dialog box	<OK> command button	Click
Cancel command	Dialog box	<Cancel> command button	Click
Get help	Status bar	<F1=Help>	Click

SCROLLING

	Location of Pointer	Point to	Mouse Action
Up or down one line	Right window border	Up or down arrow on scroll bar	Click
Up or down one windowful	Right window border	Scroll bar above or below scroll box	Click
Up to beginning of document	Right window border	Scroll box	Drag scroll box to top of scroll bar
Down to end of document	Right window border	Scroll box	Drag scroll box to bottom of scroll bar
To relative vertical position	Right window border	Scroll box	Drag scroll box to position on scroll bar relative to desired position in document
Left or right one column	Bottom window border	Left or right arrow on scroll bar	Click
Left or right one-third windowful (if document is wider than window)	Bottom window border	Scroll bar left or right of scroll box	Click
To relative horizontal position	Bottom window border	Scroll box	Drag scroll box to position on scroll bar relative to desired position in document

SELECTING TEXT

	Location of Pointer	Point to	Mouse Action
Word	Text area	Any character in word	Double-click, or click right mouse button
Sentence	Text area	Any character in sentence	Ctrl-click, or click both mouse buttons
Line	Selection bar	Line	Click
Paragraph	Selection bar	Any line in paragraph	Double-click, or click right mouse button
Whole document	Selection bar	Any line in document	Ctrl-click, or click both mouse buttons
Block	Text area	Beginning or end of block	Drag pointer from one end of block to other end

EDITING TEXT

	Location of Pointer	Point to	Mouse Action
Copy selected text	Text area	New location for selected text	Ctrl-Shift-click right mouse button
Move selected text	Text area	New location for selected text	Ctrl-click right mouse button
Choose Edit Go To command	Status bar	Any place on status bar	Double-click

WORKING WITH WINDOWS

	Location of Pointer	*Point to*	*Mouse Action*
Activate window	Window to be activated	Any place in window	Click
Size window	Lower right corner of window	Size icon (�P)	Drag size icon to new position
Maximize/ restore window	Upper right corner of window	Maximize icon (▯)	Click
Move window	Top or left border of window	Top or left border	Drag border to new position
Close window	Upper left corner of window	Close icon (▮)	Click
Split window into two panes	Right window border	Split-bar icon (≡)	Double-click or drag split-bar icon to desired position
Open footnote/ annotation pane	Right window border	Split-bar icon (≡)	Press Shift and drag split-bar icon to desired position
Size pane	Right window border	Split-bar icon (≡)	Drag split-bar icon to new position
Close pane	Right window border	Split-bar icon (≡)	Double-click

FORMATTING

	Location of Pointer	*Point to*	*Mouse Action*
Copy character format to selected text	Text area	Character with format to be copied	Ctrl-Shift-click
Copy paragraph format to selected text	Selection bar	Paragraph with format to be copied	Ctrl-Shift-click

(continued)

Formatting, *continued*

	Location of Pointer	Point to	Mouse Action
Turn ribbon on/off	Upper right corner of window	Ruler icon (⊥)	Click right mouse button
Change font or font size for selected text	Ribbon	1. Drop-down arrow of Font or Pts box	Click to see list
		2. Desired font or size in list	Click to choose
Select bold, italic, or underlined format for selected text	Ribbon	Abbreviation for desired format (Bld, Ital, or Ul)	Click
Apply style to selected text	Ribbon	1. Drop-down arrow of Style box	Click to see list
		2. Desired style in list	Click to choose
Choose Format Character command	Ribbon	Font or Pts box	Double-click
Choose Format Apply Styles command	Ribbon	Style box	Double-click
Turn ruler on/off	Upper right corner of window	Ruler icon (⊥)	Click
Move paragraph indent	Ruler	Indent mark	Drag indent mark to new position using right mouse button
Set tab stop	Ruler	Desired position of tab stop	Click
Move tab stop	Ruler	Marker for tab stop	Drag marker to new position
Clear tab stop	Ruler	Marker for tab stop	Drag marker off ruler
Change alignment of tab stop	Left end of ruler	Alignment character	Click until desired alignment character appears
Change leader character of tab stop	Left end of ruler	Leader character	Click until desired leader character appears

Appendix F

Symbols in the Scrap

Word uses the following graphic symbols to represent special characters that have been copied or deleted to the scrap.

-	Space
→	Tab character
↓	Newline mark
¶	Paragraph mark
§	Section mark
—	Optional hyphen
▣	Automatic page numbers
♣	Automatic footnote numbers
♥	Timeprint
▯	Dateprint
■	End of row in column selection

Index

Italicized page numbers indicate graphics.

Special Characters

" " (quotation marks)
  used in merge printing 246
  used in searches 275–76
$ (dollar sign) used to indicate
    compressed files 331
& (ampersand) as AND operator 274,
    275, 276
* (asterisk)
  as file marker 281
  as wildcard character 218–19, 272, 274,
    276, 341–42
, (comma) as OR operator 274, 275, 276
< (less than symbol) used in file searches
    275, 276
<> (angle brackets) used in macro key
    codes 289, 290
> (greater than symbol) used in file
    searches 275, 276
? (question mark) as wildcard character
    109, 114–15, 272, 274, 276, 341–42
\ (backslash) used to indicate root
    directory 64, 332
^ (caret)
  as running-head marker 201–2
  used in searches 109, 112–13, 114, 276
~ (tilde) as NOT operator 273–74, 276
« » (chevrons)
  used with macro instructions 290
  used in merge printing 242

A

active window 121
alignment. *See* paragraph formatting,
    alignment; tabs
Alternate (Alt) key 32, 35, 129
Alternate (Alt)-key combinations
  Alt-5, Right or Left direction key 195

Alternate (Alt)-key combinations *(continued)*
  Alt-Backspace 48
  Alt-Down direction key 93
  Alt-F5 103
  Alt-F6 80
  Alt-F8 80
  Alt-F9 58, 130
  Alt-F10 80
AND operator 274, 275, 276
annotations 106, 365. *See also* footnotes;
    View Footnotes/Annotations
    command
arrow keys. *See* direction keys
ASCII file, saving document as 211, 212
ASK instruction 250–52
AUTOEXEC.BAT file 212, 342–43, 347
automatic (soft) page break 25, 106–7,
    235
autosave feature 61, 216–17

B

background pagination 235
background shading 191–92
backing up disks 15
Backspace key 23, 46, 52
BACKUP command (DOS) 342
backup files 63, 214, 217, 330, 339–42.
    See also saving documents and files
.BAK extension 63, 214, 330
boldface 57–58, 173–74
bookmarks 106–8
borders 191–92
bulleted lists 165, 313–15

C

Caps Lock key 22, 30, 33
case of characters
  changing 22, 173, 174

Janet Rampa

Born and raised in Wilmington, Illinois, Janet Rampa studied philosophy and literature at the University of Illinois. An early enthusiast of word processing with microcomputers, she set up and managed the word-processing department at Sybex Computer Books and edited two bestselling word-processing books, *Introduction to WordStar,* by Arthur Naiman, and *Introduction to Word Processing,* by Hal Glatzer. She was a cofounder of TechArt Associates, a microcomputer software development and training group in Berkeley, California. She now resides in Los Altos, California.